CHASE DARKNESS WITH ME

CHASE DARKNESS WITH ME

How One True-Crime Writer

Started Solving Murders

BILLY JENSEN

sourcebooks

Published by Sourcebooks
P.O. Box 4410, Naperville, Illinois 60567-4410
(630) 961-3900
sourcebooks.com

Library of Congress Cataloging-in-Publication Data

Names: Jensen, Billy, author.
Title: Chase darkness with me : how one true-crime writer started solving
    murders / Billy Jensen.
Description: Naperville, Illinois : Sourcebooks, Inc., [2019]
Identifiers: LCCN 2019006718 | (hardcover : alk. paper)
Subjects: LCSH: Jensen, Billy. | Murder--United States. | Cold cases
    (Criminal investigation)--United States. | Murder--Investigation--United
    States. | Journalists--United States.
Classification: LCC HV6529 .J47 2019 | DDC 363.25/9523092--dc23
LC record available at https://lccn.loc.gov/2019006718

Printed and bound in the United States of America.
LSC 10 9 8 7 6 5 4 3 2

To the victims

CONTENTS

Foreword by Karen Kilgariff   ix

Prologue   3

1. *Bam! Pow! Screech! Zap!*   9

2. *The Body in the Barrel*   15

3. *The Murder in the Shadows*   25

4. *Have You Seen This Man?*   41

5. *A Partner in Crimesolving*   55

6. *The Absolute Worst Humanity Has to Offer*   71

7. *The Wrong Side of Broken*   79

8. *The Man in the Green Hoodie*   85

9. *The Villain with a Thousand Faces*   113

10. *Losing Jade and Finding Mariah*   143

11. *The Halloween Mask Murder*   165

12. *The Devil in Plain Darkness*   187

13. *The Girl with the Serpent Tattoo*   205

14. *The Cantina Scene*   223

15. *The Monster at the End of This Book*   241

Epilogue   265

Addendum *So You Want to Help Solve a Murder?*   269

In Conversation with Billy Jensen and Paul Holes   301

Reading Group Guide   311

Acknowledgments   315

About the Author   319

FOREWORD

by Karen Kilgariff

LOOK, I DON'T WANT TO TELL YOU HOW TO READ THIS BOOK or anything, but if I were you, I'd skip to the last chapter and read that first. Now, I'd normally never tell anyone to do this. It's illogical and bizarre. How can you grasp the meaning of an ending if you don't know who the main character is or what they've gone through to get themselves there? How can you care?

But in this book, we have a unique situation because (a) it's not a novel, it's the story of a real crime journalist and (b) if you're any sort of consumer of true crime, you're already very familiar with the last chapter's inciting incident. It involves a case now so infamous that most Americans, even the ones who "don't like" true crime, know about it. I'm just saying, how can it be a spoiler if everybody already knows what's going to happen?

———————————————

It's strange to think that I've only known Billy Jensen for about two years. It genuinely feels like twenty. So many huge, life-altering things have happened since we first met at a restaurant on Franklin Avenue.

Georgia Hardstark and I were tucked into a corner table eating dinner after a live *My Favorite Murder* show at Upright Citizens Brigade next door, and, because I was sitting on the side that faced the room, I saw him approaching first. He was an extremely tall and serious-faced man wearing a black trench coat. *Was he wearing a trench coat?* That may be an embellishment. The point is, I got a bad feeling about him. He started talking to us from five feet away. And not in the usual, sorry-to-bother-you, let-me-introduce myself way we do here in Los Angeles. He spoke like we'd already been talking, and he wasn't all that happy about it.

"Yeah, I worked on that case you guys just covered. I listened to it today."

Was he accusing us of something? Was he saying it was his case? Or that we shouldn't have done it? Who was *this guy?* I scanned the room to see if there was any type of security on duty.

"Did you hear the sheriff is going to release the original coroner's report?"

Just an FYI, that isn't literally what he said. I don't remember the real quote, but it was very detailed and specific, and it made me panic. I had no idea what he was talking about. We cover two cases a week on our true-crime podcast, but unlike actual journalists, we're much more, shall we say, casual about the details. I assumed we were being confronted by an expert about our lack of expertise. Check, please.

But Georgia did know what he was talking about and jumped right in. And when he landed at our table, I could see his eyes were sparkling with the enthusiasm of someone in a foreign land who'd found people who speak his language. It turned out he was not there to confront or correct us. He was excited to talk shop. And luckily, that conversation continues to this day.

Now that I'm thinking about it, you should probably read this book exactly the way Billy wrote it, with the ending at the end. He really knows his stuff. Take in his personal chronology. Learn about his background and his influences. Read about those early cold cases that weren't shocking, gory, or blond enough to earn mass media coverage and see how they changed him as a young reporter. See how he got fed up and came up with the idea to actually start solving murders himself. Do the legwork and get your facts straight so when you finally land at that magnificent, breathless final chapter, the author's internal fireworks display can be felt as your own.

Although, if I may say this: the end of this book isn't just the electric, live-to-laptop recounting of how a major cold case that he'd waded into waist-deep got solved. It's also the work of a seasoned crime reporter who, in the midst of the shock and unreality of such a watershed moment, had the presence of mind to write his own breaking story.

It's a movie plot come to life. After years of difficult, thankless work, a reporter obsessed with justice gets the rare satisfaction of seeing justice finally served. Who doesn't want to read that immediately?

Good crime journalists offer themselves as a bridge between the worst of humanity and those of us who want to know how bad it can actually be. And sometimes, if a crime story has no ending, then a reporter like Billy Jensen will take up the cause and dedicate their life to finding one. They'll visit old crime scenes, interview bereaved families, and walk dark neighborhoods searching for the truth. They do the rarely recognized service of filling in the blanks around these victims' identities, telling us who a person was before they became just another anonymous statistic. It's noble work. And this book is about a life dedicated to that work.

Because how can you grasp the meaning of an ending if you don't know who the main character is or what they've gone through to get there? How can you care?

CHASE DARKNESS WITH ME

PROLOGUE

IT STARTS WITH AN OVERHEAD SHOT—IN COLOR, BUT WITH no sound—of a man walking into a 7-Eleven. It's late, well past 2:00 a.m., but the scene is glowing, the streetlamps working with the store signs to give off a glimmer you don't usually see on the typical nighttime surveillance video. The nearby bars—Henry's, O'Callaghan's, Howl at the Moon, and Mother Hubbard's—are well beyond last call, and the street is a mix of those who don't want the night to end and those for whom the day is just beginning.

As bright as the street is, your eyes squint as the video quickly switches to the glaring whiteness of the store's interior. Inside, you see the back of a well-dressed man with close-cropped hair standing at the counter, purchasing what looks like a bag of chips from the store clerk. He motions to the customer to his left, and we see his face. He is handsome, but his eyes are tired, presumably from a long evening. He turns back to the clerk, completes the transaction, and walks out of the store and into the night.

The video then cuts to an overhead shot of the sidewalk, where a man wearing a green hoodie opens the door to the 7-Eleven. He is a big man, but you can't make out his face. He is barely inside the store when a security guard who was manning the door on the sidewalk comes up behind him, says something that gets his attention, and performs the universal take-a-hike gesture with his thumb. The Man in the Green Hoodie does an about-face and skulks back to the sidewalk.

Moments later, you see the customer with his newly purchased chips exit the store. In a minute, you'll learn the man's name, when a caption flashes at the bottom of the screen. He is Marques Gaines, a bartender at the Chicago Marriott on Michigan Avenue. As Marques exits the store, the Man in the Green Hoodie steps in front of him. For the first time, you can see his face, a menacing brow perched over angry eyes and an angrier scowl. You can see him yelling. He gets in Marques's face. He gets in the security guard's face. He gets back into Marques's face. Marques turns his palms up as if to say, "Why are you so mad?" then tries to walk away. The Man in the Green Hoodie follows him.

The video then cuts to a traffic camera across the street, and the images transform from a brilliantly lit close-up of animated humans to an overhead shot of grainy, pixelated ghouls. But you can still make out Marques and the Man in the Green Hoodie. You watch Marques walking quickly toward the crosswalk. Walking away from the confrontation, like everyone tells you to do. *Just. Walk. Away.*

But the Man in the Green Hoodie pursues him. Marques's walk turns into a run. He takes three strides and then for some reason turns back around to face the man. The Man in the Green Hoodie hits him in the head with a crushing right hook, sending his body backward into the crosswalk. Marques is crumpled and unconscious before he hits the ground. As he lies on the pavement, two figures run into the frame from the opposite end of the street.

"Thank God," you say to yourself as you watch the Good Samaritans kneel down next to Marques's motionless body. Your relief turns to horror and disbelief as they shove their hands into his pockets and strip them of their contents before getting up and fleeing down an alleyway. To the right of the frame, the Man in the Green Hoodie stalks away into the night.

A few seconds later, two taxicabs, one in front of the other, make right turns onto the street where Marques lies unconscious. The first one drives to the right of Marques's motionless body, narrowly missing him. The next one drives directly on top of him, crushing his chest under two tons of automobile and killing him.

The rest of the video shows the aftermath. A close-up of people in the street. On the sidewalk, one man is in complete shock. Another takes out his phone, in all likelihood calling 911.

Marques Gaines's life ended in the gutter. No one helped him until it was too late. Until they had to instruct the taxi driver to back up his car, slowly removing the front tires from on top of his body.

By the time I saw the video, Marques Gaines had been dead for three months. It was 4:00 a.m., and I was in bed in my Los Angeles apartment. After seventeen years as a journalist writing about unsolved murders, stories with no endings tend to elbow their way into your dreamscape. They aren't nightmares, just strange situations. The images and settings and characters are always slightly off, always a little different from real life. Every now and then, they trade starring roles with my dad, who has somehow clawed his way out of his grave to come visit me. That one *is* a nightmare, because I always know in my dream that he has to go back. Either way, they don't lend themselves well to restful sleep.

I clicked on the play button again, and my anger started to percolate. A few dark weeks ago, I was sitting in a bar in Boston, the dirt still on my shoes from a day of investigating the scene where a woman and three children were murdered, stuffed into two fifty-five-gallon drums, and dumped in the New Hampshire woods. I was two beers into the night when I absentmindedly looked at my Facebook messages and saw a note from a stranger. *Not sure if you heard. So very sorry*, the woman wrote, with a link to an article. I read the headline six or seven times, trying to wish the words away: MICHELLE MCNAMARA, WRITER AND WIFE OF PATTON OSWALT, DEAD AT 46.

Michelle was a partner in crimesolving. She died in the middle of her pursuit of a real-life monster in the closet, the Golden State Killer, leaving behind an unfinished manuscript about her obsession with the case. He had murdered at least twelve people and raped at least fifty women in their own homes. Michelle was driven, determined. Relentless. We would meet every month for lunch, and she would tell me about her quest. About how close she thought she was to finding him. To finding the monster.

What I had just witnessed was a monster in the street. But both were cut from the same cloth. They were masters of terror shouting in their actions "I am king here." The Golden State Killer would rape a woman in her own home while her husband was forced to lie still, lest the dishes the criminal had laid on his back make any noise and provoke him further. He would make himself a sandwich, riffle through cabinets, and then go silent, making the victims think he might have left before announcing he was still there and the terror was not over. For those few hours, Michelle's monster was the king of those people. He had their entire lives inside his palm, and he thrived on it. On the night that Marques Gaines died in Chicago, the Man in the Green Hoodie was the king of that street corner. He stalked the sidewalk, eyeing everyone in his path as prey, just waiting for someone to say something to him. Make eye contact with him. Walk down the street in a manner that just rubbed him the wrong way and be prepared for a world of hurt.

Michelle had only sketches of her villain. Sketches of a man who wore a mask. A phantom. The Man in the Green Hoodie was fully formed, preserved forever on video.

Whenever people ask me why I only write about unsolved murders, I always say the same thing: because I hate the guy who got away with it. But after Michelle died, it was different. Now I hate the perpetrator for taking over the lives of the living just as much as taking the lives of the dead. The victim's families. The investigators. The volunteers. They all gave up giant chunks of their own lives to search for an answer that someone selfishly kept hidden away.

People die before getting the answer.

As a journalist focusing on cold cases, I opened letters every day from family members desperate for justice. Some wanted to know who killed their son. Some wanted to know where their daughter was buried. Some just wanted to talk. Because everyone else had stopped listening, they came to me. I tried to help each and every one of them. But every story I wrote—the DJ shot dead on New Year's Eve in his Miami apartment, the hippie girl gone missing in the marijuana fields of Northern California, the Swedish nanny found cut in half in a Boston dumpster—had one thing in common: they had no endings. The killers had gotten away. The missing stayed missing. The Villain with a Thousand Faces continued to grow stronger. And now, as I stared at my computer screen, the Man in the Green Hoodie was the newest face in the club.

I watched the video again and again, my anger building with each play. After the tenth viewing, I made up my mind. This time was going to be different. I was going to give Marques Gaines's story an ending.

I was going to solve the crime myself.

BAM! POW! SCREEECH! ZAP!

Long Island, 1977

"THEY GOT HIM," MY DAD SAID TO ME.

He had just come home from work, but he didn't head upstairs to wash off the paint and dust like he did every other day. No, this day was different. He unfurled the front page of *Newsday*, the tabloid that was delivered to most every house on Long Island in those days, and held it up to my face. On the cover of the paper was a pasty, passive-looking man in a dingy collared shirt, the majority of its buttons opened, revealing a white T-shirt underneath.

"This is him," he said. "This is the .44 Caliber Killer."

I studied the man's face for a couple of seconds, scrunched up my nose, and said, "He looks like a turkey."

That was my first observation about a criminal: "He looks like a turkey."

I turned five that summer. In my ultrasuburban middle-class household, the fight for my family's attention was a tooth-and-nail affair between *Star Wars*, Reggie Jackson, and the New York Blackout. My two much older half sisters were charging into their teenage years, with Leif Garrett posters on their walls and starry eyes for the discos like Studio 54 they hoped to dance at one day. My dad was three years into owning his own house-painting business, and my mom was just trying to keep everyone together and get us to sit down at the dinner table to eat another creation from her McCall's cookbook.

But the shadow of the .44 Caliber Killer hung over everything. For the previous twelve months, the killer had been striking across the outer boroughs of the city, killing six and wounding seven with his trademark high-powered revolver. New York police were in the midst of their biggest manhunt in history. He was taunting them with letters. "I am the 'Monster'—'Beelzebub'—the 'Chubby Behemoth,'" he wrote. "I love to hunt. Prowling the streets looking for fair game—tasty meat." And yet they still couldn't catch him.

Girls were dyeing their hair blond (his female victims were almost all brunettes), and boys were warned not to take their girlfriends to lovers' lanes, which were his favorite hunting ground. My sisters weren't quite old enough to go to the discos, but I remember them being scared. I remember everyone being scared.

Our suburban bliss, nestled in a pocket of split-level homes adjacent to the famous Levitt subdivisions built for the GIs returning from WWII, was splintered. For the most part, I have only hazy memories of that time. Waiting by the screen door for my dad to come home from work. The action figure aisle at Toys"R"Us. "Don't Go Breaking My Heart" by Elton John and Kiki Dee playing on the tinny speakers of our light-blue VW bus. They are all fuzzy, faded, nebulous snapshots in my mind.

But I remember August 11, 1977, in technicolor—the day after they caught Son of Sam, the .44 Caliber Killer, David Berkowitz. I remember the front page of the newspaper, WE HAVE HIM in larger-than-life letters shouting across the top of the front page. *This* was the guy who was killing all those people. The guy who thought he could get away with it forever. And they got him.

What I remember most is the curious feeling of relief throughout my household, throughout my town, throughout the city. This wasn't the Muppets or superheroes. This was real. Chaos had been returned to order. Things had been set right in the world.

I liked that feeling.

———————————————

My dad never shied away from telling me about anything. He seemed like he was ten feet tall, with forearms the size of footballs, intense pale-blue eyes, and a mustache that made everyone think he was a cop (and he really didn't like cops). He was a barrel-chested brawler who had run away from home when he was fifteen, did time for punching a detective in the face, and later acquired a heroin addiction but was able to pull himself from the abyss and transform himself into a hard-working family man.

I spent every afternoon after school alone in the basement, surrounded by Chewbacca, G. I. Joe, and the Six Million Dollar Man, waiting for Dad to come home. He would arrive around 5:00 p.m., covered in dust from sanding lead paint off the houses of rich people in Great Neck or Garden City, take a quick shower, open a Budweiser, maybe take a Darvon if his head was pounding from one of his migraines, fall into his recliner, and open that afternoon's *Newsday*. At 6:00 p.m., the channel was tuned to 7, ABC Eyewitness News. He read the newspaper cover to cover with the news in the background, pausing to look over the paper at our twenty-four-inch RCA if anchorman Roger Grimsby said something that caught his interest.

I sat on the carpet, acting out adventures with my action figures and Matchbox cars: *Screeeeeeech! Zap! Pow! Bam! Bam! Bam!*

My sound effects were louder than they needed to be. With each *Bam!* I would look up to see if my dad was looking down at me. Sometimes he was, but most of the time, he was deep into a story. Usually a crime story. When he would look at me, he would tell me little bits of information, crowbarring nonfiction victims and villains into my brain alongside Scooby-Doo and the Wonder Twins.

"Billy, look at this kid," he said one day, showing me the photo of John Pius, a thirteen-year-old newspaper delivery boy who was found beaten to death in the woods behind Dogwood Elementary School in Smithtown. The autopsy discovered he had choked on pebbles that had been shoved down his throat.

"Look at these sick bastards," he would say another day, showing me the five gunmen who crashed a party in Plainview, raped two women, urinated on guests, and made off with $8,000 in cash and jewels before bashing their way into the Seacrest Diner on Glen Cove Road. There, they ordered patrons to strip and forced some to have sex with each other.

"Now look at this frickin' guy," he said a few years after that, pointing to a wild-eyed Ricky Kasso. Nicknamed "the Acid King," the seventeen-year-old stoner murdered his friend Gary Lauwers on a muggy June night in the woods of Northport. Kasso screamed, "Say you love Satan," to Lauwers as he stabbed him. "I love my mother," Lauwers whimpered back.

The tales unfolded each day—from the shock of the crime to the rush of the manhunt to the satisfaction of the arrest and the frustrations of the trial. And I sat on the carpet in between my dad and the television, riveted. Each was a cautionary tale. "Remember this," my dad would say and show me a picture from the paper.

The lessons I learned:

- John Pius was attacked by four boys whom he had run across while they were stealing a frame for a minibike. They thought he was going to tell on them, so they attacked him, shoving the rocks down his throat to silence his screams. *My dad's lesson: "Mind your business, but if you are going to say something, make sure no one can trace it back to you."*

— The five gunmen who turned the diner into a twisted rape room all fled Long Island, only to sheepishly come back and give themselves up. Why? Because inside that diner, there were some family members of some men who were "connected." They learned the identities of the gunmen and sent a message to them via their friends and family: come back to Long Island, or your family will be dead. *My dad's lesson: "The mob can get you even if you run. Don't mess with the mob."*

— Ricky Kasso turned out not to be an obsessed Satanist but an acid dealer who killed Lauwers over a drug deal gone bad. *My dad's lesson: "Be careful who you hang out with…and don't take acid."*

I didn't have podcasts or documentaries telling me about the most horrific crimes of the era. I had Dad.

2

THE BODY IN THE BARREL

New York, 1999

THE CALL CAME ON A SATURDAY MORNING. 7:00 A.M. THE voice on the other end was brisk.

"Are you working?"

Yes.

I was always working.

I needed money. Any money I could legally get my hands on. It had been sixteen months since my daughter was born. Fifteen months since my dad died. Twelve months since I had signed my life away to a thirty-year mortgage for a tiny house in a good school district. My first full year as an adult—1999. A desperate, no-safety-net adult who couldn't afford to turn down any opportunity to make money.

"What do you got?" I answered, my eyes still closed.

"Syosset. A family just moved into a house," said the voice. "They're cleaning out some junk in a crawl space and find a fifty-five-gallon barrel. They opened it, and inside was a body."

The voice was an editor from the *New York Times* metro desk. I had just started getting these calls. The *Times* was shorthanded on the weekends and needed stringers to go out and get details on breaking news. Newspapers hired us hacks to go out and do the legwork. We didn't touch a keyboard. It was all in your notebook. Canvass the neighborhood, interview sources, get color for the story. And then you called the paper and asked for rewrite. On the other end was a veteran reporter who would take all the information and build a story. John Mancini, the editor at my day job, where I wrote about hockey fights, local punk bands, and Reiki workshops for the *Long Island Voice*, knew I needed money, and twenty bucks an hour bought a lot of diapers. He gave my number to a former colleague of his at the *Times* and unleashed me with three words of guidance/warning/don't-screw-this-up: "Accuracy, accuracy, accuracy."

I had covered stories for the *Times* before. A tornado on the North Fork. A monkey stolen from a pet store.

But on this Saturday morning, it was different. I got the call I had been hoping for. I was going to report on a murder. My first murder.

I knocked on the door of the split-level house in Syosset. When the door swung open, I could tell by the look on his face that Hamid Tafaghodi, the man who had just handed over $455,000 for the American Dream on Forest Road, was not pleased with the unadvertised amenity in the crawl space.

He had been cleaning out a lot of the junk the previous owners had left behind—wire hangers, cardboard boxes, and a child's ride-on toy sat at the curb in front of the house. Then he spied a barrel under the family room. It was heavy. He told the seller of the house to remove it. Ronald Cohen had his movers roll it out to the street, but the garbage men wouldn't take it, saying there was a chance it could contain toxic waste. Unaware that the rejection was in all likelihood the start of a negotiation and a few twenty-dollar bills might have rid him of the problem, Cohen watched the garbage truck roll away. With his real estate agent next to him, he took a screwdriver and pried open the lid. Inside, he saw a shoe. Then he saw a hand. Then he called the police.

By the time I got there, the homeowner was past being shaken but was weary and not talking. Needing quotes for the story, I started questioning the neighbors.

"Did you know the people who lived in the house before?"

"Had you ever had any dealings with them?"

"Did you ever suspect something like this would happen on your street?"

I collected lukewarm memories from freaked-out residents.

"I just can't understand how this can be undetected for so long," one said. "Wasn't someone declared missing? Wouldn't it smell?"

I found a pay phone, dialed the Nassau County Police Department, and three transfers later was talking to the detective in charge of the case. He told me the barrel had been found in a crawl space underneath the family room. The body in the barrel was a young woman. And the body was well-preserved. Apart from the woman's belongings—including a faux leopard coat and an address book—there were also pellets of a dye that police had learned were used in the manufacturing of plastic flowers. The pellets filled up the empty air pockets in the barrel. Coupled with the tight seal, her body was mummified.

"Is there any idea of how she died?" I asked.

"Nothing we're ready to say," he told me. "I might have more for you later."

My notebook half-full, I called up the *Times* and asked for rewrite. But this time, there was no one available.

"Um, well." I hesitated, then asked the editor, "Can I write it?"

"Yeah," he replied. "We need it by three."

I raced the eight miles to my mom's house in Westbury and sat down in my dad's chair inside the cramped office he had built in the garage. Sales contracts to houses he never got to paint hung on the corkboard behind me. They were in his handwriting, and my mother couldn't bear to take them down.

I had the property record and phone numbers of the last three people who had previously owned the home with the dead body in the crawl space. I picked up my father's old-school beige touch-tone and dialed the number of the first family on the list. A woman answered. "I'm sorry, I can't talk right now," she said after I told her why I was calling. "The police are here."

On to the next one.

I dialed the number of the next name on my list. No answer.

On to the next one.

The last number was for the original owners. They had bought the house in 1957, when it was brand new, when Long Island had graduated from the tract housing of the Levitt homes to split-levels: a garage and a family room on the bottom level; kitchen, living, and dining rooms on the middle floor; and sleeping quarters at the top. This family had lived in the house for fifteen years, moving out in 1972.

The area code was for Boca Raton, Florida. I dialed, and a man answered.

"Hello," I said. "Can I speak to Mr. Howard Elkins?"

"Speaking."

"This is Bill Jensen from the *New York Times*."

"Yes?"

"Hi. Ah, the reason I'm calling is someone just purchased your old house in Syosset, on Long Island."

"Yes?"

"And while they were cleaning it out, they found a barrel. And they opened it, and inside they found a body."

"You're kidding," he said, drawing out the last word. "You're kiiiiidding."

"No," I said.

I read him the details I had gotten from the detective. "The body was that of a woman with long, black hair. She was four foot nine and fifty-nine pounds but had shrunk over time, with the lab later surmising that in life the woman was four foot eleven and ninety-five pounds."

18

I paused for him to say something. He didn't. I kept going.

"She was wearing a skirt, a button-down sweater, high socks, and a midheel shoe. A leopard-skin coat was stuffed next to her body in the drum, which also held residue of coloring dye that was used to make artificial flowers."

I paused and waited for him to say something. He didn't. I kept going.

"And there was a locket around her neck, with the inscription 'To Patrice, love Uncle Phil.' And she wore a wedding band with the inscription M. H. R. XII 59."

I paused for the last time.

"Do any of those details mean anything to you?" I asked.

"No," he said.

"Where was the crawl space?" I asked, steering the conversation to the house, trying to get him to say anything more than a one-word answer.

"We built a room off the kitchen to the back of the house," he explained. "A big den with a fireplace. It was built up to the level of the living room and the kitchen, so there was a crawl space.

"Unbelievable," he added. He stretched out the middle of the word. "Unbelieeeeevable."

"When was this?" he asked. "When did this happen?"

"Yesterday," I said.

I told him that a man had moved into the house, found the barrel, and told the previous owner to get rid of it. I told him that the seller and the real estate agent opened the barrel and saw a hand and a shoe.

"Unbelievable," he repeated.

"Do you have any idea how that might have gotten there?"

"No," he said.

"Did you ever go into the crawl space?" I asked.

"What for?" he said.

This answer made me pause, but not long enough. I had yet to learn the power of uncomfortable silence. As a person, you're conditioned to fill in those gaps in conversation. As a reporter, you let the last word linger. Hang in the air, weaponized and out there all alone. Waiting for the truth to meet it. I should have let it linger, but at that point, I didn't know what the hell I was doing.

"Who could have gone into that crawl space?" I asked.

"Outside of the gardeners and landscapers and the contractor who built the addition, I can't think of anyone else who had access to the house," he said. "We did have maids on and off over the years."

I thanked him for his time, hung up the phone, and opened my clunky brick of a laptop to write up the story. I was ready to send to the *Times* when I got a call from the detective.

"The woman was almost full-term pregnant," he told me.

This was now a double murder.

A missing pregnant woman would have been the lead story on the six o'clock news. Had anyone ever looked for her?

I dialed Elkins again. He didn't answer.

I furiously typed up the new details of the story, noting that the barrel was made in 1963, "and originally contained pigments used to tint plastic and paints, which were no longer made after 1972 or 1973." That at least gave the murder timeline an end date.

I emailed the story to the desk editor and called him to confirm.

"You have it," I said before adding: "Also, I know on my checks it says William Jensen, but I write under Bill Jensen."

"We don't give bylines to stringers," he told me. He apologized. The byline would read "By the *New York Times*."

My name wouldn't be on it, but I had just written my first murder story.

I swung my father's chair around and stared up at his contracts pinned to the wall. Every day since he died, something would happen that made me want to pick up the phone and tell him about it. That day,

I felt it more than ever. I could practically hear him bragging about my story to all the guys on his crew.

The next day, I bought five copies of the *Times*. It was Sunday, and I had to cradle them with two hands.

The headline read NEW HOMEOWNER FINDS BODY OF PREGNANT WOMAN IN A BARREL.

Six days after the story ran, Howard Elkins entered a friend's garage carrying a newly purchased shotgun. He crawled into an SUV and blew his head off.

My phone call had sent his thirty-year secret crashing down on top of him. Five days after my story ran, Nassau County homicide detectives paid him a visit at his Boca Raton retirement condominium community. They asked him about the plastic flower pellets. About his house. About the barrel. He said he didn't know it was there. They asked him if he ever had an affair. He finally admitted to having one.

"Who was the affair with?" they inquired. Elkins said he couldn't remember her name. "What did she look like?" they pressed. He couldn't remember. They asked him why his phone number had been in the address book found alongside the woman's body. He said he had no idea. They asked for a DNA sample to compare it with the fetus in the barrel. He refused to be swabbed. They left without arresting him. They told him they would be in touch.

My call was when Elkins began digging his grave. The visit from the detectives drove the final nail into his coffin.

The murder tale unfolded in the weeks that followed. The fifty-five-gallon drum had been manufactured in Linden, New Jersey, in March 1963 to October 1972. Writing on the drum showed that it had been delivered to the synthetic flower company Melrose Plastics, a company of which Howard Elkins had been part owner.

The crime lab then focused on the address book found with the body. Using an infrared light that could decipher indentations or faded characters on the page, they discovered a series of numbers that had been written on the first page. Those numbers corresponded to alien registration green card, which a search revealed had belonged to an El Salvadoran immigrant named Reyna Angélica Marroquín, who worked at Melrose Plastics in 1969.

Written in the book were also faded words that the lab technicians couldn't make out, as well as a phone number for a woman named Kathy Andrade. The detectives located Andrade, and she spilled the whole story. Her friend Reyna was having an affair with her boss, a man named Howard Elkins. One day, Reyna called Andrade and said she was scared. Reyna said she had told Elkins's wife about the affair and that Elkins was angry. After that phone call, Andrade never heard from Reyna again.

Howard Elkins murdered Reyna and stuffed her body in one of the hundreds of barrels he had access to at Melrose Plastics. Maybe he was thinking of taking it out on a boat and dumping it in the ocean. But it was far too heavy for one person to lift—when it was discovered, the barrel weighed close to 350 pounds, and it would have weighed even more right after Reyna's death. So Elkins chose to roll it under his house and leave the body beneath the family room. Then he and his family lived above Reyna's corpse for three years. He watched TV, read the paper, drank his coffee. He celebrated holidays and birthdays, all above the corpse of the woman he had an affair with, got pregnant, and murdered.

Elkins lived with that secret for thirty years. I thought of the blood that must have drained from his face and into his throat when I said those words: "They found a barrel. And they opened it, and inside they found a body."

Reyna's body was shipped back to El Salvador. The detectives continued to examine Reyna's address book, and the crime lab was finally able to decipher those faded words. They read "Don't be mad I told the truth."

A body was found one day. I spoke to the killer the next day, and he admitted his guilt within the week via a shotgun blast to the head.

It would never be that easy again.

Every weekend, I got to cover another crime for the *Times*: a stabbing at a high school football game. The Amadou Diallo cops coming home after their acquittal. I was on my way to becoming one of the crime beat reporters who my dad would read every day after work. And I was doing my job well enough that when an editor at the *New York Post* asked Mancini if there was anyone who could help out on nights and weekends, he offered me up again. I was going to work for the king of tabloid crime. The paper behind the relentless coverage of Bernie Goetz, the Robert Chambers murder, and the most famous headline in the history of crime: HEADLESS BODY IN TOPLESS BAR.

But my first assignment for the *Post* changed everything.

"We need you to go to Stony Brook Hospital," said the voice on the phone. Two teenage girls had been driving around Suffolk County when they encountered a pair of closing railroad crossing signals. The girl behind the wheel decided to tempt fate and go around the gates. She didn't make it, and the train smashed into their car. The girls were taken to the hospital in critical condition. The *Post* wanted their story.

I turned off my newly purchased cell phone, walked into the emergency waiting room, and immediately spotted the mother and father of one of the girls. They were the only ones who were weeping. I sat down for a minute, trying to think of what I was going to say to them. I finally walked over and kneeled down next to the man.

"Hi," I said just above a whisper. "I'm Bill Jensen from the *New York Post*," I said. "I'm so sorry. Could I ask you a few questions?"

He raised his head and gave me the most shattered look anyone has ever given me. Then he shook his head.

I found a pay phone in the lobby and called the *Post*.

"The family doesn't want to talk," I said.

The voice on the other end didn't hesitate.

"Go in and ask them again." *Click.*

I placed the receiver back on the cradle and walked around the hospital hallways for what seemed like days, trying to assemble enough courage to go back into that room. If hospitals had bars, I would have been drinking. After fifteen minutes, I approached the man and woman again.

"I'm sorry, but we are just trying to get some information. Do you think we could talk?"

The woman looked at the man, and the man gave me the same look as before. I waited a beat, then got out of there as quick as I could without running. I called the *Post* back.

"Hey, I'm sorry. They really don't want…"

He cut me off. "It's okay," the voice said. "We just got back the girl's rap sheet, and it's a mile long. It's fine." *Click.*

I hung up the phone and walked out of the hospital, earning the most shameful forty dollars I ever earned in my life. I don't even know if the girls survived the night. Limping home, something bubbled up from the pit of my churning stomach: This was not what I wanted. I was on course to be a crime beat reporter, writing rubbernecking articles about bad things that happened to people but not doing anything to help. At that moment, I was done. I wanted to write stories that actually helped change things. I wanted to try to solve murders. I wanted to get that feeling back. The feeling I got when I was a kid and my dad showed me the cover of paper with the headline WE HAVE HIM stamped over the .44 Caliber Killer's head. The feeling of solving the crime. I wanted to see some order given to this chaos.

I made the decision right then and there: I would only write about unsolved crimes.

3

THE MURDER IN THE SHADOWS

Brooklyn, 2002

THE *LONG ISLAND VOICE* SHUT DOWN IN 2000, THE PRECUR-
sor to many other newspaper shutterings to come. After two years of
toiling about at editor jobs for trade magazines, I got a call from Robbie
Woliver, the former music editor at the *Voice*. He was starting a new
newspaper—something unheard of after the crash of 2000. He had an
investor and needed to build up a staff, and he wanted me as his manag-
ing editor. I was excited to make my day job news again.

We took over the old *Island Ear*, a free music and entertainment
biweekly newspaper that you could pick up at 7-Elevens and bars on Long
Island. But we were not just going to concentrate on arts and music. We
wanted to turn it into an edgy newsweekly with hard-hitting stories, and
we needed to make a big splash. I was tasked with finding the one Long
Islander we knew would make headlines. The Long Islander who showed
up higher on Google searches than Teddy Roosevelt and Walt Whitman.

After a series of phone calls with her lawyer, Woliver and I found
ourselves at dinner with Amy Fisher, the Long Island Lolita. In 1992,
the teenage Fisher earned worldwide infamy when she shot Mary Jo
Buttafuoco, the wife of her thirty-six-year-old lover, in the head. Fisher
was now out of prison after serving a seven-year sentence, and Mary Jo

had forgiven her. Meanwhile, Joey Buttafuoco, the man in the middle of this true-crime drama, had since gone to jail for statutory rape against the then sixteen-year-old high school student. The story had captivated the nation. We wanted to know if Amy would be interested in writing a fashion column for the paper. She had told Matt Lauer in her first postprison interview that she wanted to work in the fashion industry. To prepare for the meeting, I had bought a bunch of fashion magazines to get ideas for her column, poring over them and jotting down notes. After spending hours inside *Vogue, Harper's,* and even *Women's Wear Daily,* I considered myself adequately prepared to speak to the idea and come away from dinner with a new fashion columnist who would make headlines. But before the appetizers were served, Amy told us she didn't want to write about fashion. She wanted to write about crime. Woliver and I both looked at each other and smiled. Her first cover story, in which she explained why she shot Mary Jo, got the now-rechristened *New Island Ear* on the map. News outlets from across the globe heralded the return and rehabilitation of the Long Island Lolita and introduced our newspaper to the world.

Our next big issue was the first anniversary of 9/11.

The terrorist attacks of 2001 are the most analyzed crime in American history. The *New York Times* and *Washington Post* had teams of reporters uncovering who the hijackers were, how they got into the country, and how they received their training. CNN focused on Osama bin Laden and the inevitable war that followed the attacks. Every local newspaper searched for their local angle—hijackers attending flight school in Phoenix, eating at Pizza Hut, and buying box cutters in Maine. Every news outlet would be devoting weeks of coverage to the anniversary, commemorating the worst mass murder in American history.

I had to find the gravedigger.

That's the term uttered by every editor to every reporter when they're looking for a fresh angle to a well-tread story. It comes from when the hordes of reporters descended upon Washington for President Kennedy's funeral after he was assassinated in November 1963. They were all telling the same story, except *New York Herald Tribune* reporter Jimmy Breslin. Breslin decided to tell the story of Clifton Pollard, the man who was digging the president's grave at Arlington National Cemetery. He filed a somber tale about a working man tasked with the final job after one of the most infamous murders in history.

I found my gravedigger of 9/11 in the story of Henryk Siwiak. The forty-six-year-old had lost his job in Poland, and that country's failing economy and 15-percent unemployment rate was making it impossible to find another. He had a wife and two children, one of whom was college bound. He came to New York in the fall of 2000 and took any job he could find, sending whatever money he could make back to his family.

On the morning of September 11, 2001, Siwiak was scouring downtown Manhattan, looking for work, when two planes smashed into the World Trade Center towers. He continued answering want ads and calling on businesses, even after the towers fell. When he realized that no jobs were going to be offered amid the chaos, he walked across one of the bridges connecting Manhattan with Brooklyn and got back to his apartment on Beach Street in Rockaway, Queens. Then he made phone calls to his wife and son back home in Poland.

"I'm okay," he told them before recounting the story of how he saw one of the planes fly into the towers and how he heard the rumbles when the buildings came crashing down.

At 11:42 p.m. on a pleasant tree-lined street six miles from the World Trade Center, Henryk Siwiak fell to the ground with a bullet in his chest.

There were 2,997 people murdered in New York City on September 11. The public and the authorities know who killed 2,996 of them.

A year after Siwiak was killed, I traveled to Rockaway Beach and sat at the kitchen table in the hot-pink apartment of Lucyana Siwiak,

Henryk's sister. A soap opera was playing on the television, and her brother's death certificate lay on the table in front of her.

She told me that when Henryk lost his job as an inspector with the Polish National Railroad and made the decision to come to America, he settled in the same Rockaway neighborhood as Lucyana, who had come to America six years earlier after her health food store in Poland went under. He left his wife and children behind in Poland and set out for the New World.

"He saw possibility for himself," Lucyana told me, her English aided by a handheld digital translator she had placed on the table next to the death certificate.

Though he had a fevered interest in science, Henryk failed to go to college after high school. Instead, he earned a technical school degree. He married a scientist named Ewa, who was now a middle-school biology teacher, and the couple had an eleven-year-old son and a daughter who was nineteen and about to enter college the following year.

I called Ewa in Krakow, Poland.

"He lost more than one job," she said almost with a laugh. After losing his inspection post, Ewa said Henryk "decided to go and try something else" and went to America.

Even with the language barrier, his plan to provide for his family was working. Siwiak performed odd jobs and did temp work in construction, laboring at a determined pitch. He earned close to $1,000 every month and sent half back to his family.

"Did you see the news on TV about the attacks?" I asked Ewa.

"Oh, it was horrible," Ewa said. She watched the news with her son. "We thought about our own husband and father [Henryk]."

On 9/11, they waited for two hours before Henryk finally got back to his apartment and phoned them. "We were very happy when he called us," Ewa said. Like many New Yorkers, even though he had seen the plane hit the towers, Siwiak was still unaware of the magnitude of the situation—that coordinated attacks on New York, the Pentagon, and a crash in rural Pennsylvania meant the country was under attack. Ewa filled him in, and Siwiak comforted his son.

Lucyana told me that Siwiak had settled into his apartment on the night of 9/11 when his phone rang. It was a callback from a help wanted ad he had answered in New York's Polish newspaper *Super Express*: "Men to Clean Stores in Brooklyn and Queens. English Not Necessary."

Siwiak was told by the employment agency that had posted the ad to meet a man named Adam in a white car at the Pathmark supermarket at 1520 Albany Avenue in Brooklyn.

Because he had never met the man, Siwiak told the agency he would be wearing his favorite coat, a camouflage army jacket with matching pants that he had bought at a local surplus store.

"He liked very much these clothes," Lucyana told me. "They were very comfortable."

With the entire city on edge and in chaos, not knowing whether a series of car bombs would start in the morning or a chemical attack would be unleashed at midnight, Henryk walked out the door.

He had never been to that part of Brooklyn before, and much of the transit system was shut down. But he got directions from a woman who lived in his building and went off to his new job.

The next day, his sister received a phone call from the police. Henryk's body had been found on Decatur Avenue in Bedford-Stuyvesant, nowhere near the Pathmark he was supposed to be cleaning.

"Any idea what he was doing so far away from where he was supposed to be?" I asked Lieutenant Tom Joyce, the head of the seventy-ninth precinct's detective squad.

He told me that the woman Henryk had asked for directions was actually his landlord.

"She showed him on the map where Albany Avenue was," he said. But unbeknownst to her, "the point she was directing him to was the start of Albany Avenue. That's what's so sad about this, that he was so far off."

At around eleven o'clock, Henryk got off at either the Utica, Ralph, Kingston, or Throop Street stops, more than four miles away from where he should have been. For a man with limited English in a city reeling from an attack, it might as well have been a thousand miles. "Adam," the man he was supposed to meet, told police he waited for Siwiak for an hour outside the Pathmark before giving up and going inside to clean.

Meanwhile, Henryk walked down Decatur Street in Bedford-Stuyvesant, lost.

The main thoroughfares surrounding Bedford-Stuyvesant are full of storefront churches. The Church of God of Prophecy. Pleasant Grove Tabernacle. Spiritual Israel Church and Its Army. Greater Mount Zion Pentecostal. Violent crime was down 61 percent since 1993, its "Bed-Stuy: Do or Die" reputation shrinking block by block, empty storefronts replaced by quaint coffee shops and bookstores.

The residential blocks surrounding the quiet intersection of Albany and Decatur feature brownstones and gated gardens, a stone church and a funeral home. The crack cocaine epidemic lasted longer here than in most neighborhoods, but by 2001, it had receded into the shadows.

On the night of 9/11, Bed-Stuy was like every other neighborhood in America, scared and confused.

Joyce shared the police report with me. It was sparse. I drove to Bed-Stuy, a neighborhood I had never been to, parked my car on the street, and began walking the area.

I approached every person I saw with a photo of Henryk in my hand.

"Hi, do you remember the shooting that happened on 9/11?" I asked two men walking down Decatur.

"Nah, man," one of them replied.

"Hi, can you take a look at this photo?" I asked another man on Albany. "This was the guy that was shot on the night of 9/11 in the neighborhood."

He squinted at the photo, paused for a beat, then shook his head.

"Hi, have you ever heard any stories about a guy who was shot on this street the night of 9/11?"

I received a sneering no.

I must have asked fifty people. Then I found Sharonnie Perry, the district director for the local congressman, who was working out of a storefront a few blocks away from the murder scene. She remembered the night well.

"Things were a little tense and everything," Perry told me, saying that there were "at least twenty-five to thirty people outside," late into the night.

She saw Henryk that night. In his army surplus outfit, he walked east on Decatur and found the street he was looking for, Albany Avenue. He turned south and then maybe realized how far off he actually was, as the numbers on the apartment buildings started at 6 and 8.

"He was carrying a bag and holding a piece of paper in his hands, like he was looking for an address."

Other people saw him too. A stranger walking through Bedford-Stuyvesant at night, wearing army fatigues and carrying a bag just fourteen hours after the worst terrorist attack in U.S. history was not going to go unnoticed.

Perry watched as Henryk walked south on Albany to a phone booth at the corner of Albany and Fulton. She then saw him walk back, down Albany toward Decatur.

"I saw him coming up the block," Perry recalled. "There were some guys following him."

Perry told me she saw three men. She said they had started following him south of Atlantic Avenue, home to what she called the "very desolate" Albany Projects.

She didn't see the shots, but she heard them. When she looked toward the building at 119 Decatur, she saw people scatter. Then she saw Henryk on the ground.

"He still had the paper in his hands when he got shot."

She couldn't give me a description of the three men who were following Henryk. I asked twice but knew—for whatever reason—it wasn't going to happen.

I knocked on every door within two blocks of the murder scene. Across the street and about ten doors down, I found one man who wouldn't give his name but was willing to talk about what he heard that night.

"Six, seven, eight shots, one after another," he told me. "Not a machine gun, more like a 9mm." He got out of bed and dialed 911.

"The cops came pretty quick. There was a body across the street. The guy was dressed in army fatigues, lying on the sidewalk in front of the steps. His backpack was up on the step, at the door."

He told me the police had been there a year ago and had knocked on all the doors just like I was doing. "They were talking to people. But they were almost not expecting to get a lot of information. Everyone was kind of shocked about it. The people congregating outside the police tape were asking 'Who knew him?' It was strange to see a white guy. At first, I thought he was a soldier."

Joyce told me the police responded within one minute of the first 911 call. They recovered multiple casings, all from the same gun, indicating Siwiak was fired at multiple times but was only hit once. According to the certificate of death, M.E. case No. K01–4192, death was caused by "gunshot wound to the chest with lung and musculoskeletal injuries." Siwiak's wallet, with cash, was found on his body.

Lucyana wrote to the Polish consulate, with the only result being a twenty-minute meeting and no follow-up. She contacted the police, who she said told her, "probably a black criminal shot him, that's it."

But Lucyana doesn't believe it. "Criminals stop it this evening, in New York, almost completely," she said.

"I think you see, he was in this army jacket and pants. There were many, many policemen came from other states. And probably they met him and ask him. Maybe [he was] looking like Arab. He have ID in pocket. He never understood about if police say 'hand up.'"

"So you're saying you think a police officer shot Henryk?" I asked her.

"Yes. Maybe he want to explain and show ID and put his hand in his pocket and they shot in this moment."

Ewa Siwiak agreed with her sister in-law. "Police in New York said it was a robber and nothing more. But my husband had five dollars in his pocket."

According to Joyce, Siwiak actually had close to seventy dollars in his wallet. But he swiftly rejected the idea that he was shot by a police officer.

"It was a unique caliber gun," Joyce told me. "If it was a cop, it definitely wasn't a cop's firearm."

Joyce said the police canvassed the area for three days but found only one witness who remembered seeing Siwiak walking in the neighborhood. "Do I believe there is someone out there that saw something?" Joyce asked. "Yes."

Maybe I would have a little more luck. I had already found one person who saw him walking, the same number as the entire New York Police Department had uncovered, although I wasn't sure if it was the same person or not, because Joyce wouldn't reveal his witness's identity.

I knocked on the doors along the houses of Decatur and Albany again, climbing up the twelve steps to the front door of each row house, the presence of the church down the street giving me a false sense of comfort.

Of the people who answered their doors, most claimed no knowledge of the shooting. Those who did remembered it only as "the Polish guy with fatigues on." I turned a corner, and a man in a tan sedan pulled up next to me and actually asked me if I was lost. A six-foot-four, skinny white guy with a dopey haircut walking around Bedford-Stuyvesant might very well have looked like he was lost.

I told Joyce that I had walked the neighborhood and asked everyone I could find about the murder.

"You took a really big risk," he said. "You probably talked to someone who knows who did it."

I gave Joyce all the information of the people I spoke to, hoping they might help, but no arrests came.

Lucyana brought her brother's ashes back to Krakow, where the Siwiak family and his children's schoolmates attended a funeral. "My mother tries to understand his death," Lucyana said to me. "In ocean of death, his death was just one drop more. But she can't understand. She saw the TV. She thinks he died in the World Trade Center."

Lucyana said that Ewa was coping the best she could as her children live life without a father.

"She told me about her son. He's thinking about his father's death. He keeps saying that 'I was very, very bad boy, and God said—'" Lucyana opened up her handheld translator, typed in the word *kara* and pressed translate. She showed me the word that appeared on the screen in English. "—and God said 'penalty, punishment.'"

I pleaded with Joyce to give me any information I could publish that might jostle some answers from the neighborhood residents. The caliber of the gun. The identity of the witness he talked to. The descriptions of the three men who had followed Siwiak. Anything. He told me it was an ongoing investigation and he couldn't release details.

In the newspaper, people read the story to the end. But in Siwiak's story, there was no end. It was my first of a thousand dances with the guy who got away with it.

After the story was published, I began receiving letters from people asking if I could help investigate the unsolved murder of their daughter, their sister, their son. A wave of sorrow and anger and a small, miniscule bit of hope washed over me. For five years, I had been reaching out to people to tell their stories. Trying to convince them that the story would be in careful hands. Now people were coming to me. People who had lost the thing they held most dear. It was overwhelming. But I knew this is what I was going to do for the rest of my life.

A few months later, a woman named Donna Kakura sent me a small article in the *New York Post*. The headline read POLICE SUSPECT VILLAGE SUICIDE. It was about her brother, a man named Brian Boothe. He was found dead on Christmas Day in his Manhattan apartment, the victim of a knife wound to the neck.

Kakura told me her other brother, Tommy, had committed suicide just three months earlier, pumping carbon monoxide into the car he had been living in. The *Post* and the police thought they connected the dots: a gay male spending Christmas Eve alone, whose brother had recently taken his own life... It had to be suicide.

"Brian did *not* commit suicide," Donna told me.

"We kept saying 'It's got nothing to do with it,'" his mother said to me. "Brian was the least affected by Tommy's death." He hadn't spoken to his brother in years.

His mother shared with me stories about Brian from when he was little. About him putting on song-and-dance shows in the backyard. She remembers his beekeeping phase, along with the day the bees got loose and flew away and Brian cried. She remembers him staying home on Thanksgiving while his family went to the parade because he wanted to help cook, and the time he waited anxiously as the family tried his fresh-baked cookies, only to see everyone spit them out, realizing too late that he had confused baking soda for baking powder.

And grown-up Brian seemed happier than ever. He had a good job in human resources. He was planning a family ski trip. A friend whom he had had lunch with the day before his death said Brian was gleeful and anxiously awaiting the birth of his other brother's baby girl, who they planned on naming Cassidy.

After work on Christmas Eve, Brian went to the Gap to buy presents for his two nieces. He stopped at a Rite Aid drug store, then the dollar store for wrapping paper, before returning to his apartment. He called his mother to finalize plans for Christmas dinner and then went out for a drink.

Witnesses said they saw Brian at Phoenix Bar in the East Village at 6:15 p.m. Later that night, he was placed at Wonder Bar. Brian's last known stop was the Cock on Avenue A, which he left around 1:00 a.m. The Cock is "a place you would go at the end of the night if you wanted to pick up," Brian's best friend, Tom Gestal, told me.

But no one saw Brian leave. And no one saw Brian come home. There was no doorman at his Stuyvesant Town apartment, just a buzzer system. He lived on the eighth floor.

When he failed to show up for Christmas dinner, Donna's husband, Joe, and brother Jimmy drove to his apartment. Jimmy would sometimes crash at Brian's place and used his key to get in. They opened the door and found Brian's body in a pool of blood in the bedroom doorway.

There was no sign of forced entry or a struggle. Three beer bottles were on the kitchen counter.

The weapon, possibly a knife from Brian's kitchen, was found in the apartment. Donna told me she thought that it had been found in the bag of gifts, since the family had yet to receive the stuffed animal Christmas presents back from the police.

Brian's laptop and cell phone were missing, but $160 was found in his wallet in his dresser drawer.

The *New York Post* story cited unnamed police sources who said "it was probably a suicide." The *Daily News* referred to unnamed "authorities," who said Brian "may have taken his own life."

The autopsy concluded that he had died of a knife wound to the left side of his neck, which lacerated his trachea and esophagus. The family wanted to get an investigation going. They wanted to set up a reward. They wanted to get Crime Stoppers involved. They just wanted some action. But Brian's death was still being classified, unofficially, as a suicide by the NYPD.

"We can't put up an award if the medical examiner hasn't declared it a homicide," a medical examiner's office spokesperson told me.

Brian's death was finally declared a homicide in the middle of April (I guess they realized that he couldn't have stabbed himself in the neck like that), and the family got their wanted posters by mid-May. By then, the killer's trail was ice-cold. Anyone who might have remembered Brian or who he might have been chatting with at the Cock that night was long gone.

"I am 99.9 percent sure he picked someone up at that bar," Gestal told me. "I hung out with that guy so much. I know his moves."

The niece Brian so gleefully looked forward to meeting was born seven weeks after his murder. Instead of Cassidy, they named her Brianna.

Life went on. So did his killer. A killer I was sure would kill again. A killer who might have been in town for the holidays, went to the bar, found his victim, killed him, and was gone by New Year's. I wrote the story and tried to catch him—or at least put pressure on the police to do so.

I failed. My second villain slipped away. But I was about to get a lot more chances to bring murderers into the light.

Donna introduced me to the Long Island chapter of the Parents of

Murdered Children, a group that provides resources for family members whose loved ones were victims of a homicide. She invited me to their annual luncheon at the Milleridge Inn in Jericho, where they presented me with an award for telling Brian's story when no one else would. After lunch, all the family members of all the victims went out on the front lawn, carrying balloons with the names of their loved ones written in Magic Marker. Then they all let them go into the air. Hundreds of them, flying over Jericho Turnpike and out toward the Long Island Sound. Some of the families stayed on the lawn and watched until they couldn't see their balloon anymore. I drove home shaken.

A week later, the letters started arriving, almost all of them ending with two words: "Please help."

When the mother of a murdered child writes you—a mother whose child's killer is still on the loose—it's hard not to get involved.

The difficult task of the American homicide detective is compounded by the ever-growing mountain of bodies. The five thousand murders that go unsolved each year pile on top of each other. If a detective is working on a murder investigation and five more people are killed that week, they have to drop what they are doing and investigate one of the new ones before the trail goes cold. The image of a detective taking home files every night to work that one case that haunts them is not Hollywood fiction. It happens. But it's just one or two cases. If you get killed in America, there is a 38 percent chance your killer won't be caught.

The mothers, fathers, sisters, and brothers writing the *please help* letters told me about how the police were not calling them back. They asked what they could do to get the media to pay attention. They talked about how everyone had moved on and forgotten.

I began writing about as many victims as I could. The doctor who was suffocated in her home in '96. The brunette who went missing while walking to a bar the night before Halloween in '81. The torso with the heart-shaped peach tattoo found in a state park in '97. The flight attendant who was raped and murdered while on a layover in Boise in 2000. The elderly woman who was found stabbed to death inside her burned-out Wantagh home in '85.

I talked to family members and witnesses and possible accomplices.

"He got mad and hit me in the stomach and said 'we ain't going to the law,'" Pee Wee Walton said of one of the men who assaulted Nancy Santomero and Vicki Durian before they were murdered outside a music festival in West Virginia in 1980. "We've got to clean this place up," he heard another man say. "We might want to party here again."

"I know you are watching over us," read one of the messages written on the utility pole at the intersection where fifteen-year-old Jessica Savarese was murdered by an anonymous driver in 2004. "The emptiness inside is killing me," read another.

I maneuvered from hit-and-run stories that veered into wonky government sagas to tales of unidentified remains found near the million-dollar homes on the Gold Coast of Long Island.

"In all likelihood, she was killed elsewhere and carried here," the Nassau County chief of detectives said to me as we walked through the Muttontown preserve woods to where a skull was found in 2001. A few hours after the skull, detectives found what was left of her skeleton, crunched in a fetal position between two trees.

I created a section in the newspaper—which had now morphed from the *New Island Ear* into a weekly called the *Long Island Press*—that I called "Long Island Confidential," a hat tip to the James Ellroy novel. Each week, I penned a feature story, profiled a cold case, and maintained a running list of Long Island's top ten fugitives, a subjective list chosen by me.

Every week, I hoped my reporting, my prying, or just my shaking of the trees might lead to a new piece of information to get the family closer to an answer. Every week, I came back with nothing.

The killers were still out there, not only escaping justice for the stories I told but free to kill again, believing they had the right to take someone else's life. That thought makes my teeth gnash and my lip snarl and my jaw fill with a scream. A scream that always has the same chorus. What they took away, seemingly so easily, was a person. "This was a person!"

A person who could watch a sunset and feel the wind against their cheek. Smell fresh-cut grass or listen to a Bowie song. A person who could scrape up enough money to buy themselves a hot-fudge sundae. A person who could still close their eyes and dream.

That's what the media refuses to understand. No matter how down and out someone may seem, no matter how many drugs they took or arrests they had or rock bottoms they hit—they could have still done all those things. Those things that make us human.

And one day, someone came along and took all those things away. Every single one of them. And left them with darkness.

I envy the people on TV with their hands in the air praising glory to God on high. I wish I could believe in an afterlife. More than anything. For me, death is not a door or a window. It is the most terrifying thing I can think of. It's the definition of nothing.

And no one should be given the right to deliver another into that abyss before their time. Those were the villains I wanted to chase. To make things right, yes. But also to maybe save the next person from that nothingness coming too soon.

4.
—

HAVE YOU SEEN THIS MAN?

Long Island, 1978–1998

WHEN I STARTED FIRST GRADE, I REBELLED HARD AGAINST the early bedtime that came with elementary school. I was now supposed to wake up at 8:00 a.m. every day? And for what? Nap time replaced by math? Picture books like *Where the Wild Things Are* replaced by chapter books like *Frog and Toad are Friends*? I guess I wasn't convinced it was worth it, and bedtime became a problem. My mom handed nighttime duties over to my dad. And Dad started to tell me a story. His story, beginning from when he was a little boy all the way up till when I was born.

The first night started with 1950s postwar picket-fence stuff: Cub Scouts, diving under desks for air raid drills. Then he came to the part of the story about Paul Jud.

"One day, I was out sick from school," he began. "And when I came back the next day, my friend Paul wasn't there. I asked the teacher, 'Where's Paul?' And she said, 'Paul's gone.'

"She told me he was running in front of the school bus when he dropped his lunch box. And he ran back to pick it up. The bus driver didn't see him. And the bus ran him over."

My dad's face changed.

"He was there one day. And then I came back to school, and he wasn't there anymore," he said as he tucked me in. "And it was like every-thing was normal, but my friend was gone."

Dad never took me to church. The only spirituality in my house was the two posters he had tacked on the wall of the family den. One was the poem "Desiderata," which begins, "Go placidly amid the noise and haste, and remember what peace there may be in silence." The other was a quote from Coolidge: "Nothing in the world can take the place of persistence." Heaven was not a place my dad believed in. The idea that if a person didn't believe in a certain god they would be left out of heaven, no matter how just and good a life they might have led, was something Dad could never reconcile. He wanted to believe but couldn't.

"When you're dead, you're dead," he told me.

I was six.

By the second week of the bedtime story, he told me about the day his brother convinced him to steal a fishing tackle box from Modell's department store, and how he got caught and all his friends got away and he was sent to juvie. He told me about the gangs he was in, the Asphalt Angels and the Jesters, how they would rumble with other gangs from neighboring towns, and how they would decide on the rules before each fight—skin, sticks, knives, but never guns.

He told me about the time in high school when he mouthed off to the gym teacher and the teacher actually punched him in the face. "I came home and told my father, and he took the side of the gym teacher," he said, his anger long ago replaced by his new responsibility to protect me.

Then he was caught throwing spitballs in the cafeteria and for the rest of the year was forced to sit at a table with a bunch of older girls. Each day, he asked one of the girls if she was going to finish her lunch. He finally got up the courage to ask her to a movie, one of those beach movies. But he made the date for the daytime and blushed when they arrived at the theater and realized that the matinee was different from the evening show. He sheepishly followed my mother to their seats, and they watched the cartoon *Gulliver's Travels* by the Fleischer Brothers.

By the third week, he told me how he ran away from home when he was fifteen, stealing his father's rare-coin collection, buying an ID off an older, tattoo-covered greaser named Chris Keer, and hopping on a Greyhound for Los Angeles. Halfway through the trip, he felt bad and mailed the coins back, but he made it to LA. He went straight to Hollywood and Vine, which he had heard on the radio was the center of the universe, and got a job parking cars at a restaurant. When they discovered his real age, he was fired and went to work selling encyclopedias door to door. He sold one set.

He told me how when he was in LA, he traveled south one weekend to Tijuana and went to a whorehouse, determined to lose his virginity. He remembered that, inside, there was a line of men just waiting around, yet there were plenty of available women in the room.

"I asked the guy in front of me, 'What is everyone waiting for?' He told me 'The best girls are upstairs. They are busy. We're waiting for them to come back.'" Dad told me about how he waited and picked the girl he wanted.

"Okay, bedtime."

After a month in LA, he returned to Long Island. But he was never going back to live with his family. He lived hand to mouth, on friends' couches or on the street. One night, he was walking through TSS, a department store in Levittown. "I saw a sweater that I liked. I put it on, over my shirt, and started to walk out of the store. I'm on the escalator, and this woman comes up behind me. She grabs my arm with both her hands and says"—my father clenched his teeth—"'Move, and I'll break it.'

"I stood there, waiting for the escalator to hit the floor. Waiting. Waiting. And as soon as it did, I flung her off me. Whoosh!" He threw his arm in the air. "She went flying.

"I started running toward the front doors of the store. I was twenty feet away when this guy ran up to me. I didn't think. I just reeled back and *bam*! I punched him right in the face." The guy tumbled into a rack of clothes.

"Turns out he was an off-duty detective," my dad said.

By then, I was far too wired to even think about sleep.

Dad was arrested and taken to the precinct. There, he gave his name as Chris Keer, the name on the ID he had purchased before he ran away to Los Angeles.

But the police were familiar with the real Chris Keer—he had been in trouble before and had arms full of tattoos. They knew my dad wasn't him.

He said they ran his fingerprints through the FBI and got nothing. Then they tried a different tactic: they went to the media.

"They ran my picture in *Newsday*," he told me, "with the headline Do You Know This Man?"

He said his parents saw the story and told the police that the man in their custody was actually a fifteen-year-old boy named William Jensen.

He was sent to Nassau County Jail. They offered his parents a deal—he could do a year in prison with the adults or two years at Coxsackie, which was then the youth reformatory where New York City and Long Island sent their bad boys. My dad begged his mother to let him go to the adult prison. But she refused, and he was shipped upstate.

The next week, my bedtime stories got a lot more graphic. Dad told me tales of fighting in the yard, of shivs, of fibbing that he was from Brooklyn so he would have tougher friends than the Long Island kids, and of playing a lot of chess.

He got out of Coxsackie, hid from the draft, got hooked on heroin, kicked the habit, then learned how to paint houses, married my mother, and eventually started his own business with the goal of giving me the life he had always wanted.

It was a wild tale, and it stuck with me long past those elementary school bedtimes. As a teenager, I remember going to the library to find the article of the mystery man wanted for punching a detective in the face. I believed my dad's story, but I just wanted to see it in print. I went through spool after spool of microfiche but didn't find it.

Throughout the story, one thing was clear. Dad never had a best friend. Someone he could tell stories to. Someone he trusted above all else. So he made one—me. And we did everything together.

Every carnival he saw being assembled in a church parking lot on his way home from work? We were there the next night. Every cool playground he noticed with a rocket ship jungle gym or giant slide? We were there that Sunday. Every movie that looked completely inappropriate for an eight-year-old, from *Stripes* to *Animal House*? We went. When wrestling got big, we were at Madison Square Garden when Hulk Hogan won the belt and at the first WrestleMania with Mr. T and Cyndi Lauper. We would head back home from Penn Station, Dad letting me pick out a comic book from the newsstand to read on the train. But I would never read it because we spent the ride back talking about what we had just seen. ("Did you see when Ali punched Piper!?") Because that was what best friends did. Same when we drove to Shea Stadium or Nassau Coliseum, listening to doo-wop or the Beatles. When the demented final chords of "Helter Skelter" ended with Ringo shouting "I got blisters on my fingers!" he told me about Sharon Tate and how Charles Manson's family attacked her and cut her baby out of her womb and wrote the word *pig* on the walls in her blood. The cutting-the-baby-out part turned out to be urban myth, but it all stuck with me.

My parents let me stay home alone for the first time when I was eleven. They left me with two Stouffer's French bread pizzas, the remote cable box, and instructions not to burn down the house.

They didn't say anything about what I could or couldn't watch on TV.

That first night, I sat transfixed on the floor, chewing my poorly cooked pizza and learning about my impending doom. *The Man Who Saw Tomorrow* was a documentary on HBO about Nostradamus, the Frenchman who supposedly wrote hundreds of quatrains that predicted the future. The booming voice of Orson Welles told of the rise of Napoleon. The rise of Hitler. The rise of a blue-turbaned tyrant in the Middle East, launching missiles to start World War III, one of the nukes landing with a deafening crash in the center of New York City.

But that wasn't what freaked me out that night. World War III? The end of the world? Those events, I thought, were inevitable.

What freaked me out was the man on the grassy knoll.

We got to the part about the Kennedy assassination. I watched as the president rode in his limousine in Dallas, smiling and waving to the crowd. Then I watched his head explode. Jackie climbed onto the trunk to collect pieces of his skull. But then the camera zoomed into the bushes behind her and showed an outline of what looked like a man sitting among the leaves, holding a rifle.

Nostradamus had apparently predicted that there would be an assassin in front of the president.

Apparently, no one else saw him that day. But I saw him. Or at least I thought I did.

"There's a guy with a rifle! In the bushes! He shot the president! I have to tell someone!" I yelled in my head.

That Monday, I marched into the school library and asked for every book they had on the Kennedy assassination. I spent the next forty-five minutes poring over autopsy reports.

I went back the next day. And the next. And the next.

"Can I have all the Kennedy assassination books?"

Soon, the librarian would see me coming and I didn't even have to ask. Today, that might have gotten me on a watch list, but back then, I was just the skinny kid obsessed with blood-spatter patterns and magic-bullet theories.

After a month of spending my lunch period inside Dealey Plaza, I came to the conclusion that Nostradamus was probably a fraud. It took a few more years for me to conclude that Oswald probably acted alone. But along the way, I graduated to the Son of Sam and Manson murders. I devoured Vincent Bugliosi's *Helter Skelter*, Ann Rule's *The Stranger Beside Me*, and Maury Terry's *The Ultimate Evil*, about the Cotton Club Murder and Arlis Perry's rape and brutalization inside the Stanford University church, where her attackers inserted a three-foot long altar candle inside her and shoved an ice pick in the back of her head.

My mother lent me that book after she read it.

I didn't have anything to rebel against when it came to my parents. My mom gave me true-crime books, and my dad was my best friend.

As my dad was molding and shaping his own mini me, he was certain I would grow up and take over the family house-painting business. He was so sure of it that he never thought that I would do anything else. But sitting in the seats at Shea, listening to me rattle off Mookie Wilson's on-base percentage, it occurred to him that maybe he should start saving money for college.

I never became the rough-and-tumble brawler my dad once thought he was building. Instead, I became a romantic. A devotee of the Smiths and the Cure, Sisters of Mercy and Depeche Mode. Pining after a girl, writing goth-drenched poems I would never show her. I was the boy in the back of the class with the weird haircut, a folded-up copy of Rimbaud's *A Season in Hell* slipped into the pocket of my thrift-store overcoat, which I wore over my leather jacket, which I wore over my denim jacket, which I wore over an army surplus shirt, which I wore over a *The Queen Is Dead* T-shirt.

My armor. Every layer. Anything to hide me from the world and my skinny arms from the sunlight.

I painted my room black with jagged white lightning stripes and wrote poems and song lyrics on the wall. I hated my handwriting, so I asked Dad to use his rock-steady hands to write them.

Dad looked past the melodrama. He was just a house painter helping his son fulfill his vision of sleeping in a black room with a David Bowie lyric scrawled on the wall.

My bedroom was absent of all light, save for those jagged white lines, giving it a jittery, spinning effect like I was sleeping inside one of those balls of simulated lightning you could buy at Spencer's Gifts. I would drift asleep to *The Rise and Fall of Ziggy Stardust and the Spiders from Mars*.

In the fall of 1990, I walked into a cream-colored room on the seventh floor of Myles Standish Hall residence at Boston University, lay down on the long, narrow mattress, stared up at the ceiling, and wondered what the hell I was doing there.

A few weeks later, Dad came to visit with two gallons of black paint and helped me cover my dorm room in darkness, accompanied by those jagged white lines, to make it feel more like my angst-drenched bedroom from home. He may have never understood why I was all gothed out, but he always did everything he could to make everything all right for me, including coming back up when the school year ended to paint the room back to its original, inoffensive beige.

He also didn't quite understand what his $80,000 was going to be paying for when I told him what I wanted to study.

———————————

On the first day of college, I was locked out of two of the classes I wanted to get into and wandered into a religious studies class. At the end of the first week, the professor invited anyone who was interested to listen to a talk later that evening. The topic would be "The Hero with a Thousand Faces."

From Gilgamesh to Odysseus to Jesus, every hero was following in each other's well-worn footsteps, he explained, going through the same trials, delivering the same rewards.

"Even Luke Skywalker."

"Wait, what?" I sat up. "Skywalker?"

That night, I walked into a wood-paneled room on Bay State Road along the Charles River and took a seat in the middle of a dozen or so wide-eyed undergrads and the handful of bespectacled grad students.

I sat there looking around the room, trying to figure out if the speaker was among us, when the professor walked in and thanked us for coming. He pulled a VHS tape out of its sleeve and jammed it into a VCR sitting under a boxy TV at the front of the room.

What the hell? I thought to myself. *We're going to watch a movie?*

After some cheesy synth music and 1980s-era computer graphics, an old man appeared on the screen, sitting in a chair surrounded by tall bookshelves.

"We have not even to risk the adventure alone, for the heroes of all time have gone before us."

The man, who I would soon learn was the legendary mythology professor Joseph Campbell, continued.

"And where we had thought to slay another, we shall slay ourselves. Where we had thought to travel outward, we shall come to the center of our own existence. And where we had thought to be alone, we shall be with all the world."

Holy shit, I thought to myself.

He continued on, going through Hercules and Moses and Buddha and Christ. Departure. Fulfillment. Return. And adventures in between.

His interviewer, Bill Moyers, asked him about the cantina scene in *Star Wars*.

"That's my favorite," Campbell answered. "Where you are, is on the edge… The first stage in the hero adventure is leaving the realm of light which he controls and knows about and moving toward the threshold. And it's at the threshold that the monster of the abyss comes to meet him."

I wanted in. I wanted all of it. The dragon's blood. The Iroquois princess. The song of nature. I could ring the bells of the cathedral *and* slay the minotaur.

Let's figure all this out! I shouted in my head. *Boil all this noise and religion and psychiatry and philosophy down to the essence of what we are supposed to be doing as human beings.*

Maybe I was in the middle of the existential crisis that comes with every freshman year. But I thought I had found my calling and declared classics and religion as my major, with a focus on mythology.

But the romanticism of myth could not hold back the true-crime instincts of my childhood. Four years, one bachelor's degree, and $30,000 in student debt later, I managed to shoehorn crime into my studies and found myself in grad school at the University of Kansas with a scholarship to investigate new religious movements. *New religious movements* is the academic way of saying *cults*, and I was gravitating to the cults that were posing the biggest threat to law enforcement at the time: the Christian apocalyptic movement. With names like the Covenant, the Sword, and the Arm of the Lord, the Church of Israel, and the Order, many of them shared affiliations with the Aryan Nation, had a lot of guns, and viewed *The Turner Diaries* as a blueprint for an upcoming race war.

There were a lot of these cults out there. And there were a lot more unaffiliated criminals who were going after the same thing, like the guy who blew up a truck full of weaponized fertilizer in front of the federal building in Oklahoma City in a misguided attempt to overthrow the government. Timothy McVeigh killed 168 people in that attack, including 19 children.

I was becoming well-versed in these Christian apocalyptic cults, and after the bombing, I wrote to the special agent in charge of the Kansas City bureau of the FBI, asking if they needed any help in the area.

The form letter I got back from Supervisory Special Agent William M. Chornyak asked me to fill out the enclosed preliminary application for special agent position, along with a background survey and qualifications questionnaire. It included a gentle warning that "the position you are considering as a special agent in the FBI is very competitive."

In order to apply, you had to have worked full-time at the same job for at least two years. My teacher assistant position instructing classical mythology wouldn't qualify, so I started working forty hours a week at a Play It Again Sports in Kansas City. I would study cults, teach myths, and play on the KU hockey team during the day, then sell sporting goods every night and on weekends.

I took the sample written test and aced it. The physical requirements were a different matter and had me running through Kansas wheat fields every day, trying to get my one-and-a-half-mile time down to the required sub-twelve minutes. The last stumbling block was my eyes. Agents were required to have uncorrected vision not worse than 20/200. I would have to get Lasik.

I also had to decide how I was going to answer the first question in the personal declarations section: "Have you used marijuana during the last three years or more than fifteen times?" Not that marijuana makes you paranoid or anything, but I heard they gave all applicants a polygraph exam.

In the meantime, I collected my master's degree. In the best shape of my life from running through those wheat fields and playing a full hockey season, I was deciding between PhD programs and getting the Lasik (and also reading up on how one could beat a polygraph exam) when my mother called me.

"Your father is having a problem," she said.

Dad, the man with all the energy in the world, was getting tired. One of the valves in his heart was failing. He needed open-heart surgery.

I thought the right thing to do was to go home and save the family business. I went from studying religion on the hilltop of Lawrence, Kansas, to standing on a twenty-four-foot ladder in ninety-five-degree heat, using an electric sander to scrape paint off a million-dollar house in Garden City, Long Island.

Dad's operation was a success. And it turned out that the new heart valve they installed in his chest made him feel like a teenager. It wasn't long before he was back on the job.

We drove to work together every day. After two seasons, he finally let me touch a brush. I was only painting a window in the back of a garage, but it was a start. *Maybe I was destined to be a house painter after all?* I thought. But I needed some kind of creative outlet. It was the first time in eighteen years that I didn't have a school reading list or papers to write.

I started a zine about hockey fights. I was always more drawn to the fighters, the hitters, and the agitators than the scorers. Watching Clark Gillies beat the snot out of Terry O'Reilly was the reason I started playing hockey when I was twelve.

I watched every Islander game and wrote down a blow-by-blow description of every fight: who won, who lost, who bled. Then I discussed whether the blood affected the outcome of the game. I stole some photos off the web, laid out the mini magazine on a graphics program, made fifty copies at Kinko's, and handed them out at the games, strategically placing some copies in the men's bathroom stalls. I called it the *Fight Card*.

A copy got into the hands of the *Village Voice*, the famous alternative rabble-rousing newspaper, which was getting ready to launch a new edition on Long Island. I got a call from John Mancini, the editor in chief.

"Hey," he said. "I just saw the *Fight Card*. I love this!"

He offered me $400 to write a recap of the season in punches for the first issue.

Then I stuck around and pitched any story I could think of. The day jobs of professional lacrosse players. The NYPD vs. FDNY annual ice hockey game. Extreme backyard wrestling. I tried out for a professional roller hockey team and was an Arena Football League assistant coach for a week.

My dad took my first cover story—a tale of the Mets-Yankees rivalry ahead of their first interleague series—and framed it. He hung it on the wall of his office, along with my second cover, How to Survive a Hockey Fight.

It was all fun and games and I loved it, but I still really wanted to write about crime.

Long Island had just come out of a hellish series of true-crime episodes—the capture of serial killers Joel Rifkin and Robert Shulman. Little Katie Beers locked in John Esposito's dungeon. The Long Island Railroad Massacre. The Suffolk Sniper. The Long Island Lolita. Long Island in the 1990s was like Florida is today.

I started pitching crime stories to Mancini.

"Why do you want to mess things up with the sports!? People are loving the sports!" he said in his high-pitched, staccato Queens accent. "Stick with the sports!"

My crime writing would have to wait.

At home, my father's heart was ticking along fine. My returning home to "save the family business" turned into a bit of a joke, as he would bolt up and down ladders while I asked, "Do we really have to work on Saturday?"

But one Sunday as we were working in the backyard, Dad kept needing to sit down and rest. The next day, he went to the doctor. After a series of tests, the doctor told him he had hepatitis C. He had probably picked it up from needles thirty years earlier. Maybe when he was selling his blood for food, but more likely when he was sharing needles for heroin.

In the fall of 1997, his liver began to fail. After six months of watching him get transferred from one hospital to another, I started to realize the unthinkable: my dad could actually die. His face became gaunt. His once-mighty forearms thinned and deflated.

On April 22, 1998, I sat next to him in his hospital room. I showed him the cover of my latest story for the *Voice*. It was called MY DAD KICKED YOUR ASS AT SHEA. It was all about the adventures we had together, of a father and son getting into trouble across the arenas and stadiums of New York. We watched the Mets on the TV in his room.

Before I left, I kissed him on the top of his head. "You're my hero," I said.

"Thank you," he whispered back to me.

He died the next day.

It was raining at his funeral. My wife, Kendall, held our newborn daughter in the car on the path next to the grave while I gave his eulogy. Even though I didn't believe in the afterlife, I gave my mother two things to put in Dad's pocket inside the casket: a twenty-dollar bill so he could tip the usher to get a better seat in heaven and his pocket knife in case he ran into any trouble if he ended up in hell.

5

A PARTNER IN CRIMESOLVING

Hollywood, 2013

FIFTEEN YEARS AFTER DAD DIED, I MADE A DECISION. I followed the path he had taken when he was fifteen (without stealing his coin collection or visiting a Tijuana whorehouse) and set out for Hollywood. I had one goal—make a TV show about solving unsolved crimes.

I had already seen the writing on the wall when it came to the future of newspapers. In 2006, I had reinvented my day job. I started building websites and blogs and honed a particular talent of getting millions of people to click on web links to read stories or look at photo galleries. I tripled my paycheck, but my life became filled with analytics, spreadsheets, marketing strategy, and revenue goals, leaving little brain time for what I was still searching for—that first murder solve. The job did afford me the chance to start a national crime blog called *True Crime Report*. I staffed it with a writer and also built what was then the nation's largest unsolved murders database that could be accessed by anyone. But it wasn't enough. So I left the six-figure job behind to pursue a dream of becoming a Jack-Webb-meets-John-Walsh for the reality TV generation. *American Idol*, *Keeping Up with the Kardashians*, *Duck Dynasty*, *Hell's Kitchen*—that was where the public's attention was directed. Why not use the reality format to try to solve murders?

So I went to LA, with the plan to fly back to Phoenix every weekend to see Kendall and our son and daughter, who were now both teenagers, back at the homestead. Figuring a hotel room for four nights a week was cheaper than an apartment, I checked into the Hollywood Historic Hotel, a ninety-nine-dollar-a-night accommodation boasting a 1920s bathtub, a 1980s mini fridge, and a far-reaching view of the Hollywood sign.

Before I walked into the long, brooding building poised over Melrose Avenue, a Google search yielded tales that the hotel was haunted. The story didn't say whose ghost it was, but a few months after I arrived, it had gained a friend when the woman down the hall hanged herself in her room. The hotel was cheap but clean, and when it was available, the night manager would give me the room on the top floor with the vaulted ceiling and secret compartment under the bed where I hid a bottle of vodka between stays.

With my housing settled, I then needed some type of income to keep me afloat as I worked on creating the TV show.

My friend Lenora Claire, a redheaded Vargas pinup girl come to life, told me about a job opening where she worked casting reality TV. I took it. During the day, I tracked down people with peculiar habits or uncommon occupations—like a woman who couldn't stop eating the stuffing in her couch cushions or the girl who opened a business where lonely, fully clothed men paid to cuddle with her for a hundred bucks an hour. At night, alone in my hotel room, I investigated crimes. For *Boston* magazine, I wrote about Maura Murray, the UMass coed who had gone missing in the snowy New Hampshire woods in 2004, launching a thousand theories from amateur sleuths. For *Rolling Stone*, I investigated how animal-rights citizen detectives used their web smarts to track down kitten killer Luka Magnotta in Canada. They pleaded with authorities to take their information and make an arrest, warning them that this guy would one day kill a person. No one listened until human body parts began showing up in the mail.

Down the street from the casting office was a start-up company called TradioV. The idea behind it was to bring in interesting people from all walks of life, put them in front of a microphone and a video camera, and live stream whatever they had to say. C-list celebrity Andy Dick had his own show. So did actor Eric Roberts, Jane's Addiction guitarist Dave Navarro, and the tattooed-and-pierced models of the Suicide Girls. Lenora had a show, too, called *The Obscenesters*, where she interviewed a rotating cast of Hollywood eccentrics.

She told me they were looking for more content, and I pitched them a true-crime show. They liked the idea. It wouldn't pay anything, but at least I could scratch the itch to bring some of the cases I was looking into to light while I was trying to get a traditional TV show off the ground. They ended the meeting with a suggestion: "You should find a cohost."

I did a Google search for "Los Angeles" and "true crime" and found a site called *True Crime Diary*, which I had run across before. I read a few of the blog posts—one about the Zodiac Killer, another about serial killer Israel Keyes—and then clicked the "About" link.

"True Crime Diary began when Michelle McNamara, a writer, decided the investigating she was doing on unsolved crimes to satisfy her own curiosity might be better shared."

The name sounded familiar. I googled Michelle, clicked the first link, and discovered that I had read a story she published in *Los Angeles* magazine about her quest to find a serial killer who had eluded authorities for decades. I remembered reading the story and saying to myself *Damn, I wish I wrote this.*

"By day, I'm a forty-two-year-old stay-at-home mom with a sensible haircut and Goldfish crackers lining my purse," Michelle wrote. "In the evening, however, I'm something of a DIY detective."

I sent Michelle a message asking to meet up and included links to my work in an attempt to assure her that I wasn't a psychopath.

A couple of days later, I woke up staring up at the bright white cathedral ceiling of the very best room of the Hollywood Historic Hotel, pulled on my leather jacket, walked out of the hotel, and headed toward the cemetery, where I had left my car.

I passed the Paramount gates that Norma Desmond crashed to see Cecil B. DeMille before a writer ended up dead in her swimming pool at the end of *Sunset Blvd.*, then turned north on Gower, walking along Hollywood Forever Cemetery and the remains of DeMille, Bugsy Siegel, Jayne Mansfield, Rudolph Valentino, and even Lana Clarkson, the actress Phil Spector was convicted of killing. Reminders of mortality on every side. It wasn't the death that was getting to me but the length of time that they lived—I was actually older than every single one of those legends when they checked in to the cemetery. Every tick on my watch was a march toward failure, four lines and a slash on the wall adding up to a death without purpose. And becoming a cliché? That was a punishment worse than failure. I had to make something, anything, happen.

I got into my car and drove to Los Feliz for the meeting. Walking into the Coffee Bean on Hillhurst Avenue, I got a text from Michelle McNamara.

I'm on patio, dark hair, black-and-white outfit.

I walked out to the patio and spotted Michelle in her black-and-white outfit straightaway. She was the only person not sitting in front of a laptop.

I sat down, and we immediately began sizing each other up, dancing around like two prizefighters in a ring, trying to see how much the other knew about this murder or that. The laptop people surrounding us were arguing over scenes with their writing partners. "This is the character's arc." "And *then* that's when he gets his superpower." Michelle and I were talking about the specific ways Elizabeth Short's internal organs had been dissected and removed from her body.

We clicked.

We lamented the media's insatiable hunger for retelling the same five crime stories over and over again. For the networks, true crime had turned into a fossil-rock concert experience—everyone just wants to hear the hits. "Play Manson!" "Play OJ!" Meanwhile, thousands of unsolved murder stories went untold.

Michelle was game for doing the show, and we decided to call it *The Shadowpulp True Crime Radio Hour*. The first episode would be about the serial killer she wrote about in that *Los Angeles* magazine story, the East Area Rapist/Original Night Stalker (EAR/ONS), the closest thing to the boogeyman the United States has ever had.

Unlike Son of Sam, who killed people on lovers' lanes, or John Wayne Gacy, who murdered young boys living on the margins, EAR/ONS attacked people where they felt most safe—in their homes, with their lovers beside them in bed and a loaded gun in the drawer. He would break into a house, empty the gun of all the bullets, and then leave undetected. He would return the next night, slink his way through an unlocked window, creep down a hallway, and present himself in the darkness with a blinding flashlight in his victims' eyes. Then he terrorized them for hours, tying up the man. Raping the woman. Making himself a sandwich in the kitchen. Stealing a personal item or two. Then slithering away. In the beginning, he left his victims alive. After fifty rapes, he evolved into a killer, murdering at least twelve people.

Michelle had first written about the case in 2011 on *True Crime Diary*. Her wonder at EAR/ONS's elusiveness bled through each sentence. He left so many clues behind. He was luckier than he was good. He "wasn't a supervillain," she wrote. "He was a man, a guy with habits and traits and preferences that, with enough examination, should shine like Hansel's breadcrumbs in the woods."

She believed one of the reasons he hadn't gained traction in the public consciousness—and the main reason he was still at large—was due to branding. The man was responsible for two separate series of crimes at opposite ends of the state that had not been connected until years later via DNA. So he had two names. The one he earned in Northern California was the East Area Rapist. Not as flashy as the Zodiac, the Ripper, or the Florida Sex Beast. It was an incredibly provincial name. East of where, exactly? The one he earned in Southern California was the Original Night Stalker, "Original" to differentiate him from the more famous Night Stalker, Richard Ramirez, a qualifier which would be comical if you weren't so terrified by the realization that there were two serial killers called the Night Stalker operating at the same time in the same metropolitan area. Michelle believed rebranding the criminal might lead to more information to uncover his identity, so when she wrote her feature story, she introduced EAR/ONS to a broad audience and swiftly christened the monster with a new name: the Golden State Killer.

We live streamed the first episode of the *Shadowpulp Radio Hour* in front of a two-camera set up at the TradioV studios on Santa Monica Boulevard. Fewer than a hundred people watched. We received one phone call from a viewer calling himself "Frank from Burbank." Frank from Burbank was in actuality Patton from Los Feliz, Michelle's husband, the comedian Patton Oswalt, who was watching the live stream from home.

Despite the lukewarm reception, they asked us back for another show. Michelle and I went back and forth on which case we would dig into next.

"Bauerdorf/Christa Helm, Hollywood Starlets unsolved in general," Michelle texted me. "Or Zodiac? Or the additional murders linked possibly to Manson family? Whatever you feel like, I'm flexible."

Every murder she suggested we cover was an unsolved case. I was really starting to like her.

We settled on the unsolved murders that surrounded the Manson family. While the Manson tale is the most infamous American true-crime story ever told, there were still secrets to be uncovered. Beyond Gary Hinman, the victims at the Tate and LaBianca houses, and Don "Shorty" Shea, who was killed at the Spahn ranch, true-crime buffs have speculated for years that the family was responsible for more than a dozen bodies that were found across Los Angeles in the late 1960s, including Marina Habe's, who was found near Mulholland Drive on New Year's Day in 1969. The seventeen-year-old had been kidnapped from her mother's driveway, beaten, and stabbed multiple times. Another, Jane Doe #59, was dumped in the heavy undergrowth of Laurel Canyon in November 1969, within sight of where Habe had been left less than a year earlier. The teenage girl (identified decades later as Reet Juvertson), had been stabbed 157 times in the chest and throat. The bodies of fifteen-year-old James Sharp and nineteen-year-old Doreen Gaul were found in an LA alley on November 22, 1969. The teens had been active in a Scientology splinter group called the Process, which Manson had flirted with. They were both stabbed to death. The bodies of Nancy Warren and Clida Delaney were found near Ukiah on October 13, 1968. They were strangled to death and beaten with leather thongs. Members of the Manson family were among the suspects, but no one was ever charged. Proving any kind of connection between Manson's family and these victims would have been a huge accomplishment for the show.

We divided up the cases and began collecting material. We both got to talk to Vincent Bugliosi, the district attorney who not only convicted Manson but also wrote one of the bestselling true-crime books in history, *Helter Skelter*. We shared the internal fanboy and fangirl squeals after hearing the voice of a legend on the other end of the line. Bugliosi politely declined to appear on the show, his voice weakened by the cancer that would lead to his death two years later, but we had more than enough facts to stuff into the hour-long episode.

For the filming, Michelle brought in her Manson family Russian nesting dolls, which began with a large Charlie Manson and ended with a small refrigerator, a miniature version of the one from the LaBianca residence with the misspelled words "Healter Skelter" scrawled in blood across the door. The dolls sat between us as we discussed how Manson once bragged about committing more than thirty-five murders, and we wondered whether his charismatic reach could have extended from Venice and the supposed Russian roulette "accident" of John Haught to London and the supposed "suicide" of family member Sandra Good's boyfriend Joel Pugh. Scott Michaels of Dearly Departed Tours, a company that takes curious tourists to infamous Manson sites across the city, called into the show to add his own insight. So did Frank from Burbank.

A week later, we decided to take on the Zodiac Killer.

"I could certainly get a few interesting callers for that one," Michelle texted. "People LOVE their pet Zodiac theories."

For the Zodiac show, Michelle brought in a small piece of artwork Patton had commissioned. It was a cartoon of Michelle holding a cup of coffee while confronting the Zodiac Killer, who was wearing the hooded uniform from the Lake Berryessa murder. To roll in and out of commercial breaks, I played the Beatles' "Wild Honey Pie," "Do it Again" by Steely Dan, and Gerry Rafferty's "Baker Street," completely breaking copyright laws, which is probably one of the reasons you can't find the episodes on the web anymore.

The Shadowpulp True Crime Radio Hour was *kind* of like TV, but I was ready to start pitching my first real television show. I called it *The Murder Circle*. The idea was to take seven individuals who had all devoted their lives, in one way or another, to crime. There was a hard-edged female former prosecutor, a former FBI agent, a tough-but-likable ex-con, a young crime-scene investigator, a former homicide detective, an investigative journalist (me), and a citizen-detective housewife

(Michelle). We would convene each week in a small town stumped by a cold case and put the investigation on steroids. In each episode, we were going to pick through all the evidence, reinterview the major players, and invariably fight with each other until we found the right guy.

I found five people to fill the other roles of the show, filmed interviews with them all, and built a sizzle reel. Each individual introduced themselves and explained what they would bring to the circle.

"During the day, I'm the mom to a four-year-old," Michelle began, talking directly into the camera from her daughter's playroom. "But at night, it's autopsy reports. It's googling gruesome details. And it's all about trying to solve unsolved crimes. Everyone has their cause, and this feels like what I was born to do."

Michelle and I would meet for lunch once a month at places like the Tallyrand in Burbank, Fred 62 in Los Feliz, or the 101 Coffee Shop in Hollywood and talk almost exclusively about crime, welcoming any chance to bounce ideas off each other. She was working on a proposal to turn her Golden State Killer investigation into a book, while I was continuing to write features on unsolved cases.

I texted her after watching the sizzle reel we built for *The Murder Circle*.

"It came out great," I said and told her we would be shopping it around as soon as we could set up some meetings.

"Cool!" she texted back. "And I think I sold a book to HarperCollins :)"

I met with a production company who said they liked the idea of *The Murder Circle*, but the back-and-forth and lawyer fees were just the first of many throat punches Hollywood would land. I would get close to producing a show, then get it pulled at the last second for the same reason over and over again—I couldn't guarantee a solve by the end of each episode.

"Our viewers want a resolution," each network executive would say.

"But look at all the people who are discussing unsolved murders online," I countered. "They can be a part of solving the mystery."

"Yes, our market research says our viewers want to watch more unsolved stories," one network executive said to me. "But we know that they actually just really want to see things solved in the end."

Trying something I could have slightly more control over, I decided to throw my hat into the ring when the South by Southwest Interactive (SXSW) Festival, the Austin, Texas, conference where tech nerds converge to talk about the next big things in digital, announced their call for proposals to present sessions at their annual conference the following March.

I had just started working on that story for *Rolling Stone* about the citizen sleuths who used their considerable skills and tenacity to find the kitten killer, Magnotta. I wanted to show how that type of crowdsourcing could be replicated and used to solve all types of crimes. Michelle was not only a top researcher but had also written an excellent story on her own digital sleuthing methods while searching for the Golden State Killer. Those were two positives on the amateur detective front. But I would also have to address the negative. The citizen-detective community was still reeling from the crowdsourcing failures in the aftermath of the Boston bombing, when amateur sleuths were drawing circles around bulging backpacks and misidentifying the bombers responsible for the blast.

Citizen sleuthing was ready for its close-up, and Michelle was the perfect partner to help deliver the message.

I created a presentation that I hoped would catch the attention of the hipsters, digital nerds, and other assorted riffraff who voted on which panels should be presented at the conference. The slides featured statistics and examples of private individuals who had used the internet to solve crimes: The *Gawker* commenters who fingered a New York City mugging suspect after they identified the fraternity sweatshirt he was wearing while committing the crime. Blogger Alexandria Goddard, whose quick-thinking screenshots of social media posts of high school students boasting about the rape of a sixteen-year-old girl in Steubenville, Ohio, provided crucial evidence. And the citizens on Websleuths who dug up incriminating information on DeeDee Moore, the woman eventually convicted of murdering Abraham Shakespeare, the part-time garbage collector turned lottery winner.

It would be the first-ever crowdsourcing crime presentation, designed to show the tech world that crimes could be solved by regular people. But with more than three thousand entries for SXSW and only a few hundred slots, we needed a title that would stand out from the crowd.

I texted Michelle. "I was thinking Catching Murderers with Social Media."

"That's good," she wrote back. "Some others: @murder: Internet as Dragnet. Catching Serial Killers with Search Engines. Okay, I'm done :)" she finished. "Your first one is clear & understandable."

But having seen the other entries, I knew the winning panels often had names that were a bit over-the-top. I came up with a header, typed out the title, cringed a little, and pressed send.

"How does this sound: Citizen Dicks: Catching Murderers with Social Media."

"Like it though idk about the 'dicks' part :/" she replied.

Michelle relented, and thanks in part to Patton tweeting out the link to our proposal, it got enough votes and was selected.

In March 2014, Michelle and I traveled to Austin and ran through a PowerPoint deck detailing examples of crowdsourcing crimesolving and how regular people can aid investigations if they have specific knowledge.

We talked about Michelle scouring eBay looking for cuff links that were taken from a crime scene by the Golden State Killer, buying a pair that fit their description, and mailing them to one of the detectives on the case.

And we discussed the Boston bombing aftermath, how web users throwing out the names of suspects on social media was damaging to the crowdsourcing effort, but also highlighting how the crowd did produce two key pieces of information. Redditors swiftly identified the logo on the hat Bomber #1 was wearing in the grainy video released by the FBI (it was a Bridgestone Golf hat), and a Facebook user produced the only clear photo of Bomber #2 walking away from the scene of the crime.

The panel was a success, and *Shadowpulp* was fun, if under the radar. But in between the time we launched *Shadowpulp* and when we presented the panel in Austin, Michelle went all in on the Golden State Killer. From Sacramento to Goleta to Irvine to Walnut Creek, she bought lunches for retired detectives, hustled police reports, and talked to survivors, putting together material for her book.

We still met for our monthly lunches. She would tell me how hard-nosed detectives were opening up, sharing information not only with her but with each other. The Golden State Killer had committed crimes in multiple jurisdictions, and either red tape or blind ego halted the exchange of vital clues between the departments. Michelle used her unassuming charm to break down those walls, and my eyes would widen and my jaw would drop whenever she told me about the pieces of info she was able to squeeze out of her contacts. We talked about how we both couldn't sleep sometimes and would wake up in the middle of the night and grab the computer to compare multiple angles of blood spatter photos from a crime scene in Orange County or google photos of tread patterns of Adidas jogging shoes manufactured before 1979.

We talked each other up from every rabbit hole we jumped down. She had an early sample of the Golden State Killer's DNA profile and was entering it into public DNA databases like Ysearch to try to find some distant cousin who could lead to the killer. She thought she came close a few times, but they were false alarms. We were both sure there would be a familial DNA match inside 23andMe or Ancestry.com, but those were closed databases—the public and law enforcement were not allowed to access them due to the privacy terms of each company.

In between discussing our obsessions, we dreamed long term. Although I hadn't been able to get *The Murder Circle* TV concept off the ground, I wanted to start a group in Hollywood that would meet once a month and attempt to solve an unsolved crime. It would be a casual, unconventional squad, filled with detectives and forensics scientists and prosecutors and psychologists, but also writers and actors and people who had both the brains and the instinct to think a little differently than the average person on the street.

It would be loosely modeled on the Vidocq Society, a group of select law enforcement types who meet once a month in Philadelphia and investigate cold cases. Individuals would work on different parts of the case—DNA extraction, witness interviews, facial reconstruction—then return the next month and present their findings to the group. If we felt we had a case—and enough evidence of who might have committed a crime—we would present it to the local police department in charge of the investigation.

Michelle was interested and wanted to host the group at her house. But first, she had to finish the book. "Once the book is done" became a constant refrain, which led to me giving her gentle pushes every time we met. I would quote Steve Jobs to her, "Real artists ship," trying to impress upon her that at some point, she needed to let the manuscript go and send it into her editor's hands. But there was always one more lead to track down, one more witness to call.

"Please finish the book so we can start our West Coast Vidocq Society," I texted her near the end of 2015. "You can pick the name."

"Michelle McNamara and her Dicks," she wrote back, finally embracing the name of our SXSW panel.

"I can already foresee the lazy porn parody," I answered back.

"Srsly though," she said. "West Coast Vidocq is really the only project I'd do right now after my book."

At the end of March 2016, we made plans to meet at the Golden Road Brewery, a brewpub next to the railroad tracks in Glendale. "Just a head's up," she warned. "Turns out I found out EAR or GSK, whatever I'm calling him, possibly wrote a letter taking responsibility for the bombing at LaGuardia. While I was researching it, I saw that you wrote about it! He claimed that it was to kill a girl that had rejected him. I'm pretty sure it's bullshit but just would love to talk to you about that case." There was always another lead, and I was happy that this time I could help a bit more than usual. A decade earlier, I had spent months going through the dusty facts of the still-unsolved 1975 bombing at LaGuardia Airport, interviewing everyone from the lead detective on the case to the main suspect's girlfriend for a *Long Island Press* story.

At lunch, she grilled me about the case. Killing eleven people, it was the third most deadly terrorist attack in New York history, behind 9/11 and the 1920 bombing of Wall Street. We quickly dismissed the idea that there was a connection to the Golden State Killer, just more unfounded boasting from unstable people in the heydays of madmen.

When it was my turn, I told her about my latest case. I was investigating the Bear Brook murders, four unidentified bodies found in barrels fifteen years apart in the New Hampshire woods, also known as the Allenstown Four. I just didn't understand how a family unit—a woman and three children—could disappear, be murdered, and still remain unidentified.

She knew the case well but had never written about it. It was just one more murder that had to wait until the book was done. She told me she was planning on shipping the manuscript to HarperCollins by the end of the year, and then we could start our crimesolving group. I pulled out a notebook and showed her a list I'd scribbled of a few people who could take part. At the top was John Mulaney, a comedian whose specials I had been binge-watching. He was a great storyteller, did a brilliant bit about *Law & Order*, and his parents were lawyers; maybe he would want to look into some murders?

Michelle looked at the notebook. "Oh my God, I just met with him!" she yelled. Turns out he was into true crime. Michelle and I were on the same wavelength. This was going to happen. We were going to bring people together and solve murders.

We finished lunch and walked to the parking lot. I hugged her goodbye and drove away.

Over the next couple of weeks, we texted bits of crime news to each other.

"Another true-crime fan: Kesha," I texted, half jokingly. "She took the Manson tour yesterday with that guy we interviewed."

As soon as I learned that one of the Manson girls had gotten parole, I sent Michelle a message.

"Leslie Van Houten Ok'ed for parole," I wrote on April 14.

"Holy shit," she wrote back.

I would be in the middle of one of my stories when an idea would pop into my head about the Golden State Killer, and I would immediately text Michelle. "Have you ever looked into anyone who was killed in a home invasion by a homeowner around the time EAR/ONS stopped?"

"Yes!" she wrote back. "I did a lot of combing back through media etc. for that very thing, and also suicides in the year after. We have a pretty good suspect right now. Fingers crossed. Unfortunately, he's a world traveler who doesn't seem to come back to the US very often (not surprising) but they r tracking him down. If it turns out to be him, his getting away will be what I suspect: weak elimination based on Chinese Whispers between agencies. One agency who had eyes on him said he had an ace bandage. Somehow Sac [Sacramento] is told crutches and

69

cast. He was a '10' on Sac's suspect numbering system of 1 (weak) 10 (strong). Then I found out he transferred to UCSB at exactly the right time. Among a bunch of other tiny details in his favor. We'll see. Have been here before. But God would I be so happy."

A week later, on April 20, I texted her again. I had just gotten a call that A&E was going to order a pilot for a new show I had created on DIY citizen detectives. And I was preparing to fly out to DC the next day to begin filming my investigation into the Allenstown Four.

"I think I just sold a show," I wrote. "Want to do lunch or dinner next week?"

6.

THE ABSOLUTE WORST HUMANITY HAS TO OFFER

New Hampshire, 2016

I HADN'T RECEIVED MICHELLE'S RESPONSE BY THE TIME I landed in Washington, DC. I was there to interview Joe Mullins, a forensic imaging specialist at the National Center for Missing and Exploited Children headquarters. He was the artist who had worked on reconstructing what the Allenstown Four, the woman and three little girls found in barrels in New Hampshire in 1985 and 2000, might have looked like when they were alive.

With dark features, a dapper orange-and-blue-striped tie, and a high-top haircut split in two by a shock of white hair, Mullins looked like the kind of character a CBS crime drama would cast as the "forensics guy."

He sat down at his computer and opened a file containing a 3-D rendering of the smallest victim's skull.

"We are looking at the absolute worst that humanity has to offer," he said as he maneuvered his stylus to rotate the skull 180 degrees so we were looking at the back of the child's head. A series of cracks and holes came into focus on the back left side. "A two- or three-year-old little girl who looks like a brick has been used to smash her head in." He ran his pinky along the cracks in the skull on the screen.

The cracks in the back of the skull were jarring, but I was determined to show them on *Crime Watch Daily*, a syndicated daytime true-crime show I had started working on as a producer and investigator, which landed me a steady paycheck so I could move out of hotels and into an apartment in Burbank. No one outside of law enforcement had ever seen the wounds of the victims before. Maybe the images would tug at someone's conscience.

Mullins spun the skull of one of the other girls on the screen so that it was staring straight at us, and I watched over his shoulder as he began to add each layer of digital flesh to the bone. The image on the monitor transformed from a skull to what looked like a baby doll to a clay version of a little girl. Then he added digital pencils, layering flesh tones and hair. But it was only when he added the eyes that the girl looked like a person, like someone somebody might remember.

"It's devastating," he said, "but you have to turn that devastation into motivation, and I want to give her her name back."

That night, I flew to Boston, and the next morning, I drove to Allenstown, New Hampshire, to the park where the bodies in the barrels were discovered.

There I met Ronda Randall. Ronda didn't grow up in Allenstown. She never lived there. But she knew every tilt in the landscape, every placement of every skinny tree, every home—and most every occupant—on every lot in the trailer park that sat a quarter mile west of the woods. She started working on the case in 2011 and became an obsessed citizen detective, just like Michelle. They were both fortysomething Irish-American women. Both dedicated to cases that had baffled investigators for decades. Both seemingly unrelenting.

I followed Ronda down a narrow trail into the woods. About one hundred yards from the road, she began to veer us off the path. Twenty feet later, we stood in a small clearing.

"Right here," Ronda said, pointing to a bare spot on the ground.

In November 1985, two brothers were out hunting when one came across a fifty-five-gallon barrel on its side, up against a birch tree sapling. Spilling out of the barrel was a plastic bag.

"One of the brothers told me that he saw a small human foot sticking out of the bag," she said. Ronda was standing right in front of where the barrel had been, but I could tell she was being careful not to step on the exact spot where it had sat thirty-one years ago.

The brothers called the police. The police had nothing to work with. No clothes or jewelry were found with the remains. And they were careful to say "remains." This was not an intact skeleton but a jumble of bones inside a bag inside a barrel. At first, they thought it was one victim. Then they looked closer.

AUTOPSY: TWO VICTIMS read the headline in the *Concord Monitor*.

GIRL AND WOMAN WERE MURDERED, POLICE SAY.

The locals were stunned. Two bodies? And one a little girl? (They didn't know that fifteen years later the horror would multiply, when two more bodies would be found just a hundred yards away. For now, it was just the Allenstown Two.)

Dr. Henry Ryan, the Maine chief medical examiner, crossed state lines into New Hampshire to help and brought in Dr. Marcella Sorg, a forensic anthropologist from the University of Maine. Over the course of an eleven-hour examination, they deduced that:

The little girl was between 5–11 years old, 4'3" tall, with light brown to blond hair, and had been beaten about the head. The adult woman 23–33 years old, was 5'4" to 5'7" with light brown curly hair. She was cared for at some point in her life, as her teeth showed numerous dental work. Eye color and weight were undetermined.

The bones were "commingled," but Ryan stated that the difference in ages between the two victims meant reconstruction was fairly simple.

Their forensics team told them the remains had been there anywhere between six months to three years. That was a lot of time for a killer to get away.

Authorities checked records from elementary schools, campgrounds, and missing-persons reports, looking for names that might belong to the woman and little girl. They followed a lead about a mother and daughter who had gone missing from an Indian reservation in Maine. That turned out to be a dead end when they were found alive and well. Another pair that was brought to the attention of law enforcement were found alive in Arizona. Sketches were created of the two females, whom everyone assumed were mother and daughter.

In 1985, DNA testing for criminal investigations was one year away from its first case. (DNA evidence was first used in 1986 to identify a seventeen-year-old attacker in two sexual assaults/murders in Leicestershire, England.) The best bet to identify the woman and girl was going to be through their teeth. They brought in a forensic dentist, but no records matched.

In May 1987, the two bodies were finally laid to rest, buried together inside a steel casket in a corner plot in St. John the Baptist Cemetery in Allenstown. A local donated a headstone. HERE LIES THE MORTAL REMAINS KNOWN ONLY TO GOD OF A WOMAN AGE 23–33 AND A GIRL AGE 8–10. MAY THEIR SOULS FIND PEACE IN GOD'S LOVING CARE. Below the words was an image of a woman and little girl, holding hands.

Thirteen years went by. In 2000, the case was given to State Police Sergeant John Cody. Cody knew the area where the barrel was found had been picked over time and time again, but he wanted to get a sense of the place, and he followed the trail from the road down to where the remains were found fifteen years earlier. All he saw was a small, empty clearing in the forest. As he walked back toward the road, he spotted a few fifty-five-gallon drums, around one hundred yards from where the barrel with the woman's and child's remains were found.

He walked up to one of the barrels and gave it a push, just to see if it felt full. It did. He peeled off the lid, and in a split second, the mystery in Allenstown multiplied.

Inside, he saw the remains of two little girls. The first aged between one and three. The second two to four.

Had the second barrel been there since 1985 and was just overlooked? The police were cautious about declaring whether the two "new" remains were connected to the two remains found in 1985. But they knew. All they had to do was look at the heads of the two new victims, which both had gaping holes in the back sides of their skulls. The same injuries as the woman and little girl found fifteen years earlier.

The earlier victims' remains were exhumed, and the now-routine DNA tests revealed that one of the newly discovered victims was related to the woman and child from the first barrel.

Now they had three victims who were biologically related to each other, who were murdered and dumped in fifty-five-gallon drums, accompanied by one victim who was not related but still shared the same fate.

And that's all they had.

It takes a special type of person to devote their life to trying to solve a murder of someone who is unidentified. There are no mothers calling you in tears saying they just buried their babies. No candlelight vigils filled with friends and families asking for answers. There is no support system. You are the only voice of the dead.

Today, there are anywhere from 40,000 to 60,000 unidentified remains sitting in police storage lockers or anonymous graves across the country. And there are about 110,000 missing persons on the books at any given time. The trouble is, there is no single database where the information and samples of their DNA live. NamUs, the National Missing and Unidentified Persons System, tries its best to capture this information, but most police departments are not required to enter every set of remains they find or every missing person who is reported to them, and many don't bother. A year earlier, I had worked a case where a woman lost her son. Every year, she put up flyers looking for answers. Three years after he went missing, she learned that his body had been found just six months after he went missing only a half mile from her house. As she put up flyers year after year, her son's remains were sitting on a shelf in an evidence locker just down the block.

Pulling DNA from unidentified remains and running it through ancestry databases looking for familial matches would lead to thousands of answers. Answers to the identity of the remains. Answers to the fate of the missing. And for those who died a violent death, answers to who might have killed them. But every time I ask, authorities give me the same answer: "We just don't have the money or the resources to do the tests."

Ronda, who had dedicated years of her life to the Allenstown Four case, just wanted to find out the names of the woman and the three little girls.

"The case hooks you," she said as we walked out of the woods. "It's so impossible to understand how they just dropped off the face of the earth."

Blunt-force trauma to the back of the head? Of an entire family unit? This was not some crime of opportunity. It had to have been committed by a friend or family member. If no one had reported them missing, he had to have set up a plan. Maybe he told people that he and the woman were moving out of town and would contact them as soon as they were settled. This was before social media. People didn't keep tabs on each other like they do now. People could get lost. Disappear.

I left Ronda and Bear Brook and traveled to the state capital in Concord to talk to New Hampshire assistant district attorney Jeff Strelzin.

Strelzin was supportive of Ronda and her blogging about the victims. "In a case like this, there is really no harm that you can do by putting information out there," he told me.

Strelzin had crystal-blue eyes and kept details close to the vest. He said the case was still active and he wasn't going to tell me much. But it was his answer to my last question that shocked me.

"Do you ever think this will be solved?" I asked.

"I think the chances are pretty slim," he replied.

Driving back to Boston, I kept thinking about those words. I guess it was easier for him to say the "chances are pretty slim" for this case, because the victim's family wasn't banging on his door every day searching for an answer. The victims were nameless. He wasn't stealing hope from a living, breathing person with that statement.

But there is no way in hell Ronda or Michelle would ever say that. I saw Michelle's despair when a promising lead didn't pan out or a juicy clue turned out to be a red herring. She ate a lot of frustration. But she never once thought the Golden State Killer case would forever stay unsolved.

I got back to Boston around 8:00 p.m., enough time to grab some sleep before an early morning flight. But I was restless. I called up some old newspaper friends and made plans to meet up for a drink. Taking an Uber to the Back Bay neighborhood, I got out near the entrance to the Public Garden and hiked the length of Beacon Street, which had officially shaken off winter and was already in bloom.

I walked past Marlboro Market, where two months after I arrived in Boston twenty-five years earlier, I stumbled in with a girl who lived down the hall in my freshman dorm. We had drunk four tequila slammers each and were there to rent a movie to finish off the night. We secured the VHS tape and went back to a friend's apartment to watch our find. With the dialogue of *Beetlejuice* as our soundtrack, we had our first kiss. We were married five years later.

I then walked past the Wishing Tree, my name for the giant oak that hunched under the overpass at Charlesgate East road, which I would sit under and think about the world and my place in it and all the other things you wonder about when you are eighteen years old and in a strange city, and it's a weeknight, and you're too young to buy alcohol. Two decades earlier, I had placed a guitar pick inside the folds of the tree's bark, and I gave a cursory glance over where I thought it might be.

I passed by Myles Standish Hall, my freshman-year dormitory at Boston University, where my dad came up and painted the walls of my room black for me to make it feel more like home. I continued walking west, under the blinking Citgo sign, behind my first apartment across from the Victory Gardens, and straight into a waking nightmare.

7.

THE WRONG SIDE OF BROKEN

Hollywood, 2016

MY SHOES WERE STILL CAKED WITH DIRT FROM THE WOODS in Allenstown as I stood at the bar of the Verb Hotel behind Fenway Park. I was surrounded by my former colleagues from the *Boston Phoenix*, an alternative paper I worked at for a couple of years after I left Long Island. We were swapping stories and laughing, the commiserating foxhole-type of laughter writers share when lamenting late nights and late edits.

I was two beers into the night when I absentmindedly scanned my Facebook messages and stopped at a note from a stranger. *Not sure if you heard. So very sorry*, the woman wrote, with a link to an article. I stared blankly at my phone, rereading the headline of the article six or seven times, trying to wish the words away:

MICHELLE MCNAMARA, WRITER AND WIFE OF PATTON OSWALT, DEAD AT 46.

I looked back up from my phone and excused myself, stepping outside to the hotel's pool deck. I made a few phone calls and searched for more information, hoping it was a hoax, that someone was somehow messing with me. The first thing I thought of was the Golden State Killer.

Had he won? Then I thought of Michelle's young daughter, Alice. Then I didn't know what to think. I didn't know what to feel. I just knew to order another drink.

Three drinks turned into ten. I have no idea how I got back to my hotel that night, but a check of Facebook the next morning showed I had logged on and posted a status update a little after midnight. It was two words: "Fucking devastated."

On the plane ride home the next morning, I read a bunch of articles relaying the news, all saying Michelle died in her sleep, all referring to her in the headline as the "wife of Patton Oswalt." I opened the Notes app on my iPhone and began writing.

Michelle McNamara, True Crime Writer

Michelle McNamara was dogged. Fiercely dogged. Don't-take-no-for-an-answer, don't-leave-any-stone-unturned dogged.

She was a mother and a wife, but after she took her daughter to school or put her to bed, she spent seemingly every waking moment working on her book about a series of unsolved rapes and murders that took place across California in the '70s and '80s. Her ultimate goal? To identify the villain, to give the real name to the unknown assailant who goes by the monikers "the Original Night Stalker" and "the East Area Rapist." She had written about the case in *Los Angeles* magazine—where she rechristened him "the Golden State Killer"—and on her site *True Crime Diary*.

Every month or so, we would meet for lunch or drinks, where she would tell me about the latest clue she had uncovered—some bit of information that had been missed all those years ago. Her eyes lit up like Christmas as she walked me down the path of how the new clue might fit into the ever-expanding jigsaw puzzle she was putting together.

Then we would meet the next month, where she would excitedly tell me how that piece fit into the picture...or how it sent her down one of many rabbit holes.

She was unearthing an intense amount of information—boxes and boxes full of documents and police reports, old phone books, news articles. The kind of stuff you just can't google. She went digging—into dusty archives, newspaper morgues. She knocked on doors. Shoe-leather work.

But her most amazing skill—what set her apart from any writer I have ever seen—was getting grizzled detectives from different police departments and law enforcement agencies to talk to each other and share details about their individual cases, something they never did at the time of the crimes. If they did, they could have helped solve the case and brought this serial killer to justice. But they are doing it now, because of Michelle. It's not always easy talking to detectives about a cold case they worked on. It's their unfinished businesses. Imagine if someone called you up to get you to talk about a project you failed to complete forty years ago. Now imagine telling that person no. Now imagine that person not going away until you talked to them about it. Now you have an idea of Michelle.

She knew more about this case than anyone, and I truly believe she would have solved it. Hell, I bet she already has solved it. I bet she has the name of the bastard in one of her thousands of pages of notes. She texted me earlier this month saying she had a real good lead on a suspect. "A lot of tiny details in his favor," she wrote. "We'll see. Have been here before. But God I would be so happy."

I don't know what is going to happen to the book, but if asked, I would do my damnedest to help get it out there.

After the book was finished, Michelle and I were going to start a cold case group, a sort of Los Angeles Vidocq Society, where we would invite the smartest people we knew from Hollywood, law enforcement, and journalism to a dinner one night a month and review an unsolved murder case. We would then give each person a task, and at the next meeting, they would present their findings, which we would deliver to law enforcement before introducing the next case.

Michelle was really excited to do this, as was I. We were building a list of people to invite and a list of cases to work. The only thing we didn't know was what to call this little group. The Vidocq Society was named after the French criminal-turned-detective who is credited with ushering in a new era of detective work. Michelle was ushering a new era of citizen sleuthing, and her investigation is going to illustrate what a dogged woman who wouldn't take no for an answer could do for justice. If I can ever muster up the strength to start this group without her, I guess I now know what it will be called.

I posted the story on my website and tweeted out a link. On the day she passed, Patton had posted two photos of Michelle with the words "A beautiful friend/She opened up her heart and let me in…" but had since gone silent. He was still looking at Twitter, however, and saw my post and retweeted it. For the first few days, what I wrote became the de facto memorial for Michelle, and journalists began sending me messages asking if I could comment on her death. I could not and would not. I forwarded the requests to Michelle and Patton's nanny. She got back to me a day later, saying Patton wanted me to call him at noon on Sunday.

I had barely spoken with Patton, but he had made me laugh a thousand times with his whip-smart observations about comedian magicians, Stella D'oro Breakfast Treats, and the *Star Wars* prequels. What do you say to someone who just lost his copilot in life?

That night, I didn't sleep. And the next morning, I was so anxious waiting for the call at noon that I couldn't stay at home. So I went to Target.

I walked around aimlessly through the action figure and cereal aisles. After an hour, I dialed his number.

A man on the wrong side of being broken answered. My hands started to shake.

"I am so, so sorry," was the only thing I could think to say. Then I said the only thing I could think of: "I will do anything I can to help finish the book."

We talked about all the work Michelle had done and how it had to see the light of day. Of the giant amounts of police reports, witness statements, and other documents she had collected in banker's boxes in Alice's playroom and the thousands of files on her computer. But also that so many of the dots to be connected in the case were in her head.

"I feel like Sherlock just died," Patton said to me, "and I'm Watson and I have to solve this mystery."

I just about lost it in the office supplies aisle of Target.

I was going to help finish the book. I had no idea how much Michelle had written, but it was going to come out to the world. But there was something else at play. Patton sounded just as concerned about finishing her investigation and actually catching the killer as he was about making sure the book would be published.

I bought a pen, a notebook, a box of Lucky Charms, and walked out of Target, thinking one thought: *How am I ever going to help solve a case that Michelle worked on nonstop for half a decade when I can't even help solve any of my own cases?*

8.

—

THE MAN IN THE GREEN HOODIE

Chicago, 2016

IT WAS A FEW WEEKS AFTER MICHELLE DIED WHEN I FIRST saw the video of the killing of Marques Gaines on that street in Chicago.

In bed in my Los Angeles apartment, I watched it over and over and over again. I began to learn every step like it was a dance. I knew every inch of that street corner. Every mannerism of the Man in the Green Hoodie. When Marques was punched, I still winced as he fell to the ground. When the two thieves ran over to rifle through his pockets, I still shook my head in disgust. When the cab drove on top of his chest, I still looked away, focusing on the other cars, the bystanders, anything but what was right in the center of the screen.

The homicide of Marques Gaines isn't the type of true-crime story most people gravitate toward. It's a street crime. There was a think piece to be written about the bystander effect on the crowd as they rubbernecked from the sidelines, a Kitty Genovese redux unfolding in 2016 America. But most true-crime addicts don't want to hear that. They want twists and turns. They want love gone bad. And most of all, they want solves.

People read and watch and listen to true crime because it restores order from chaos. That's the answer to give when someone asks you why you like hearing about real-life murders. It's the comfort of watching everything be put in its place after an episode of outright, sickening bedlam. Read along with me in your best Keith Morrison, true-crime voiceover voice: "Everything is perfect (a sleepy town, high school sweethearts, a loving marriage), then everything goes wrong (a love triangle, a missing woman, a body found in the woods), then everything is right again (the killer is caught and convicted, and society is back to where it should be)." True crime satisfies the same urge as watching blackhead-popping videos: there is a foreign element in an otherwise perfect environment, and it must be removed. Then everything resets to normal.

I spent my life writing stories that begin with those first two parts, the perfect-then-chaos parts. It was the third part that I was always missing. But that missing piece was what had compelled me to work on the stories in the first place. People don't like stories without endings, but I wrote them anyway. Because families pleaded with me to. Because I felt like I might be able to help. And because maybe, just maybe, I might be able solve one. But so far, I hadn't.

I watched the video again, trying to block everything out except the Man in the Green Hoodie. I was trying to find something distinctive beyond his imposing frame. A crooked nose? A scar on his chin? A neck tattoo? I scanned his body, looking for anything that stood out.

And then I found it. Peeking out from underneath his hood was a distinctive hairline, a widow's peak, giving off a kind of Dracula vibe. I peered down at his clothes, and they didn't look dirty, and his white sneakers showed few scuffs, leading me to believe that this wasn't a guy who slept on the street. He had an address. Bottom line: he was identifiable.

"Why the hell haven't they found this guy yet?" I asked the darkness.

The police couldn't identify him; otherwise, they wouldn't have released the video to the media asking for help. The media couldn't identify him; all the local TV stations, the local newspapers, and even a few national broadcasts had run a story about the crime. Admittedly, their motive was less to help identify the suspect and more for the eyeball-grabbing nature of the footage. SHOCKING VIDEO SHOWS CHICAGO MAN LEFT TO DIE IN THE STREET read the headline of the NBC story. It was the kind of video that forced a viewer to look up from their morning corn flakes.

Yet no one knew who the Man in the Green Hoodie was.

Thirty years ago, having your story run on every local TV station and in every newspaper in your city would be tantamount to sending a text message with a picture of the wanted man to everyone within a twenty-mile radius. If a body was found at noon, people heard about it first from their local anchorman, then read the fleshed-out version the next day in the morning paper. If a body was found at night, it was the newspaper that first delivered the story, and they waited until the evening news for the accompanying video. If the story was interesting enough, the locals talked about it with their coworkers, the clerk at the deli, and later with their family over supper. The half dozen television stations and the multiple newsstands speckled across the city made sure that information reached every person, every day, in some way, shape, or form.

Then the internet happened.

By the time I was watching the video of Marques Gaines being attacked, people had been cutting the cord to their cable boxes for years. Newspapers were a shell of their former selves. Most people under forty—the kind of people who would be out on the street at three in the morning—were getting their news from the internet. They chose what they wanted to watch, as opposed to having to wade through a series of local crime stories to get to the sports highlights or the weather. Before the internet, if you wanted to hear about anything that was going on around you, you were forced to sit through stories you wouldn't look at today, including the crime story showing a picture of a wanted man.

The American media diet has gone from a fixed menu to an all-you-can-eat buffet. People are just not seeing the news anymore.

But there is one thing almost everyone is seeing: social media.

There are more than two billion active Facebook users. Twitter has more than three hundred million tweeters. Most every person under forty visits Facebook or Twitter or Instagram at least once per week. It is where you find news and where the news finds you. But even if you are following the local news station's Facebook page, you will not see every story they publish. Most stories that are posted by a media publisher reach only 7 to 10 percent of their fans or followers. Of those that are reached, it's another small fraction that actually clicks on the link and reads the story or watches the video. If you are a TV station airing a video showing a man getting murdered and asking people to identify his killer, most people are not going to see it. How is the public ever going to help with solving the crimes if they never even see the news?

The death of old media meant the people who might recognize the Man in the Green Hoodie would never know someone was even looking for him.

But here's the thing: I knew all this. It's been written on the urinal wall of every newsroom and tattooed on my brain for a decade. And not only did I know all this, but I was an expert at it.

"This is *my* job," I said to myself, sitting up in bed. *I'm* the guy who finds the people who don't read the newspaper or watch the news anymore. I travel to where you now live. Your Facebook, Twitter, and Instagram feeds. As you're scrolling through *Family Guy* memes and pictures of your nephew's new baby, I'm the one interrupting your bliss with FRESNO GANG MEMBER'S HOT MUGSHOT GOES VIRAL, 32 MOST MEMORABLE JUGGALOS WE SAW AT THE GATHERING, or MOM CAUGHT ON CAMERA POISONING YOUNG SON TO DEATH IN HOSPITAL. I try to make it so irresistible that there is no way you are not going to click on the link, come to the websites I work for, and see the story alongside the accompanying ads. The evisceration of newspapers forced me to create this particular set of skills for myself.

I have directed dozens of social media editors at newspapers and TV shows to post at least a million stories, photos, slideshows, and videos. And every time before they hit *publish*, I forced them to ask them themselves two questions: "Will this post stop someone from scrolling long enough to grab their attention?" and "Will that person think the post is interesting enough to share with a friend?"

"Learn it. Know it. Live it." I had the rules posted on the wall like All American Burger in *Fast Times at Ridgemont High*. After not messing with cats (people on the internet are very protective of cats; you just don't post anything negative about cats, or there will be hell to pay), these were the two most important rules of the internet: get your users' attention—and then turn those users into sharers.

What if I used the same strategy to find someone who might recognize the Man in the Green Hoodie?

The video of Marques Gaines's homicide would surely grab people's attention—it was as compelling as it was gruesome. People would watch. But that wasn't enough. I needed to get it in front of a specific person: the person who would recognize the attacker. Fifty thousand people across the country sharing the video *might* get it in front of the right set of eyeballs, but it would be like tossing a bunch of darts at a map while a hundred feet away and blindfolded. I had to reach people in a very specific location—to make them care enough to watch and try to identify him. "A squirrel dying in front of your house may be more relevant to your interests right now than people dying in Africa," Facebook founder Mark Zuckerberg once said. You might watch the video, but unless the crime happened near you, you're not going to care as much. But watch a video of someone dying at an intersection right by your house, and your ears prick up, your face leans in, and you scan each frame to see if you recognize the street, the stores, and maybe the man they are looking for.

To find the Man in the Green Hoodie, I would have to reach people who not only lived in Chicago but lived, worked, or played in the neighborhood where the crime occurred, River North. People who would see the story and share with their friends: "Look what happened outside that 7-Eleven we always go to after the bar." If I could get the video in front of everyone in a three-square-block area, I thought I could find him.

My day job and my night job were about to crash into each other. I was going to solve this murder myself.

———————————————

I set the alarm on my phone for 6:00 a.m. and was able to grab a few hours of sleep. In the morning, I rolled over, opened my laptop, and began my quest. I started with Marques's cousin Drexina, who was on a YouTube video speaking at a press conference at the scene of her cousin's homicide, pleading for anyone with information on the man who attacked him to come forward.

Drexina was really more like his sister than a cousin, as Marques's mother and father had both died when he was nine years old, and he had gone to live with his aunt Phyllis and Drexina in Atlanta. A quick search revealed that she ran a beauty parlor in Atlanta. I called and identified myself as an investigative journalist.

"I saw the video of Marques. I am so sorry for your loss," I said. "Have you heard anything new in the case?"

"No," Drexina replied. "The detectives don't even call me back anymore." Her voice revealed a level of frustration I have become accustomed to when talking to family members of victims.

I told her I wasn't sure who I was going to write this story for—or if I was going to write a story at all—but that I wanted to try some new techniques to attempt to identify the man in the video. "Would that be okay?" I asked. I could tell she didn't really believe it would go anywhere, but after months of no answers, Drexina sounded willing to accept any help she could get.

Before I start reporting any story, I always contact the detectives in charge, not only for information but to make sure they don't have a suspect in their sights. If they do, I back off. I don't want my digging to spook a suspect into running. But if law enforcement didn't get back to me, the case was fair game. I would follow the same code in this endeavor.

After my conversation with Drexina, I called the detective in charge of Marques's case and left a message. Chicago homicide detectives are a busy bunch. The murder rate skyrocketed in 2016 to 762 homicides, up from 496 the year before. The department simply didn't have enough detectives to cover all the investigations as thoroughly as they needed to. A few days later, I left another message and sent a couple of emails. Nothing. There was also another factor I was aware of: some cops like dealing with journalists, some don't. Chicago cops don't. I had given them enough time. I had the family's blessing. I was moving forward with my plan.

I opened Facebook and began building a new community page. I named it "River North Puncher," using as the profile pic the cleanest screenshot I could grab from the surveillance video of the Man in the Green Hoodie. All the images of the attacker were shot from above, which was going to make an identification difficult. I had gone through a few hundred mugshots on a public Cook County database, but the image I had was just too distorted. I was hoping his distinctive feature—the widow's peak hairline—would be that one detail that would make the difference between someone recognizing him on Facebook or passing on by.

Then I had to build a post. That was what would show up in people's Facebook feeds.

The post needed to stand out and away from the same tired "Information Wanted" posters law enforcement has been distributing—and the media have been echoing—ever since they were searching for John Wilkes Booth in 1865. Always fact-heavy, leading with heights and weights and age ranges, the bulletproof native language of cops. "Just the facts" was not going to be effective. I needed to tell a story. I selected eleven screenshots from the video—all different angles of the Man in the Green Hoodie. And then I wrote the post in the killer's voice, speaking directly to the reader.

> This is the video where I punch a stranger—a stranger who later dies. It was taken 4:20 a.m. on Sunday, Feb. 7 outside the 7-Eleven on State and Hubbard in River North, Chicago. I am the man in the green hooded jacket and white sneakers. (The man who died is in the blue shirt. He just went to the store for some chips.) If you know my name or anything about me—anything at all—please message me here or leave a comment. If you don't have any information, but have friends in Chicago, please share. His family desperately wants answers.

The next part of the plan would be geotargeting—identifying the location where I wanted to share the photo of the suspect and delivering content directly targeted to the people in that location. Even if I had a million fans on my own personal page, I would never get the video in front of the people I needed to reach: the people from that neighborhood. The right people. That meant I had to break out my credit card.

As I wrote the post—the same way you would write any post on Facebook—I was asked by Facebook if I wanted to "boost" the post. I clicked on that button and was met with a series of options. Depending on how much I spent, I could target a certain number of people based on a certain set of characteristics. Under the audience section, I entered the location of the incident—418 North State Street in Chicago—and drew a circle around it encompassing a two-mile radius. I kept the age range the boosted post would reach at eighteen to sixty-five plus. I did not select any interest targeting. (In later campaigns, I would narrow down the reach to the most specific of groups, say "Females, ages thirty-five to forty-five, who are interested in the Oakland Raiders and Martha Stewart." Yes, you can get that specific.) For the budget, I entered $100, a number I would soon realize was paltry. With a hundred bucks, I would reach 4,400 to 12,000 out of the 240,000 Facebook users who lived or worked in the area. If I added more money, I could reach more people. This is how Facebook has become a $328 billion company.

With the photos, caption, and geotargeting parameters set, I pushed *publish*.

Comments immediately began to trickle in.

Hope there's justice.

I hope they catch the mfer.

People just let him lie there in the middle of the road and walk off? What is wrong with these people?

One woman volunteered to help make the man in the image more identifiable.

Ima do a 3d on this photo and also google the address and blow this photo up it will give me a clear message. I will post this after turned in to police. Take 3 days...and yes I am a computer geek.

I was hoping it would be the start of a crowdsourcing relationship. I reached out to the woman, but she never produced the image.

Another woman wrote:

This depicts the death of a beloved coworker of mine. Marques Gaines was a beautiful human being and he deserves justice.

The post was undeniably hitting the right neighborhood.

With the Facebook boost set, I moved over to Twitter. I edited the video down to forty seconds and shrank the text to fit Twitter's frugal 140-character limit at the time: "Chicago, corner of State+Hubbard. Please help identify man in green hooded jacket. #JusticeforMarques."

I purchased a boost of thirty-five dollars to reach Twitter users within a one-mile radius of the 7-Eleven. That first night, I got a handful of retweets but little else. I had to get resourceful. Who did I know in Chicago with a lot of followers who could retweet the video and get it in front of more people?

The crime happened in the middle of an assortment of sports bars, so I went back to my origins. The first time I was in Chicago was when my dad took me on a vacation to Wrigley Field to watch the Mets play a four-game swing against the Cubs. We shouted loudly for New York, Dad relishing being the lone dissenters surrounded by thirty-four thousand rabid Chicago fans. Chicago is a sports town, and the sports writers, bloggers, and TV personalities have passionate followers on social media. I reached out to a dozen of them, but they didn't know me from Adam, and for them to ask their Twitter followers if they recognized a killer wasn't exactly on brand. But there was one sports guy I knew who might be willing to help.

I sent a direct message to @FanSince09, a snarky sports blogger from Philadelphia whom I had interviewed a few months earlier when he helped solve a crime. @FanSince09 is a sports social justice warrior who anonymously fights the good fight against hatred.

When he heard about a gay couple who were brutally beaten in downtown Philadelphia, with one of his followers tweeting a CCTV video of the alleged assailants, it made him mad. Over Twitter, he teamed up with All-Pro Eagles lineman Evan Mathis and a Philly detective. The unlikely trio retweeted surveillance video images of the attackers—who looked like upper-middle-class college kids out for a night on the town— and asked for help identifying them. The crowd then jumped into the fray and searched the Facebook pages of restaurants and bars in the area. They looked into every person who had checked into every restaurant on the night of the assault and found a woman who had posted a group photo of a bunch of upper-middle-class college kids inside one eatery. Some of the males in the photo matched the males in the surveillance images. The information was sent to the detective. The suspects were arrested. This was crowdsourcing at its finest.

His Philadelphia connections wouldn't help with this one, but sports tweeters are an incestuous bunch. @FanSince09 said he knew a guy and reached out to Dan Katz, a.k.a. @BarstoolBigCat, who ran the *Barstool Sports* Chicago blog. BigCat gave me a retweet, which in turn garnered a dozen more retweets. But by 9:00 p.m., I still had no leads.

I was $135 in the hole. The money didn't matter, and I was used to the frustration. But I had thought I was onto something and was dismayed it wasn't working. I kept monitoring the Facebook page and the Twitter feed throughout the night, racking my brain for the right scheme to reach that one person who could help. I drifted off to sleep about midnight.

I woke up at 3:00 a.m., reached for my phone, and opened Twitter. The Man in the Green Hoodie was staring right at me.

Someone had seen @BarstoolBigCat's retweet and replied to him and me with an image of the puncher, almost a portrait of him, wearing the same outfit from the night of the assault.

"Hope this helps," he wrote.

Holy shit, I said to myself. *What the hell is this?*

At first, I thought it was a mock-up—that this guy had done some sort of 3-D rendering like the woman said she was going to do earlier in the day. It was a clear, front-facing picture of the Man with the Green Hoodie looking directly into the camera.

I immediately tweeted back at him: "Thanks. Did you make this?"

I needed to talk to him right away. People are predisposed to be more truthful at 3:00 a.m. than at 3:00 p.m. Besides, my mind was spinning. Where did he get that photo? Was he there? Did he witness the attack? I followed him on Twitter and asked him to follow me back so we could have a private conversation. He finally responded.

He told me that one of his friends was at the corner of Hubbard and State that night and had taken the photo. I asked if he could put me in touch with the friend. And I waited. I waited for what seemed like forever. The next day, he responded. "He doesn't really want to talk to anyone about it so it doesn't sound like he is going to reach out."

Dammit.

Now, I'm not a cop. I can't subpoena someone's phone records or bring someone into an interrogation room or make deals for less jail time or better TV privileges. I don't have many weapons in my arsenal. I resorted to one of the few tactics at my disposal: I begged. "If you could plead with him," I wrote back. "His name won't be released—hell, he doesn't have to use a name at all. We just need more information, such as if he heard the puncher talk, what the argument was about, and if he had an accent."

The next day turned into night as I fell asleep waiting for an answer. I woke up at 3:00 a.m. (again) and checked my phone. It was him.

Hey man, FYI, I took a screen shot of this and sent it to him and haven't heard back. I did find something that might help. This was from a saved snapchat he took that I found in the archives of a group message. You can hear the puncher yelling in it and get a better look at his face.

Below the message was an image with a white-and-blue play button in the center indicating to me it was made with the Snapchat app. Behind the button was a still image of a man lying in the street, his arms at his sides, his eyes closed. It was Marques Gaines.

His friend didn't just take a photo—he shot a video.

I sucked as much oxygen as I could gather into my lungs. Then I pressed play.

The camera begins focused on Marques passed out in the crosswalk. If I didn't know any better, I would have thought he was sleeping. In a split second, the camera pans up and swings counterclockwise to the sidewalk. There, staring right at me, is the Man in the Green Hoodie. His hood is now off his head. Both fists are clenched. He walks straight toward me, stopping inches before the camera, his face filling up the entire screen. He yells something I can't quite make out. Then the video ends.

I was frozen. It was like someone had just sent me a Super 8 movie of Oswald skulking away from his sniper's nest at the book depository in Dallas.

I now had a clear, face-forward photo of the Man in the Green Hoodie that I could compare against the database of mugshots.

I played the four-second video over again. In addition to a clear image, I also now had another detail that I needed: the man's voice. He did not have an accent. He sounded like a U.S. native. But what was he saying?

I closed my eyes and tried to isolate his words. After the fifth try, I finally got it.

Over the buzzing commotion following the assault, the Man in the Green Hoodie walks back toward Marques lying in the street and yells "Get your faggot ass up."

I knew they might not be able to get him on murder—they might charge him with aggravated assault or, at best, manslaughter. But with this audio, there might be proof that this was a hate crime, which carries a stiffer sentence when coupled with an assault. It also showed why the initial group of people dispersed so quickly after the punch. The Man in the Green Hoodie had frightened them away.

Sending the video to Drexina cold—the last image of her cousin, lying helpless in the street just before a taxicab runs over him—would be devastating. I needed to wait and show her in person.

And I had mugshots to go through. Luckily, Cook County, Illinois, releases all its mugshots to the public. This has created a cottage industry—basically an extortion racket—in which websites publish the name and mugshot of everyone who is arrested for all the search engines to find. If your mugshot keeps showing up when a future employer or prospective lover googles your name, you can contact these sites, and they will take it down—for a substantial fee, of course.

This is where the investigation would get decidedly old school. I was not in possession of facial recognition technology, and while that software is becoming more advanced, it might not have been effective in this case. I was going to do this one photo at a time.

I was looking for a black man with a scowl, a heavy brow, and a widow's peak. I reached out for help from a production assistant who was helping with the citizen-detective TV show I had created, which was going to be called *Crowdsolve*, and we split up the digital pile as best we could, working into the night to try to find the puncher in the haystack. Over the course of forty-eight hours, I went through more than three thousand photos. Every time I saw a widow's peak, I set the photo aside.

That left me with fifty. From there, I looked for the scowl and brow. That left me with three.

I placed each of them on my screen next to the Snapchat video of the Man with the Green Hoodie. They all looked good, but each one had something going against him: one was too old, one was too pudgy, and one was too tall.

The older guy just looked too...old. The pudgy guy was a little too short, as the puncher didn't look like he was smaller than the people around him. I liked the tall guy, but he was listed at six foot four, and the puncher didn't look exceptionally tall on the video. I'm six foot four, and when I see myself on video, I'm always alarmed by how freakishly gigantic I can look next to an average-sized person. I wasn't getting that sense from this guy.

But he looked *a lot* like the man in the video. We ran a background report on him.

His name was Marcus Moore, and his rap sheet was considerable:

Obstruction of traffic 8/28/2013. Possession of cannabis (2.5–10 grams) 7/25/2013. Two counts of criminal damage of property, reckless driving, eluding police, speeding, and driving with a suspended license 2/21/2012. Panhandling. Reckless conduct.

Most importantly, two of the arrests took place within a few blocks of the incident with Marques.

I was maybe 75 percent sure he was the man I was looking for. The height was still bothering me, but he was for sure a big guy.

Then I found him on Facebook. I scrolled through his pictures: Marcus Moore wearing a Chicago Bulls cap, throwing up a peace sign and a sly smile. Marcus Moore wearing a Chicago White Sox cap, sneering at the camera. Marcus Moore wearing a stocking cap, grinning.

Then I saw a selfie from December 15, 2015. Marcus Moore wearing a wifebeater and a scowl, his brow furrowed over his dark eyes. This time, he wasn't wearing a hat. His widow's peak was in all its V-shaped glory.

It was him. It had to be him.

I talked to the production company in Los Angeles that wanted to film my citizen-detective show. Each episode was supposed to begin with me visiting with an amateur sleuth and helping shift their investigations into high gear by offering up multiple resources—DNA testing, facial reconstruction, sonar searches in lakes and rivers. But this would be a different show—just me. And the Marques Gaines case would be the first episode. After looking at the pictures, they agreed that Marcus Moore was most probably the guy who punched Marques Gaines, and we should go to Chicago and see if we could connect all the dots and prove it.

I flew to Chicago in August, film crew in tow. Drexina and her mother, Marques's aunt, Phyllis, would meet me there. Before I could start the investigation on the ground, the crew had me re-create some moments that had already happened in order to craft a cohesive narrative. The scene of me watching the Snapchat video of the puncher for the first time had shifted from me lying in my bed in LA to me walking across the DuSable Bridge over the Chicago river.

I met with Drexina and Phyllis, and they told me stories about the type of guy Marques had been. Happy-go-lucky. Electric smile. They told me about their frustrations with the case, about how much they had cried. I couldn't tell them about my suspect yet. I still had one more thing to do. I wanted to confirm that the guy I found online was the guy we were all looking for. I wanted as much evidence as I could get before I contacted the police with the name of the suspect. And I knew my luck would multiply if I waited until dark. With time to kill, we walked together toward the scene of the crime.

During the day, the corner of Hubbard and State pulses in the heart of a thriving business-meets-tourist district. There's a bar or restaurant every twenty feet. It's bright and sunny, nothing like the ominous and unpolished location in the video I had watched dozens of times. I stood in the spot in front of the 7-Eleven where Marques was confronted and walked in those final steps he took before he landed in the crosswalk. I saw how the slope of the sidewalk aided in the devastation of the punch; Marques was running away, but when he turned to face the puncher, his momentum took him down the slope toward the road. When the Man in the Green Hoodie reeled back, he planted his foot into the downslope and landed his right hook. The momentum of a man that big, walking swiftly downhill, made the punch that much more ferocious. Placed in the right location, it was enough to knock any man out.

Standing in the middle of a scene I had experienced only in photos and videos was like the first time I stood on the grassy knoll in Dealey Plaza or peered over the fence into the Brentwood courtyard where Nicole Brown and Ronald Goldman were murdered. Everything seemed smaller and closer together. I looked up and saw the camera that filmed the punch, perched above the traffic light at the intersection of State and Hubbard. I took photos and measurements of the area for a pseudo-scientific experiment to see if I could compare my height with the puncher's when I reviewed the video back at the hotel.

But mostly, I found myself looking down at the ground.

I stepped off the curb and bent down in the street, touching the part of the black asphalt where it met the thick white paint of the crosswalk. This was no place for anyone to die.

I wanted to grab every single person who was walking past me and show them the photo of the Man in the Green Hoodie that I was holding in my back pocket. To see if they had seen him, knew his name was Marcus, or maybe even knew where he might be. But it was still daytime, and at this intersection, daytime was a whole 'nother planet compared to what happens at night. I went back to the hotel and spent the next two hours rewatching the video.

My plan was to wait for the sun to set, then walk down Hubbard and show the photo to every valet, bouncer, and beggar I came across. The film crew would follow fifteen feet behind me, along with two armed, plainclothes former Chicago police officers, which the crew insisted on hiring.

With fifteen minutes to kill before darkness, I shuffled aimlessly around the block, circling past the 7-Eleven and the gutter where Marques died, past one of the two alleys where I believed the guys who scavenged through his pockets might have escaped, craning my neck to find every security camera that might have caught their faces.

The search for more cameras sat at the bottom of just one of the thousands of rabbit holes I've jumped down. The angle of the grassy knoll, the coded letters of Son of Sam, the cell phone records of a murdered DJ in Miami, the 1979 Merrimack County, New Hampshire, Yellow Pages looking for the names of the victims in the barrel. The unreturned phone calls. The no-outlet dead ends. Every editor telling me I'm too deep into the story and to wrap it up. Every detective telling me to just let it go. Every reader asking me how the story ends. "How does it end?" "I hope they catch the guy?" "How does it end?" "They catch him, right?" "But seriously, how does it end?"

But you keep going. No matter what is thrown in your way, you keep moving forward. Because these crimes, crimes like the Marques Gaines case or the Golden State Killer, they don't solve themselves. They sit in boxes in evidence lockers collecting dust until someone comes along and says, "I'm not going to stop until I catch this guy." And it's probably not all that healthy to say that. But often, it's the only way it will get done.

————————————————

With the sun finally down, I was ready to begin, prepared to cover three square blocks starting down Hubbard. I walked at a brisk pace, the camera crew following discreetly, noticeable only if you were explicitly looking for them. I approached a valet in front of a steakhouse at the corner of Dearborn and Hubbard, pulled out the photo from my back pocket, and asked if he recognized the man. He didn't. I approached the doorman standing in front of the Howl at the Moon bar next door. Another blank.

I was halfway to State Street when I saw an older man wearing soiled, ill-fitting clothes and a weathered face walking toward me.

"Sir, I was wondering, could I ask you a question?"

"Okay," he replied in a gravelly timbre.

I leaned in close and pulled out the still image from the video.

"Do you recognize this guy?" I asked.

He looked at it and didn't wait a beat.

"Yeah, that's Big Dummy," he told me. "Real name's Marcus."

A bolt of lightning went through me, cracking me in the chest and coming out my fingers, which started to shake. *Keep it together. Keep. It. Together.*

"Do you think we could move over here?" I asked him, wanting to get out of the way of passing pedestrians. He asked if we could go somewhere else to talk. I had no idea who this guy was or what he could do. For all I knew, he was a friend of Big Dummy's.

Thankfully, he followed me away from the street, and we stopped in front of the window of a bar called Rockit. I huddled next to him, leaning down to make sure I caught every word. In that moment, he was

Gandhi, Buddha, Jesus. In that moment, he was telling me the secrets of the universe.

He told me Big Dummy spent his days in the caverns of Lower Wacker, a tunnel that travels underneath the skyscrapers just a few blocks away. At night, he came out around Hubbard and State. He hadn't seen him for a while, but he was sure: "Big Dummy, real name Marcus."

I handed him a twenty-dollar bill and thanked him for his help. I would have given him a thousand if I had had it on me. Within five minutes, I had gotten confirmation for my first solve. Marcus Moore was the puncher, the Man in the Green Hoodie. Now I wanted to find out where he was. I talked to a dozen more people in the streets and down Lower Wacker. I learned that Marcus liked to refer to himself as "the King of the Streets." That he hadn't been around the neighborhood for a few months. And that he might be holed up at a shelter north of the city.

I got back to my room around 10:00 p.m. on a high, seventeen years of scratching and clawing and I was so close to finally getting a result. I finished building the dossier on Marcus Moore that I would deliver to the detectives. It contained Moore's background information, arrest record, known addresses, family members and associates, Facebook profile, and a description of how I had come to the conclusion that he was the man they were searching for. I was also running through my head how I was going to tell Drexina and Phyllis that I had discovered the identity of the man who had caused Marques's death.

I reached for my phone to text Michelle what had just happened. I had just scrolled past the *K*'s on my contact list when I remembered.

The next morning, I met Drexina and Phyllis along the Chicago Riverwalk. We sat on a park bench in the bright sun, and I spelled out the entire investigation to them in detail: the Facebook page I had created, the boosted posts, the sports blogger I had reached out to, the retweets I got in Chicago. Everything leading up to the Snapchat video. Then I took out my phone.

"It's not going to be easy to watch," I warned them.

Drexina said she understood, but they needed to see it.

I handed the phone to her and pressed play.

The moment she saw Marques on the ground, she let out a wail and turned her head away from the screen while at the same time pushing the phone back into my hands.

I didn't think I could hate this Marcus guy even more.

She took five seconds and a deep breath, then turned back around and reached for the phone. I pressed play again. We watched as the camera panned from her cousin lying motionless on the street to the Man in the Green Hoodie snarling at the camera.

She only needed to watch it once.

"He's just a big bully," she said.

I showed them Marcus Moore's Facebook page, presently featuring a new girlfriend and changed relationship status. Now that the villain was fully fleshed, seeing him in real life—or at least as real life as Facebook can be—was maddening for Drexina. I showed her the dossier I would be giving to the detectives, and then something struck me.

"I wish I could go have a drink with Marques," I said to her. "I just wish I could tell him about it. About how everything came together. That's what we should be doing tonight." My first solve was not what I thought it would be. It was elation swiftly followed by a numbing, hollow comedown.

We hugged each other, and I told them I would do everything in my power to aid the police in apprehending Marcus Moore.

I called the detectives to try to arrange a meeting to tell them what I had found. I left a message. I went to Drexina's lawyer's office and dropped off the dossier with all the information I had gathered, then had a courier drop off a duplicate to the police department, addressed to the detective in charge.

All I got back from him was a confirmation that he had received the information.

———————————

Back home, I continued to monitor Marcus Moore's Facebook page. In the fall, he changed his "current city" to Holbrook, New York. And in September, he posted a photo of himself in front of what looked like a work truck. From his background check, I knew his brother lived in Bloomington, Minnesota. Zooming in on the logo on the side of the truck, I could see a *T* surrounded by a red circle. A web search of businesses and city trucks in Minnesota revealed that the same logo was found on many transit vehicles in the Minneapolis/St. Paul area. On September 14, Moore posted that he was in a relationship with a woman whose profile listed her as living in the Twin Cities area. Posting that he was living in Holbrook, New York, was a ruse. He was in Minnesota.

I sent emails to the detectives with this information. I heard nothing back. I had to remember the mantra I always told victims' families they needed to recite when dealing with law enforcement. "The squeaky wheel gets the grease." When a police department has an ever-growing mountain of unsolved cases, the ones that scream the loudest are going to get the most attention. I needed to continue to be the squeaky wheel for Marques.

I would call or email the detectives around once a week. I instructed Drexina to do the same. We also reached out to the state's attorney's office, the local alderman, the two former Chicago cops who were my security the night in Chicago when we got confirmation of Marcus's identity—everyone we could think of. I searched on LinkedIn for people with Chicago Police Department contacts and cold messaged a bunch of them. I needed to get someone, anyone, who might be able to move the ball forward on the investigation and put out a warrant for Marcus Moore's arrest.

Come Christmastime, I sent a plea to the police: it was the holidays, and there was a good chance that Marcus Moore could be back at his mother's house in the Chicago area.

Nothing.

I called Drexina, and we mulled over options. She continued monitoring Marcus Moore's Facebook page, getting more livid every time he posted a new photo of himself laughing, smoking, or showing off the new beads he was sporting in his hair.

Right before the new year, I received a lifeline. A retired detective I had found on LinkedIn was willing to listen. He made a round of phone calls to his old contacts, then called me.

"I found out something," he said. "There's a stop/arrest alert for Marcus Moore." That meant that if he was picked up for anything in the Chicagoland area, he would be questioned about the Marques Gaines homicide. But if he was arrested in another state—like Minnesota, where I was pretty sure he was hiding out—that information would not come up in a background check and he could walk.

I kept pressing. January 20 brought another call from my retired detective source. He told me that within the last seventy-two hours, an arrest warrant had been issued for Marcus Moore. The charge was aggravated battery. Chicago police were working with the U.S. Marshals Service, searching for him in an "upper Midwest state." It felt like it was heating up.

A week later, I was at the *Crime Watch Daily* newsroom, working on another case, when my phone rang.

It was Drexina. I ran to the makeup room and answered the call. She didn't even say hello.

"They got him!" she exclaimed. I could hear her smiling.

I felt like jumping up and down. I felt like screaming. But I tried to play it cool and instead punched the air as hard as I could as the word "Yes!" erupted out of my gut and echoed through the empty room.

Marcus Moore was found in Minnesota. He waived extradition and was shipped back to Illinois. In his mugshot, he clowned for the camera, contorting his face into a slanted, grotesque snarl. The men who had robbed Marques in the street were still unidentified, but the Man in the Green Hoodie was king of the streets no more.

Nine whole months had elapsed between the conception of the plan and getting him in handcuffs. Nine months plus nearly two decades of trying and failing. But finally, finally, it worked. My first solve was behind bars. I was over the moon.

But once the euphoria subsided, I have to admit, all I could think of was the word *rip-off*.

When someone would ask about my dad and I would say he was dead, that was the word that always came to mind: *rip-off*. It was just a rip-off that he had invested so much creating and molding and shaping me, and he would never see the end of my stories. Now, I had finally done it. The story he might have read in the newspaper would have a bow on it, neatly wrapped up. "Look at this," he might have told the eight-year-old me. "This guy tried to solve crimes for seventeen years and finally got one. Remember, the lesson is nothing in the world can take the place of persistence."

But he wasn't here, and it all just felt like a rip-off.

I once read an interview with comedian Mike Myers, where he talked about his dad dying, and he gave me some better words to articulate what I was feeling whenever something good happened to me.

"Things only became real when I would tell him," he said. "And much of the work I was doing was for him, to make him proud, to make him happy. My dad was kind of like the cashier window at the casino. Things that would happen were just chips, but when I told my dad, it would turn into money. And that went away."

That was just my own selfish thought. Drexina and Phyllis were dealing with a far bigger rip-off. The arrest was not going to bring Marques back.

The day after I learned the Man in the Green Hoodie was caught, I flew back to Phoenix. My wife, Kendall, turned to me in bed that night and asked me how it felt. I reminded her of that quote from Mike Myers. Then I shrugged. "I don't know what to feel," I said. "I just know I want to find another one."

I opened my laptop and began scanning the headlines of other cases I had been collecting. Hit-and-runs and drive-bys and botched robberies and sex worker slayings.

These were not the cases people built podcasts around. They were "ordinary" murders. Blink-of-the-eye murders. No twists. No turns. No one was going to be debating their theories about these murders over brunch.

The world didn't need another story about the Zodiac Killer or Jack the Ripper. The murders in the shadows add up to a hell of a lot more than the murders in the spotlight. The shadows are where I needed to tread, because that's where the problem lay. The blood of the forgotten was just as red as the "famous" victims.

There is one common thread between the shows that grabbed America's attention in the true-crime renaissance of the 2010s. *Making a Murderer, The Jinx, O. J. Simpson: Made in America, The Staircase.* They all centered around white female victims.

Their murders all needed to be solved. And there were a lot of people out there trying to solve them. The cases I was working on at night were not the types of stories that "rated" for crime shows like *Crime Watch Daily* or *Dateline* or anything on ID. There were none of the kinds of "oh, shit" moments that make Keith Morrison's eyebrow raise or Karen tell Georgia, "Don't worry, it gets worse!" on *My Favorite Murder*.

Most of my victims were not suburban soccer moms. They were males of color. Or white female drug addicts. Sex workers. Or people in the wrong place at the wrong time. No love triangles or fancy intrigue. They were the victims who make up the bulk of the murders that go unsolved every year. Lives worth no less than JonBenét's or Nicole Brown's.

There were few clues left behind by the killers I was going to be chasing. No intricately knotted pieces of rope. No coded letters. No DNA. Nothing that people like me—and everyone else who has ever swum in someone else's blood while reading a true crime tale—could hang a clever theory on.

What I did have with most of them was an image. Grainy, blurry, blown up, distorted. But still, an image. Taken outside a liquor store or above the counter of a pawn shop. Inside a parking garage or down a garbage-strewn alley so foul you could smell it through the screen.

These were the neighborhoods where I would need to set up shop. Not an upscale block of million-dollar Tudors in Boulder or million-dollar condos in Brentwood. My victims would not be getting their own Lifetime movies. But their stories all deserved an ending. All two hundred thousand of them.

That's how many unsolved murders there are in America since 1980. We add five thousand more to that number every year.

And I had just solved one.

One.

I scanned the files of the unsolved murders I had been collecting over the years, the villain now with 199,999 faces smiling back at me. All sorts of manner of death—stabbings, drive-bys, hit-and-runs, brutal beatings, arson. But I was excited. These were going to get knocked down one by one, I thought. I separated them into piles, the ones with surveillance footage of the suspect going to the top of the list. Lurking in another pile was the Golden State Killer, sitting atop just a fraction of Michelle's files.

9

THE VILLAIN WITH A THOUSAND FACES

West Hollywood, May 2016

KENDALL AND I ATTENDED THE MEMORIAL FOR MICHELLE AT the Largo Theater in West Hollywood. Waiting for the program to begin, the snare drum entrance of David Bowie's "Five Years" crept up through the speakers, and it felt like a piano was sitting on my chest. It was crystal clear from the vibe in the theater that Michelle had so many people who loved her.

Afterward, as family and friends and celebrities spilled past us in the lobby on their way to the reception, I spied a man with short blond hair and piercing blue eyes. It was Paul Holes, an investigator for the Contra Costa district attorney's office in Northern California. A cross section between detective and crime-scene investigator, Holes had worked on cases ranging from the 1991 kidnapping of Jaycee Dugard to the Northern California serial killer Joe Naso. But for the last two decades, he had been working day and night to discover the identity of the Golden State Killer.

Michelle had told me about Holes. He was sharp and confident. And a little dreamy. They shared information about the case, and he had placed a lot of trust in Michelle.

After I wrote the tribute to Michelle, I had received an email from Holes. Michelle wasn't exaggerating about the extent of their collaboration.

> I read your tribute—very true. Michelle earned our trust—it wasn't just given. She proved over and over I could tell her something in confidence and she kept it that way. Between that trust and her tremendous natural investigative mind she was accepted into a very close-knit group. Quite frankly, I'm not sure anybody else could have pulled it off to the point she did... I didn't know her at the same level as you but I feel like I've lost a member of my family.

"I really considered Michelle my detective partner in this case," he told me in another email. "We just didn't ride together, but constantly were in communication. I would get excited about something I found out and would send it to her and she would also get excited."

I approached him, and we shook hands. I told him I was going to work with Patton to make sure Michelle's book was published. And then I tried to show my bona fides by talking about some other cases I was working on, in a clumsy attempt to impress upon him that the book was in competent hands.

"I just worked on a story about the Allenstown Four," I told him. "Four bodies found in barrels, a woman and three little girls, still unidentified."

"Have they run DNA?"

"Yes," I said. "Nothing. They could be from Canada. Or overseas. They just can't find anything..."

I paused for a second.

"They still haven't tried familial yet."

He knew what that meant. Michelle had told me about her and Paul's conversations about using familial DNA searches to catch the

Golden State Killer. By entering DNA from a crime scene into a public database of DNA samples submitted by genealogical buffs across the globe, you could find a relative who could then lead you to the person you were searching for. Since Kendall, a neuroscientist, was with me, I steered the conversation toward how we might be able to get the GSK's sample into a database like 23andMe or Ancestry. Paul was up for it, if they could get the okay from the companies.

But he also mentioned that there was only so much of GSK's DNA to go around.

"We don't have a ton of it," he said.

"Have they tried doing whole genome amplification?" Kendall asked him. "It's pretty cheap. And you could get enough material to work with to do a lot of tests. You could do whole genome sequencing. Exome capture. SNP arrays." If you could sequence the whole genome of a person from a sample found at a crime scene, you could map out every base in a person's genome. Every change that makes them different from all other people. Other tests cover just parts of the genome, specific chromosomes (Y chromosome), or small single nucleotide changes. Unique identifications can be made using any of these strategies; they just differ in their completeness. But whole genome was the whole enchilada. If you were able to map the whole genome, you could enter it into the public DNA database. And it would connect not just with brothers and uncles but third and fourth cousins.

If it could be used, thousands of cold cases could be solved. Rape kits sitting in storage lockers could be sequenced and compared with the samples in the database, and detectives could track down the thousands of attackers who thought they got away with it. The people spending ninety-nine dollars, spitting in a tube, and sending it off to 23andMe and Ancestry could hold the keys to unlocking so many unsolved crimes.

Kendall and Paul talked geek for a little longer. I was focused on the task of getting the book done. But getting a solve for Michelle would be an amazing bonus.

———————————   ———————————

Every night around nine o'clock, I took a break from my cases to work on Michelle's manuscript. It was less than two months since Michelle had died, and Patton was still in rough shape. But he connected me with Paul Haynes, whom Michelle referred to as "the Kid" in her *Los Angeles* magazine article about her search for the Golden State Killer. Michelle had met Paul (who was not a kid at all but a twenty-nine-year-old writer and cinephile living in Florida) on one of the East Area Rapist/Original Night Stalker message boards and was impressed with his ability to mine data and find virtually anyone who was living in the neighborhoods where the attacker was hitting in the mid to late '70s. She offered him a job as her research assistant, and he moved out to Los Angeles. She called him "the case's greatest amateur hope."

Haynes sent me Michelle's hard drive. "The total number of files I transferred over from Michelle is 4,296, totaling 38.33 GB," he wrote. "That was on top of the 35 Bankers Boxes, and 2 outsize Sterilite-type bins of case files and evidence that we cajoled from the OCSD [Orange County Sheriff's Department] January of this year. This feat represented the greatest development in our work on the case to date, really. Michelle and I considered this acquisition to be the 'mother lode.'"

I began sifting through the documents, each bearing a tantalizing file name: "Goleta Dog Stabbing," "Remaining Questions," and "I hunted the serial killer from my daughter's playroom." There were emails from Michelle to her book editor from the very start of her journey.

I'm heading up to Contra Costa County (suburban area just east of San Francisco) for a couple of days. My sense is that Paul

Holes, chief of the crime lab up there, is going to be an essential source for me, and he's able to dedicate a day and a half for my visit, taking me to the crime scenes, to the lab, introducing me to some of the old-timers who were there back in the day. I'm thrilled. It's a real mix of old and new, which is exactly what I'd hoped for.

There were maps and graphs and photos of sneaker treads and diamond knots left at the crime scenes. And a very, very long list of suspects. In one file was an inventory of all the items the East Area Rapist took from the houses he attacked: "Binoculars, scientific calculator, salt and pepper shakers, champagne, butter dishes," with the heading "Unusual things to take in my opinion."

"Paul [Haynes] and I are going through the major holes that are left within the narrative and seeing what we can find to fill them with her words only," I wrote to Patton and Michelle's agent. "I have an idea for Part 3. I was thinking it is very organic to just show some of the threads she would have kept following by going through her computer."

Michelle had written a lot of chapters, but they were not in any kind of order, and we had to lay them out to create a coherent narrative. We settled on starting in the past with the Original Night Stalker murders, then on to the tale of the series of rapes in Sacramento by the East Area Rapist. These two seemingly unrelated story lines would converge in the "holy shit" chapter when the Orange County crime lab discovered that all the crimes were committed by the same unknown assailant. Part 2 would pick up with Michelle traveling to the crime scenes, meeting with investigators and victims' family members. Interspersed throughout were stories about her home life and her motivations for telling crime stories. She never intended on covering all forty-nine rapes and twelve murders in the book, but there *were* some events that we needed to include, which we pieced together from her notes, emails, and early drafts of her *Los Angeles* magazine article. There was so much material to work with that the book could have been twice as long.

Haynes not only knew where the bodies were buried but also their state of decay and the alkaline percentage of the soil on top of them. We split up the chapters and went to work seeing where we could fill in gaps with her writing—plugging a hole with a note she had written in one document here, filling in missing details from an email there.

Part 3 would be written by myself and Haynes. Patton gave us one word of guidance when it came to the section we wrote: mechanical. He wanted just the facts and theories, free from emotion. We focused on the two methods Michelle believed would eventually lead to identifying the villain, geographic profiling and familial DNA.

Haynes had become adept at geographic profiling, or geoprofiling, a method used by law enforcement to map out a series of connected crimes to attempt to nail down where the offender might live, work, or spend significant amounts of time. He had compiled an impressive collection of 1970s phone books and census records from the neighborhoods where the East Area Rapist had struck. As he hit so many houses within such a small area, we thought for sure the attacker either lived, worked, or had some other reason to be close by, possibly in a "buffer zone," close enough to where he was attacking to know the streets but far enough away to not be easily recognized.

With Paul writing about the geography of the attacks and the probability that the Golden State Killer was very familiar with the area, I focused on the other identification method Michelle thought would lead to a solve. Investigators had entered the DNA found at the Golden State Killer crime scenes into the Combined DNA Index System (CODIS) database, searching for either an exact match or a familial match. But CODIS records only thirteen sites in the genome, which means that matches can be made only to close relatives—parents, children, and siblings. And CODIS only included the DNA from criminals.

Michelle had been corresponding with a volunteer genealogist named Colleen Fitzpatrick, and they had entered the Y-STR DNA profile of the killer into a public database called Ysearch. Ysearch only had a few hundred thousand samples, as opposed to the millions in closed databases like 23andMe and Ancestry. Michelle thought she had found GSK once when his DNA had matched more than twenty markers of a man with a unique British or Germanic surname. The match was far away—maybe eight generations. But it was a lead. We went up and down the family trees of that surname, pulling up old British census records, trying to connect him. It went nowhere. But Michelle knew the answer was undoubtedly sitting behind the locked doors of 23andMe and Ancestry. A third or fourth cousin of the killer who wanted to learn about his family history, who paid the ninety-nine dollars and spit in a tube. His spit would be processed on a genome-wide set of single-nucleotide polymorphisms or SNPs, which are little changes in a single nucleotide, one of the three billion pairs of nucleotides that occur in a precise location in the human genome. They are known areas of personal variation. Multiply those variations by the millions of places that those changes occur in your genome, and you get the differences between people. Everyone is different, but if you find a sample with enough similarities to the sample you uploaded, it could mean that the two people are related. If Michelle was able to enter the GSK's DNA into a large database, the service would send her an email with all the cousins they found who were related to the killer. She would then have to build a family tree, eliminate individuals based on age and location and other factors, and eventually land on the Golden State Killer. But 23andMe and Ancestry's databases are fiercely guarded by the companies' terms of service, which guarantee privacy against outside elements looking to exploit the data. For instance, if DNA profiles were accessible to a health insurance firm weighing the likelihood of people getting sick, it could cost users billions of dollars. So they remain closed.

Every other night, I would bang my head against the wall, knowing that the answer to this horrendous riddle was sitting inside the databases of 23andMe and Ancestry. All the time Michelle and Holes and dozens of other people spent looking into clues, like a piece of homework or shoelaces left at the crime scene, could have been saved if these databases would simply let us open the door to their DNA warehouse, find a good match of a second or third cousin, then search to narrow down the findings till we zeroed in on the perfect suspect. It was enough to drive you to drink. And I drank a lot of bourbon sitting in my living room, computer at my lap, working on *I'll Be Gone in the Dark* while the TV played reruns of *The Office*.

True-crime podcasts were coming on like gangbusters, but I wouldn't listen to any of them. The only time I spent away from crime was when I was in my car driving to work, and Sal and Richard's buffoonery on Howard Stern's show was what I required to keep me somewhat human. I might seek asylum by opening a prize inside a cereal box or sneak a read about Walt Disney and his Imagineers creating imaginary worlds at Disneyland. Things that didn't take up much time, because whenever I would go astray for more than an hour, I would get trapped in an existential maze where every signpost was scrawled "Keep trying to solve the next murder," right next to "How will Michelle be remembered?" Her legacy was lurking inside her hard drive, a living, breathing behemoth to be trimmed, organized, and then unleashed into the world. Not only for the words and work that could lead to an arrest but for Alice, the little girl who could hold onto her mother's book forever. If this book failed, Michelle couldn't write another one. This was her only shot. And at the same time all this was going through my head, there was a killer in the shadows needing to be identified, standing only slightly in front of the more than two hundred thousand other killers who needed to be brought into the light.

But no matter how many brilliant chapters she might have written— and they were intense, sparkling chapters filled with facts and empathy and a little frustration—the book was still not going to have an ending. He was still out there. Then I came across a file titled "Letter to an Old Man." After ten thousand hours of hunting and one hundred thousand words, the letter is Michelle speaking directly to the killer. Just him and her. She begins with reminding him of the details of his crimes from so long ago, of the pain he caused, the things he stole, and how he got away. But then the letter morphs from a reminiscence to a plea for him to show his face, to give himself up. And then it mutates again, this time to a prediction bordering on a warning to the killer.

"You excelled at the stealth sidle. But your heyday prowess has no value anymore. Your skill set has been phased out. The tables have been turned. Virtual windows are opening all around you. You, the master watcher, are an aging, lumbering target in their crosshairs. A ski mask won't help you now."

My hairs stood on edge. It was as if she knew she would be gone and this would be her coda. And it was one of the most intimidating things I had ever read. Her prose had turned the hunter into the hunted. To be honest, I could barely write a word of my own for six months after I read it.

———

I was tinkering with my new solving-crimes-with-social-media method, looking for the next case to tackle, confident that the success of the Marques Gaines case after so many years of frustration was going to open the floodgates of justice. But life was also going on around me. My daughter graduated high school. For her present, she wanted to go to Disney World. We hadn't been there since she was seven.

"The crimes can wait," Kendall said to me.

What? I had finally solved my first crime. After almost two decades of trying. And I'm supposed to go on a vacation? I didn't want to hit pause. And this was the Magic Kingdom we were talking about, but I didn't care. I wanted to dive headfirst into every case I'd ever come across and use this new technique to try to solve them all. But there was one fact I knew above all else. *My dad would move mountains to take her*, I told myself. So we booked a trip.

When you have tattoos, people ask you what they mean. I have a Tonka truck bulldozer on my back, with my son's name on it. It is driving up from my side and recreating the scar my son got from the heart surgery he had as a baby. On my right triceps is a quill pen, because no matter what job I am doing, I will always identify myself as a writer and story-teller first. On my left forearm is a magnifying glass, because I am an investigator and am forever attempting to uncover a mystery. And on my lower left leg is the monorail coming out of the Contemporary Hotel at Walt Disney World.

I can explain the first three pretty easily, but the fourth is the one that raises the most eyebrows. "Why would you get a tattoo of a monorail and a Disney hotel?"

When I was little, my dad worked a lot. As a painting contractor who owned his own business, he had to go out on nights and weekends to do estimates—look at rich people's houses and give them a price for what it would cost for him to put "colored liquid on their houses," as he once called it. Then during the day, six days a week, he would paint them.

Because the meetings for the estimates were often at the whim of the homeowners, I never knew what time they were happening. So when I would ask my dad if we could do something—go to Toys"R"Us for a new G.I. Joe figure or go to the rocket ship playground—he would always reply "Maybe." The maybes almost always turned to yeses. But there was always this uncertainty. I was always having to share my dad with his work. Except at Disney World.

He first took me there when I was two years old. And we went back every February break. At Disney, my dad was all mine. When I would ask "Can we go on the Pirates of the Caribbean?" the answer was always yes. "Can we go to the hotel arcade?" Yes. "The Mystery Fun House?" Yes.

I was twelve the last time he took me to Disney, and for the first time, we stayed at the Contemporary Hotel—the hotel that the monorail rides straight through. We rode every ride. We played every game in the arcade. And there were no maybes.

For me, that tattoo is my dad saying yes. Yes, there is no work to be done. Yes, it's just me and him.

When the kids were toddlers and I was making $27,500 a year at the *Long Island Voice* and Kendall was a PhD student, we had no dispensable income, but I *had* to take the kids to Disney. I went on eBay and sold one of the few things my father had left me when he died: a Lionel Mickey Mouse train set. That gave us enough money to scrape together for the first trip. Now, fourteen years later, we were going back.

We arrived in Orlando and started out in Epcot, eating an obscenely priced dinner with the princesses before heading to Hollywood Studios and challenging each other at the Toy Story Mania ride.

The next day, we woke up at the Animal Kingdom Lodge, looked out our window at the zebras and giraffes, and went to breakfast.

On our way to the restaurant, I checked Twitter and read the news. Twenty people were reported dead at a shooting at the Pulse nightclub in Orlando, twenty miles from where we were staying. All that was known was a man carrying automatic weapons walked into the club, one of the biggest gay clubs in Orlando, and started shooting.

We sat down to breakfast at the happiest place on earth, and you would never know anything bad had happened. Cast members were still smiling, loading carved ham onto our all-you-can-eat plates. Families were either unaware that twenty people had been slaughtered less than twenty miles away or trying to forget so their kids could enjoy their vacation. Me? I felt sadness and anger.

But one of the redeeming things about being a journalist is that when something horrible happens, one emotion you rarely feel is hopelessness. When something horrible happens, as a journalist, you have a job to do—even if it seems insignificant in the grand scheme of things. You can go tell a story.

Amid all the pain, there is always a story of hope or heroism that can—and should—be told. Flashing through my mind that morning while reading the news was the quote from Mr. Rogers: "When I was a boy and I would see scary things in the news, my mother would say to me, 'Look for the helpers. You will always find people who are helping.'"

Crime Watch Daily had wrapped up its first season just two days before I left for Florida. But our sister show *Extra* was still filming. I sent my producers a note saying that I was down in Orlando and wanted to help in any way possible.

In the time it took to send the note and check the news again, the death toll had climbed from twenty to fifty. It had become the largest mass shooting in American history.

My producers asked if I could go to the scene at Pulse and work the story for *Extra*. I checked my family into the Contemporary Hotel and took a Lyft to the crime scene. The Magic Kingdom would have to wait.

I got to the club around 2:00 p.m., twelve hours after the shooting had started and nine after it ended. I met my crew and searched for anyone we could talk to.

In an effort to speak to anyone whose story hadn't already been told, we went down a side street and walked to the closest spot to the club that we could. Our sound technician snapped a photo of the holes the SWAT team had poked into the wall to breach the building and get people out. The police had put up temporary fencing to cover the parking lot of the club. We were alone, save two international photographers taking photos of the dead as they were being wheeled out in white sheets. For a split second, my first reaction was that this was exploitative. But that moved quickly to more anger, to wanting people to see what happens when guns get into the wrong person's hands. Instead of their thoughts and prayers, every lawmaker should be forced to tour the inside of the club to see firsthand what these guns can do.

Two white vans carrying the dead drove past us.

I found a man who lives near the nightclub, who heard the first shots and spent the three hours of the siege watching from his balcony, closer than any news crew. He showed me the video he took on his phone of the final raid. It was nothing but flashes of light and a cacophony of bullets.

I went back to the Contemporary, the images banging around my head, but still wanting to ride the monorail and spend some time with my son. I was trying to capture the same feelings I felt with my dad when I was on the cusp of being a teenager, hoping they would transfer over to my son. It felt a bit forced—I was that dad dragging his too-old-for-this kids in front of every Chip and Dale and every other costumed character for the perfect photo. But there were some great moments. We had as good a time as we could, and I went to sleep at midnight.

I woke up at 5:00 a.m., took the elevator downstairs past the monorail station, and climbed into a Lyft to take me back to the murder scene.

I talked to a man who was at the club the night of the shooting. He told me he dropped to the floor when a clubgoer next to him was shot. After he escaped, he helped a man who had been shot in the arm, using his bandana to apply pressure to the wound. Then he saw the bullet hole in the man's back. He had no idea if he survived but said he would never forget him. I couldn't help but hug him after we talked. It wasn't professional, but I really didn't care at that point. He didn't need the hug, but I did.

I spoke to a woman outside the hospital, visiting her cousin who had been shot, and a man who was at the club alone and had managed to get out. I even spoke with a man who had grown up with the shooter.

The details began to emerge about the shooting. Pulse was hosting its weekly Latin night, and there were roughly three hundred people in the club at 2:00 a.m. A man walked into the club at 2:02, armed with a semiautomatic rifle and semiautomatic pistol. He began shooting anyone and everyone and held siege for three hours. People hid from the gunman in bathrooms and dressing rooms inside the club, sending text messages to their loved ones as the madman stalked around the building, plotting his next move. At around 5:15, a SWAT team using an armored vehicle broke a hole in the building, tossed flashbang grenades inside, and engaged the gunman in a firefight. He was shot eight times and died at the scene.

The news mentioned that the gunman had declared allegiance to ISIS before he started shooting. But only one person I spoke with mentioned the word *terrorism*. Every person I spoke with mentioned the words *hate* and *guns*. *Easy access to guns*. They were all resilient. And almost all of them had a message to deliver: at the end of the day, love would trample hate.

I went back to the happiest place on earth, and we spent the next day at the Magic Kingdom. We left before sundown and took the monorail to the Polynesian Hotel on the Seven Seas Lagoon. We put our feet in the water and watched a thunderstorm roll in. Maybe it was the strong cocktails from Trader Sam's Grog Grotto and Tiki Bar talking, but I looked at Kendall and smiled and said to her, "For the first time, this feels like a vacation."

We got back on the monorail and glided past the Grand Floridian Hotel. From the space-age cars, we saw the flashing lights of fire trucks and ambulances and police cars bouncing off the white walls of the hotel. We got back to our room, turned on the TV, and learned that a two-year-old boy playing in the lagoon behind the hotel had been snatched by an alligator.

A fucking alligator. Three hundred feet from where we were standing on the shore of the lagoon. We didn't see or hear a thing.

They searched for the little boy through the night. Two days later, they would find his body, in murky water six feet deep, just fifteen yards from where he was last seen. It was covered in puncture wounds.

I wanted to go home.

Once the school year started, Patton was ready to start meeting regularly and read what Paul Haynes and I had put together. Every other week, I would take a long lunch from *Crime Watch Daily* and drive to his house, where Haynes and I would update him on our progress. After two hours, I would go back to the show and produce more crime stories. I would drive home at six, pop a frozen dinner in the microwave, eat over the sink, pour a glass of Bulleit, then work on my own cases. At nine, I would take a break and work on Michelle's book until midnight. Then I would go back to my cases and usually pass out by two.

I missed my family like crazy, but the good and bad news is that I'm married to a scientist, who between lab work, grant writing, and speaking at conferences might just be busier than I am. My daughter started college, and my son was engulfed in playing *League of Legends* and *World of Warcraft* on his PC, shouting at the screen to his digital cohorts into the wee hours of the morning.

I'm not sure if I could have handled the crime load when the kids were smaller. But now I had the time (meaning every waking moment) and the energy and a little bit of spending cash. And I had gotten a taste for it. I desperately wanted my next solve. But although I had been able to achieve success on my very first social media investigation, I was about to learn the soul-crushing lesson that beginner's luck is no myth.

"I loved him so much," Alicia Lopez said shakily as the television camera zoomed in on her face, which she had partially covered with her well-manicured nails, trying in vain to halt the tears. She dropped her hand and sucked in a breath. "I still can't believe he's gone."

Lopez was talking about her friend Timothy Croskey, who everyone called Pacman. They'd known each other since they were teenagers. Pacman was a father of two, a never-a-dull-moment twenty-five-year old who worked his fingers to the bone at his construction job during the week and cheered for his beloved Washington Redskins on Sunday.

"He was hilarious," Lopez continued. "He would just make you laugh, the first moment you meet him." A smile started peeking out through the tears. "And that's how I met him. He just made me laugh." On that last line, you can see she's picturing Pacman in her mind. And he makes her laugh again.

On the afternoon of August 17, 2016, Pacman had just taken a shower after work and was walking out to his car in front of his house in a residential neighborhood in Chesapeake, Virginia, on his way to go pick up one of his daughters. He was found in his driveway by police, dead from gunshot wounds.

The police couldn't find his killer. But there was a major clue—a fifteen-second color video of a lanky man wearing a black T-shirt, black ball cap over dreadlocks, and black pants, walking with a purpose through a quiet intersection. Halfway through, the video cut to the same man now running back the way he came. Police said this was the killer.

"Not only was he my child, but he was robbed of being a man," Pacman's mother said. "He was robbed of having his family, of seeing his sister, his brother, the other family members. [The murderers] get to talk to their parents every day, relatives, kids, to say I love you. You know, just to talk. I will never be able to talk to my child again. They all should be punished for what they've done, and I will accept nothing less."

The police released the video of the suspect to the media. It was daylight. In color. Very clear. This crime was solvable.

I reached out to the family and contacted the police. The family wanted all the help they could get. The police wanted little to do with me—but they didn't tell me to back off.

You couldn't make out the man's face on the video, but his gait was distinctive. As a tall, lanky guy, I knew people could pick me out in a crowd just from my walk, which has been described as everything from Travolta in the opening scene of *Saturday Night Fever* to an ostrich on holiday. I started a campaign, running the ad on Facebook with the video accompanied by this caption:

> Watch the way this man walks. Look at his thin frame. He is a murder suspect, wanted in the killing of a good man in the South Norfolk neighborhood of Chesapeake, VA, in early August. Do you recognize him? Maybe someone who you haven't seen around for a while, who left town in August? Please message with any information, no matter how small. Please.

The video of the man's distinctive stride, propelled by a $300 advertising boost, caught people's attention, reaching 121,000 people in the five-mile radius around the crime. The comments came in thick and fast and introduced me to the eight archetypes that continue to pop up during virtually every one of my social media investigations.

There was the trying-to-be-helpful comment: *Looks like he may be wearing a McDonald's uniform, hard to tell though.*

The why-are-you-so-focused-on-*this*-murder? comment: *Fun fact… people get shot ey' day.*

The cops-are-trying-to-frame-someone comment: *Not really good evidence. He could of been running away from the actual shoot up don't know.*

The tips-on-how-to-get-away-with-it comment: *Well…looks like somebody is getting a haircut.*

The it-might-be-a-female comment: *Kinda moves like a girl to me even though there is a flat chest.*

The ever-popular complaining-that-the-video-isn't-clear-enough comment: *All the up to date technology & y'all can't get a clear image of this guy's face?*

Which came hand in hand with its partner, the pessimist comment: *Good luck on finding him with these images.*

And finally, the most difficult to read, the friends-and-family-of-the-victim comment: *That boy killed my best friend smh r.i.p Pacman Gorilla Mane they will catch his ass i promise u that if they dont sombody will…*

There were also a few of the racist and just-want-to-watch-the-world-burn comments that seem to come with most every story about a crime posted on Facebook. I won't repeat them, but let's just say proper spelling and grammar are kryptonite to racists.

I tried not to be cynical, weighing my desire to get answers for Pacman's friends and family against the urge to throw my phone out the fucking window.

The comments kept coming, but there were no tips. Then late in the day, I got a private message:

CHASE DARKNESS WITH ME

I recognized that man in the surveillance video his name is Darrius Copeland... I have pictures of the suspect and the getaway car.

The tipster included photos of a tall, thin man with dreadlocks. He looked promising.

Two hours later, I got another message from another tipster:

That boy name Darrius Copeland.

This time, the tipster included a link to a music video. The suspect was walking down the street to the music, matching the gait from the man in the surveillance footage.

I immediately interviewed both tipsters. I looked up Copeland's Facebook page, ran a background check, and within twenty-four hours had a dossier built and sent off to the detective.

"The victim, Mr. Croskey, was involved in a relationship with Darrius Copeland's sister, Dequashia," I wrote. "Based on information from reports and individuals I have spoken with, I have reason to believe that the relationship between Timothy and Dequashia was quite volatile. I also have reason to believe that Darrius Copeland may now be in Georgia and more specifically in the LaGrange or Columbus area based on recent people he has added on Facebook and also having family in that area."

Facebook had all the connections right there in front of me. By this time, some police departments were seeing social media as an effective tool in a murder investigation. If the victim was active on Facebook or Twitter, a good chunk of their social circle was at the investigator's fingertips. I included links to all the accounts in my letter to the detectives.

All they did was acknowledge the receipt of the information. It was frustrating for me, but that was nothing compared to what Pacman's friends and family were feeling. If I had identified the right guy, we were just going to have to wait until they could build up a case against the suspect. After the unknown, the waiting is the hardest.

———————————
        ———————————

Summer turned to fall. *Crime Watch Daily* hired Chris Hansen, best known from *Dateline*'s *To Catch a Predator* series, as host for the second season. Child-predator investigations were added to the small-town beauty murders and love-triangle homicides that were proving to be just as appealing to daytime viewers as their nighttime counterparts. I was dedicating every waking moment to crime. Murders during the day. Murders during the night. Chasing. Chasing. Chasing. Just endless chasing with no end in sight.

I was adding a new case every other week. I couldn't wait for just one case to get solved. Justice is a slow-moving beast, and I needed to have as many irons in the fire as I could afford so I wouldn't go insane. And then in November, I saw the story of White Boy Q.

Quinton Langford's mother died in a car accident when he was five. He was raised by his grandmother and then his aunt. He worked hard in school and earned a scholarship to Florida A&M University, where he majored in construction engineering technology. He moved from his hometown in Plant City to Tallahassee and immediately gained a bunch of friends in the mostly black FAMU community, who took to calling the friendly, generous Quinton "White Boy Q." He loved both hip-hop and country music.

On homecoming weekend, October 22, 2016, the twenty-year-old was on the street outside a party with a group of people when shots rang out. Everyone scattered. Quinton's friend Landsey Elisson was shot in the face. He survived. Quinton did not.

Quinton and Landsey weren't targeted, the police felt. It was just a case of wrong place, wrong time.

"He was a great young man," his father said to me. "Smart. Full of life. Put others ahead of himself. He was going somewhere in life. I just don't get it."

But the police did have a lead—a video of a woman and man walking near the area of the shooting. They created a montage of different camera angles. In the first scene, you see a woman with long dark hair, wearing a light, sleeveless top and tight, white short shorts, cutting across a parking lot, walking away from the camera. It then cuts to a color shot of the same woman now on a sidewalk, jogging away from the camera. Then we see her walking toward the camera but far enough away that her facial features are hidden. In the next cut, we see her walking away from the camera again—only now there is a large man in a white shirt walking a few steps behind her. The video ends with a green Nissan driving through the frame, believed to be driven by one of the suspects.

You couldn't see their faces. But the woman with tight, white short shorts was identifiable for sure. She was a head turner. She was going to be what the campaign would focus on.

I set it up for a mile radius around the murder site. I got a few tips here or there. Then I thought I hit the jackpot.

"I've seen these people around this complex," a tipster wrote. "And that car with the damaged bumper. And that boy's name is [redacted]. I know that him and his girlfriend live here and were both using that car." The tipster said it was the boy's brother. "The girl I can't tell, cause I can't see her face."

"Can you tell by her legs?" I asked.

"She lives in the dorms. I know that walk."

I was doing cartwheels. I sent the information to the detective. And I waited.

I called him repeatedly. No response.

I was finding suspects. Suspects who looked good. Real good. But the police weren't acting. Were they too busy? Did they just not care? Or were they right there with me but couldn't make a move because they didn't have enough evidence to get a conviction? It's no use arresting someone without enough evidence, spending tens of thousands of dollars to prosecute, and then watching them walk free, never to be tried for that crime again. That's the thing many true-crime watchers and internet sleuths sometimes don't understand. Detectives want the bad guys just as much as you. You might have done work identifying the perpetrator, but building a rock-solid case against them is a whole 'nother matter.

Sometimes it comes down to the district attorney. Some are confident. Some are timid. And the detectives know what each attorney needs to take on a case. You see this with missing-persons cases. Sometimes you see a suspect you are confident was responsible for the person going missing and had probably murdered them. Sometimes they are charged. Sometimes they continue to walk free.

I just had to build another case page and move on. I found a new one while scrolling through videos on Facebook. And I hadn't seen an image so chilling since the Marques Gaines case.

———————————

Teddy Grasset was a thirty-year-old fashion designer from Los Angeles. He grew up in a small town in the south of France, but he dreamed of America and came over in 2005. He cofounded the vintage denim brand Dr. Collectors, which he ran out of a shop called the Trading Post in Hollywood with his father, Oliver. The store was included in *GQ* magazine's "2015 Ten Best Menswear Stores in America" list.

With wavy disheveled-for-effect hair, often covered with a flat cap, a scruffy beard, thin frame, and tatted arms, Teddy put forth a very European persona in the middle of the Hollywood fashion scene. But he did have a playful side, as evidenced by the tattoo of Raccoon Mario from the *Super Mario Bros. 3* video game on his right butt cheek.

In September 2016, Teddy traveled to Nashville with thoughts of opening a store in the music city. He was walking with a friend behind the Country Music Hall of Fame when a car pulled up behind them. It was late. The car must have made Teddy's senses tingle. The surveillance video shows Teddy and his friend start to run. Two men get out of the car and start to chase them. They all leave the frame. Off camera, Teddy is shot and killed.

The video is the stuff of nightmares. Boogeymen creeping up slowly behind you in the dark, inching their car close enough that Teddy felt something was wrong, a feeling strong enough to tell him to run.

You can't make out the killers' faces, and the car was a Chevy Impala, one of the most common cars on the road. But the car did have something distinctive. The license plate was unreadable—because it was surrounded by an eerie blue glow, most likely an aftermarket neon lighted plate frame. The car also had a sunroof and a spoiler.

The cops had initially held back the information about the blue light plate frame, not wanting to tip off the killers as they continued their investigation. But they were stalled and finally put everything out to the media.

A memorial service for Teddy was held on October 3. The dress code called for everyone to wear indigo or blue. No black.

I launched a campaign.

See these two men walking? In a few seconds, one of them will be dead. See that car pulling up behind them? Do you know anyone who recently drove a Silver Chevy Impala with a glowing blue license plate holder? Watch the two men get out of that car. Do you recognize them? This happened behind the Country Music Hall of Fame in Nashville on Sept. 25. Please message with any information. And please share.

The campaign reached 109,000 people.

I got one tip from a guy saying he saw a silver Malibu near the Douglass dorms on the Nashville Auto Diesel College campus.

Another said he saw an Impala and took down the license plate.

The next day, another saw an Impala and actually took a photo of the car and plate.

The next day, another guy saw a gray Impala pass him on the road. "Young black man texting and driving. Damage to plate fastener." And gave me the plate.

Another saw a car with the blue light plate cover on Burkitt Road.

I funneled all the tips to the police. The noose was tightening. It seemed like everyone in Nashville was looking for a Chevy Impala.

They found the car on Friday at a Nashville auto body shop. The bumpers had been removed, along with the spoiler and that blue light license plate holder. After inquiring about the owners, the police were sure it was the right car. Andy Francisco Nunez and his girlfriend, Daniela V. Cruz, were arrested in Raleigh, North Carolina.

But it turns out that there had been three people in the car that night, which meant there was one more suspect at large. I changed the campaign to focus on finding twenty-five-year-old Joseph Santillan, who police said was the final suspect.

Have you Seen This Man? Joseph Santillan, 25, is wanted in connection with the Nashville murder. Targeting Antioch, where he is from, and North Carolina. If you see him, please message us. And please share.

His photo showed his soft features, close-cropped hair, and a faded neck tattoo.

I'd never seen so many responses since I started. A thousand shares. Pages of comments, and most importantly, dozens of tips.

One tipster wrote in saying he went to middle school with Santillan.

Another was more on point: "His sister and him are pretty close so there's a good chance he might be at that address or she might also be helping him stay hidden." Another tipster directed me to another family member's house where he often hung out.

The technique was working.

I messaged William Ashworth, the detective in charge of the case. "We amped up ads in the Antioch area and NC to help find the 3rd suspect. A lot of people writing saying they know him, but one person wrote that he might be at his little sister's house."

The campaign was plastered across everyone's feed in Santillan's hometown. A digital posse a hundred thousand strong. Facebook, Twitter, Instagram. Santillan's picture was everywhere.

The pressure must have gotten to be too much for him. Santillan turned himself in. Finally, a result—my first since the Marques Gaines case. The campaign may not have ID'd the suspects, but it got close and was able to put the screws on the last man standing. For his efforts, Detective Ashworth was awarded the Nashville Police Field Operations Bureau investigator of the year. It was well-deserved. Ashworth used everything at his disposal to solve the crime—including working with a guy he had never met who had a crazy idea about using Facebook to flush out the killers.

In December 2017, Teddy's mother, Beatrice, made a post on Teddy's memorial Facebook page. The poem was translated from her native French.

My sentence is infinite as teddy's path now.

He fell, smiling as always, but this time life didn't smile at him in return.

The head in the stars, he liked to be in the desert alone with his books.

Humanist and a dreamer, he liked to think that human is naturally good. He made his heart open to the world and to the others.

Without malice or hatred, he loved animals, children, their common innocence no doubt. Teddy was passionate about music. He was a tender and happy being in what he was doing.

And then…

"He liked to think that human is naturally good" hit me hard. We all like to think that. But Teddy was gone. I reached out to the next story.

Tips on murder and violent assault cases were often difficult to get detectives to act on. But missing persons had an edge. There was a definite urgency with missing cases. And there was often a lot of public activity and support. If I was able to get information, they might jump. I wasn't getting discouraged about solving murders—I was still on the high of solving one, but I saw missing persons as an opportunity. I hadn't attempted a missing-persons case since 2003, when I searched for a Catholic-school-girl-turned-Deadhead from Long Island who traveled to California and went missing in the scrub brush of Trinity County a decade earlier. Back then, I was just reporting for newspapers. Facebook and Twitter hadn't been invented yet. This time was going to be different.

There are thousands of missing-persons Facebook pages on the web. They contain pictures of the missing person, information about where they were last seen and what they might have been wearing, and a missing-persons poster that they implore people to share on Facebook or print out and plaster on lampposts and in local businesses in their towns.

I needed to create a page that would stand out. But the case of Morgan Bauer would also bring with it a unique challenge. There was someone close to her saying she wasn't really missing.

Morgan Bauer was a pretty, freckled nineteen-year-old who left her home in Aberdeen, South Dakota, for the big city of Atlanta on February 12, 2016. Her mother said she just wanted to make it on her own. She met a man through Craigslist and made arrangements to live in his house rent-free in exchange for housekeeping duties until she could find something full-time. The arrangement didn't work out, and Morgan found herself out on the street in a strange town. But she was headstrong and refused to retreat. She started staying in hotels, and while she had worked as a waitress in South Dakota, she decided she needed more money to survive in her new city and started dancing at a club in Gainesville, Georgia. She was last seen on February 28, 2016, the same date when all her social media posts stopped and her cell phone stopped pinging.

A missing person, thousands of miles away from home. No fixed address. No fixed job. Morgan was a transplant and had no support system looking for her in Atlanta.

I asked her mother if she had a video of Morgan I could use in the campaign. There are numerous advantages to using video when trying to locate someone. For one, the Facebook algorithm favors videos more than pictures and will get it in front of more people. But more importantly, you can see the person's mannerisms and hear their voice, things that don't change with a new hair color or different clothes.

But here was the challenge. Morgan's sister had posted on social media that her sister was not missing but was trying to escape their "domineering" mother. There were Facebook pages with the names "Morgan Bauer Is Not Missing" and "Morgan's Safe Haven." Posts on Reddit claimed that she was safe. There was a fake page someone set up for some unknown reason, called "Bauer Morgan," that had people messaging me with false leads once I posted the ad targeting the club and the hotel where she had stayed. There were also stories about Morgan trying to buy a driver's license from a fellow dancer so she could show proof of identity to get another dancing job—a requirement in Georgia.

I contacted anyone I could find who was affiliated with the club she was supposedly working at, from dancers to doormen to anyone who had used social media to check in or post photos of the club. I got nowhere. In July, a body was found in a suitcase along I-985 in Gwinnett County, just northeast of Atlanta. A lot of people thought it could be Morgan. The woman inside was in her twenties, five foot one to five foot five. But she looked to be Asian or East Indian and did not have tattoos matching Morgan's.

At the time of this writing, Morgan was still classified as missing. At the request of Morgan's mother, I took down the page to avoid confusion with a new Facebook page she had started, which has attracted more than seven thousand followers and a small army of volunteers who consistently hang flyers and send out mailers looking for Morgan all across the United States, from Vegas to Florida to Maine. In November 2017, Morgan's mother posted three photos of her daughter with the caption "My name is Morgan Bauer. Please call and ask why they aren't searching for me," along with the number for the Atlanta police department.

The woman found in the suitcase is still unidentified.

I was late to the game on Morgan's case. But for the mystery of Jamie Harroun, I was right in the middle of everything.

On Halloween night 2016, Harroun, a forty-year-old blues-rock singer, cut from the same cloth as Janis Joplin and Stevie Nicks, went missing in Southern Illinois.

Jamie's sister Gerri told me that the previous two weeks had been a whirlwind for Jamie. She had gotten a Facebook message from a long-lost friend, Blu—a man she hadn't seen in twenty years. They made plans to go for a drink one night.

The day after that drink, Jamie told her boyfriend, Brian, that she was moving out—and moving in with Blu. Now she was gone.

I launched a campaign, targeting Galesburg, the southern Illinois town from which Jamie went missing, along with the nearby city of Peoria. I learned Jamie's cell phone had pinged north of town, so I targeted there as well. The ads I built included pictures of her truck, a black Ford F-150. I mocked up her license plate and found an image of the racing sticker she had stuck on her back window.

Blu told Gerri he had no idea where her sister was. He had last seen her at 6:00 p.m. on Halloween night. She was going to go back to Brian's place to pick up some more clothes—and a boat—and was going to come right back. Blu said she had talked about going to Florida to swim with the dolphins, and that was where I should look.

I contacted the police to make sure there was a missing-persons report in place and that everyone was on the same page, that this was being looked at as a missing-persons case. They confirmed a report had been filed.

There was no one with a Facebook account within ten miles of Blu's apartment who didn't see the campaign looking for Jamie. I talked to dozens of locals. The ex-boyfriend, the new boyfriend, the sister, the guys at the diner, and the workers at the gas station. There were so many scenarios of what could have happened. Everyone was worried. People were pointing fingers at each other, and tensions were fevered. And everyone had their own theory. The investigator in me wanted to think I was putting the pieces together. That she didn't just leave. That there was something nefarious at play. It was a sick notion. I wanted to think that there was a monster at the end of the story, that Jamie met with some end that I could help figure out. It was a shameful feeling. This wasn't a movie. There was a woman missing a sister. A man missing his ex who he had lived with. And another man who thought he had just reconnected with the love of his life.

I wanted to see a happy result. I wanted to find her in Florida swimming with the dolphins. I wanted a homecoming.

Jamie was found dead behind the wheel of her pickup. She drove into a ditch right outside town that was covered by heavy foliage, making it invisible from the road. It looked to be an accident.

What the hell am I doing? I asked myself. I had just spent the last week entwined in the drama of these three people. And the result was still the same. No answers. Just death.

But unlike the other cases, I was living this all in real time. When I started, everyone I spoke with was hoping Jamie was still alive. And when she was found, the page I had built to find her morphed from one looking for a missing woman to one giving details about where and when her friends could attend her memorial. It wasn't anything like the first missing-persons case I tried to solve.

10

LOSING JADE AND FINDING MARIAH

Humboldt County, California, 2016

JENNIFER WILMER LIKED TO QUESTION AUTHORITY.

In grade school, she'd yell at the nuns when they picked on students who didn't know the answers. In fifth grade, she asked her mother if she could have a Halloween party.

"Someone else in her class was having a party," her mother, Susan, told me, "and Jennifer wanted to invite all the kids who weren't invited to the other party. That was Jennifer. She hated inequities."

So it came as no surprise that the Camaro-infested, big-haired mainstream of late 1980s Long Island drove the teenage Jennifer toward a kinder, gentler counterculture.

In 1993, at age twenty, she bolted for California, trying to, in her mother's words, "make it on her own." She left her full scholarship at St. John's University for the seaside town of Arcata, two hundred miles north of San Francisco.

She tried registering at the two-year College of the Redwoods but was too late to get into any classes. She waitressed and lived on welfare for a spell, mainly hanging out in Arcata Plaza with the hundreds of other street people who had made the pilgrimage from all points east. Everybody around the plaza had some type of nickname. Skinny Bob. Ragman Pete. Jennifer had come to be known as Jade.

But not all was awesome in the city by the sea. Jade had bouts of depression and had started to see a therapist. Then, toward the end of the summer, her roommate announced she had to bail the scene, and Jade was forced to vacate her apartment.

Susan said Jade was ready to come home. So much so that she had purchased a return plane ticket for her, which she could have picked up and activated at any travel agency.

But Jade wanted to give California one last chance. "It's so beautiful here," she said to her mom. She left Arcata and told her mom she was moving in with some friends "out in the country." The country meant Trinity County, thirty-five hundred square miles of mountainous desolation and marijuana crops.

She moved in with her boyfriend, a local named Tro Patterson. They shared a rented house in Hawkins Bar with a guy named Opie, another guy named Mingo, and a girl named Rebecca. But Jade still needed work. A friend told her about a farm up the road. They weren't looking for any help at the moment, but maybe she should still go down and introduce herself.

At 7:30 in the morning on Monday, September 13, Jade set out to hitchhike the nine miles into "town" along Route 299. She left a note to her roommates:

Bye everybody,

Went to my 1st day at the farm. Wish me luck! Good luck to you, Mingo, and see you in a few months. If someone could give food to the kitten as needed, I'd appreciate it. Hopefully I'll see you folks later.

Jade

She was never seen again.

A week later, Jade's housemates went to visit the farm, where they were told she had never arrived. Susan Wilmer got a phone call from Jade's boyfriend, Tro.

"I knew she wasn't alive," Susan said. "I knew."

Frantic, Susan Wilmer called the county police. She FedExed a picture of Jennifer. It sat in the sheriff's mail slot for days. The police wouldn't help.

"You have to understand that her adult daughter was a walkaway," said Martin Ryan, chief of the California Bureau of Investigations. "There is no evidence of foul play, other than the time that's gone by."

"Initially, I wasn't convinced that [there was foul play] and I had my reasons," said Trinity County under-sheriff David Laffranchini, alluding to Jennifer's counterculture lifestyle.

But the evidence didn't support their theory. Jade left all her identification at home. She left her clothes. Her address book. Her Bible. Her bank card. But most importantly, Jade left her sleeping bag.

"No self-respecting hippie leaves her sleeping bag!" screamed a furious Susan.

She felt helpless. She called her local congressman. His office called Trinity and got the excuse that she was a runaway. She contacted her local police department, where Nassau County PD Detective George Doherty checked the law enforcement database National Criminal Information Center. Jennifer's name was nowhere to be found. It was Doherty, three thousand miles away, who filed the missing-persons report. (Laffranchini claimed that Trinity had filed a report, and Wilmer filing another one left two reports with two different case numbers.)

That was the last straw. Susan and her husband, Fred Wilmer, made arrangements for their fourteen-year-old son to stay with a friend and caught the next flight to California.

The Wilmers were familiar with the caravan of New Age hippies Jade traveled with. A few years earlier, their daughter had asked her mom if a bunch of Deadheads could sleep in the backyard while the band was playing a set of shows at Nassau Coliseum. Unlike many arenas, Deadheads were not allowed to sleep out anywhere near the Coliseum parking lot. Susan agreed and woke up the next day to a "street full of VW buses" and "wall-to-wall sleeping bags" in her yard.

"They were so quiet," remembers Susan. "My neighbors didn't even know they were there. They were very sweet."

So when the Wilmers entered the house in Hawkins Bar, sixty miles west of Eureka, and were met by three Deadheads, they weren't shocked—even with all three having shaved their heads, ditching their dreadlocks a few weeks earlier. The house was dirty, but Jennifer's housemates, just like the Deadheads who had slept in her backyard in Baldwin, were "sweet" and pleasant.

The kids at the house showed her a picture of Jade. It was the same one she had FedExed to the sheriff's office. The police, for some reason, had delivered it to the house.

"It was like a message," Susan told me. "'Here, take the picture back. We're not taking the case.'"

The Wilmers met with detectives at the police station, whose lobby is presided over by a large painting of the sheriff, a big six-gun on his desk, a "don't mess with me" look on his face. Susan, a tough-talking Long Island woman with a missing daughter, tried to get answers. She spied the manila envelope case file marked "Wilmer" in one of the detectives' hands. It was empty.

Months passed. Then years passed. Susan kept pressing. She got loud.

She started a letter-writing campaign, with seemingly the whole town of Baldwin, Long Island, sending thousands of letters to anyone who would listen. They got the ear of the California Justice Department.

But it was far, far too late.

When I talked to Susan in 2003, I was writing a series for the *Long Island Press* I called "Long Island's Lost Girls," about three women, in three different decades, who left Long Island never to return. Susan was nine years and $20,000 in private investigator's fees into her search. She was not going to give up, even though she had just made a crushing decision.

"I just had Jennifer declared dead," she told me from her Baldwin, Long Island, home, referring to Jade by her birth name. "Two weeks ago. I did that for my children, for the rest of the family. The therapist said it was a good idea. But it's not changing anything in my mind."

She was in the process of preparing a memorial for Jade, something that she hoped would provide closure for her children. She gave me a handful of photos to accompany the article. There was that serious-looking photo of her from St. Mary's, pictures of Jade at a party with friends, and one photo that showed her in transition from Catholic school girl to a Deadhead flower child. She was on a beach, holding a little girl—her niece Jessica. Jennifer had a gargantuan smile—the kind that could swallow darkness.

Susan had lost all faith in law enforcement. I have never had a family member refer to the person who was supposed to be looking for their loved one with such disdain.

"I don't want to bad-mouth anyone," John Mohon, the Wilmer's private investigator, told me. "But they did mishandle some things."

Susan was more to the point. "He's an idiot," she said of Under-Sheriff Laffranchini.

I needed to talk to Laffranchini.

I got his number and called him. He knew what Susan thought about him and was sorry he had no answers. He told me that sometimes when he's driving across Route 299, the east–west road that connects

Redding, Hawkins Bar, and Arcata, California, that he would ask himself one question.

"If I was going to dump a body, where would I do it?"

Sometimes he got out of his car, walked along the mountainous terrain, through the pull-off areas where the grass is worn out by impromptu piss breaks taken by weary travelers during the hour-long ride to the coast.

He was looking for any signs of Jade—or more specifically, Jade's body.

"This is the type of county where it would be easy to kill and dispose of a body," he said. He believed in his gut that Jade was dead.

There was some hope—if you want to call it that—for an answer in 1998. Wayne Adam Ford, a truck driver from Arcata, walked into the sheriff's department in neighboring Humboldt County and pulled a plastic bag from his pocket. Inside was a woman's severed breast. Ford preyed on hitchhikers and confessed to killing four women, including the one whose breast he carried into the station that day. Could he have any answers?

Negative. Ford said his earliest kill was 1997. He said he knew nothing of Jade. Mohon, Wilmer's private eye, learned that Ford was in the Midwest during the time of Jade's disappearance.

Around the same time, a young woman entered an abortion clinic and signed her name as Jennifer Wilmer. The missing-persons infrastructure was set in motion. Could it be her?

It wasn't. The woman was a scared fourteen-year-old girl who was trying to hide the pregnancy from her parents. She had seen Jennifer's missing poster and chose the name as an alias.

The $20,000 the Wilmers had spent on private investigators produced only hazy possible scenarios.

One focused on a man named Happiness, whom Susan went looking for in the Nassau Coliseum parking lot at a recent Grateful Dead show on Long Island. Happiness was thought to be able to provide the true identity of a Deadhead regular known as Cowboy Fred, an older man who Susan says "was obsessed with" Jade. "He may well be who murdered her," she told me.

"Cowboy Fred was a dude Jennifer was scared of for some reason; no one knew why," Mohon, the private investigator, told me. "He was an older guy and would follow her around Arcata plaza."

Arcata police chief Randy Mendosa tossed another theory at me. "It could be totally innocent," he said. "She could have stumbled into somebody's grow, and they got threatened." It was an interesting definition of "totally innocent."

Or Jade could have been hitchhiking to the farm. Maybe she got a ride but in the car had second thoughts about going—they had said they weren't looking for any help right away. Maybe she said to herself, *You know what, I'm gonna go to the coast and meet up with Tro.* Tro usually spent the weekends in Arcata and would stay until Tuesday to watch *Monday Night Football* in town. So maybe Jade took the ride all the way down Route 299 to Arcata and something happened along the way.

I tried to track down Tro Patterson as best I could from afar, pre-social media. Without the budget to fly to California, that meant a series of dead-end phone numbers, calls to ex-girlfriends, and leaving messages at dive bars. I couldn't find him. I did find his father, Jay Patterson, who claimed he didn't know where he was.

"He's up north," he told me. "I was hoping that we could get over this calamity, rather than open up a festering old wound."

"But the wound has never been closed," I told him. "Jade is still missing."

Immediately after Jade disappeared, Jay Patterson was in constant contact with the Wilmers. But that December, he became connected to another heart-wrenching situation. One of his employees' children had been kidnapped. Polly Klaas was a twelve-year-old girl who was abducted from her bedroom three hours south of Trinity just eighteen days after Jennifer had gone missing. After that, according to Susan, Patterson stopped talking to the Wilmers.

I pressed Jay Patterson again, and he stuck to his claim that he had no idea where his son was. Tro and his cohorts were living in one of the places in America where people run to get away from society. They specifically did not want to be found. Even after the story was published, I kept looking.

Five months later, I found him.

On August 29, 2003, Tro Patterson was found dead in California. He had committed suicide.

Again, I had written a story with no ending.

Jennifer would be the first member of the Humboldt Five, a name coined by California missing-persons activist Brenda Condon. Five women who went missing in what is considered one of the most dangerous swaths of land in America, filled with marijuana crops and biker gangs, where the drugs were plentiful, the trees hid secrets, and the locals distrusted any semblance of authority. People running away from their lives found themselves in Humboldt, five hours north of San Francisco. Humboldt made its own rules under the redwoods and could turn on a dime from heaven on earth to a forest of hell.

Google "Humboldt Five" and you'll find a map, with photos of each of the women superimposed directly above the locations where they were last seen.

Jennifer Wilmer is in the top right corner, her frosted Long Island locks and serious Catholic school pose from the St. Mary's High School yearbook a stark contrast to the other missing girls, who portrayed more of the free spirit that she would later become in Northern California. On the map, she seemed so separate from the other girls—in geography (she was last seen in the town of Willow Creek, forty miles from the others), looks, and, most noticeably, timeline. The date she was last seen was printed below the photo: September 13, 1993.

On the left side of the map by the coast are Christine Walters, November 14, 2008, and Karen Mitchell, November 25, 1997. They both went missing from Eureka, California, a port town about halfway between San Francisco and Portland.

In the center is Sheila Frank, February 2, 2014. Sheila was thirty-seven when she disappeared, standing five foot five, 120 pounds, strawberry blond hair, blue eyes. She was last seen in Fortuna, eighteen miles south of Eureka, at her boyfriend's house. The boyfriend, a man named Jim Jones, said Sheila had gone for a walk, and he never saw her again.

Next to Sheila in the center of the map is Danielle Bertolini. Underneath her picture reads February 9, 2014, seven days after Sheila went missing.

With blond hair, pencil-thin eyebrows, freckles, and a bright smile punctuated by a diamond stud pierced above her lips, Danielle had a magnetic personality and didn't shy away from speaking her mind. She grew up in Maine and loved being outdoors. Camping, fishing, hunting, the ocean. She loved any kind of water.

In May 2010, twenty-year-old Danielle was six months pregnant when a doctor gave her the devastating news. Her unborn baby boy, who she was going to call Xavier, had Edwards syndrome, in which an extra chromosome 18 disrupts normal development. Danielle knew he would not survive. But when she couldn't dilate, the doctors had to do emergency surgery. They had to "take him out piece by piece," her mother, Billie Jo Dick, told me. "Danielle freaked. That's when her world changed forever."

Two months later, she moved to California and began trimming marijuana crops on a mountain in Humboldt. She spent four years on the mountain. Billie Jo pleaded with her daughter to leave Humboldt County and come back home to the East Coast. Danielle said the same thing Jade had told her mother two decades earlier: "It's beautiful here, Mom."

Then in February 2014, Danielle disappeared.

She was last seen near Highway 36 in the Swains Flat area, forty miles southwest of Eureka. The police had learned that her ride into town that day in February never showed up, but she was picked up by a man who said he dropped her off by her house and never saw her again. The man's name? Jim Jones.

Missing-persons posters went up. *Missing: Danielle Bertolini, 24. Five foot two, 105 pounds, blond hair, blue eyes. Last seen in Fortuna. Goes by "Nellie."*

Nellie talks to her sister almost daily, the poster read, *but has not contacted family members since the 10th of February, which is totally out of character for her.*

A year went by with no sign of Nellie.

A month later, in March 2015, a local man was heading home on his ATV from a day of fishing along Eel River near Ferndale when he spied something white buried in the sand. He quickly recognized it as a human skull. The mandible was gone, along with all the teeth save two molars in the upper right of the jaw.

The county coroner's office collected the skull and searched the surrounding area for more remains or clues. They found none.

Danielle's mother, Billie Jo, was back in Maine when she got a phone call telling her about the skull. She says they told her they had compared dental records and said it wasn't Danielle's. But Billie Jo knew. She just knew in her gut it was her daughter's skull. Two months later, they called her back. This time, they had compared DNA of tissue that was preserved in the skull against Danielle's. It was a match.

Fortuna Police Department chief William Dobberstein told the local NBC affiliate "we have identified a person of interest in both cases

[Sheila Franks and Danielle's], and it's the same man. We aren't releasing his name at this time."

I knew what that name was. I was investigating the Humboldt Five cases for *Crime Watch Daily*. While the police didn't have enough to make an arrest, that wasn't going to stop us from paying Jim Jones an unscheduled visit and asking him some questions.

We sent a crew to Humboldt in the spring of 2016 for a story to air in the fall. By the time we got there, the police were ready to name names. "James Jones was involved with Sheila and was the last person to see Danielle," Fortuna police officer Brian Taylor told us. But they still didn't have enough evidence to make an arrest. We tracked Jones down, and our correspondent Andrea Isom knocked on his door, coming face-to-face with the man many believe has information about the last moments of Danielle's and Sheila's lives. A bald and hulking Jones answered the door wearing a bright orange shirt and a confused expression. He refused to talk. We would all have to wait for a break in the case.

Billie Jo's younger daughter, Mariah, had just gotten a tattoo on her left thigh in her sister's memory—Danielle's name written below a cross with angel's wings.

Billie Jo continued to talk to her daughter in death through the "MissingNelly2014" Facebook page she created.

Oh Nellie why does everything we do for you have to be so hard? You're in a better place now and I get that part. What I don't get is how this monster gets to roam around looking for others to do the same thing too... I just want this over with and him behind bars where he belongs.

—Oct. 24, 2015

A week later, she posted:

153

Been a very long and rocky path Nellie that we have been down honey. Please open up the eye's and hearts of people there, baby girl. We need to bring you and Sheila home, honey… Point us baby girl in the right direction… Nana sends big hugs. I love you to the moon n back

Then on April 4, 2016, after Danielle's skull was found:

I'm already not liking the idea of having to make funeral arrangements for you… Momma just wants you to know how very special you are to me. Please baby girl try and make this as easy on me as you can because I already am a basket case. Hugs and kisses baby girl. All my love momma

Billie Jo wanted to bring her daughter home—all of her daughter.

Then on Friday afternoon, November 11, 2016, I got a message that Billie Jo couldn't find her daughter Mariah. Danielle's sister was now gone too.

She had been missing for three days. She had cancelled a scheduled visit with her son and was last seen at her grandmother's house in Medford, Oregon, on November 8.

I immediately contacted Billie Jo. She was three thousand miles away at her home in Maine, her nightmare on repeat, only now with the added horror of knowing that the last time one of her daughters went missing, a year later, they found her skull in a riverbed. Billie Jo told me Mariah might be with some guys in Medford. She mentioned a white truck they might be in. Or possibly a black car.

It wasn't much to go on. I started a page, "Missing Mariah Bertolini," and posted the missing flyer that had already been made: photos of Mariah smiling, of Mariah holding her toddler son, of Mariah with a horse, and of the tattoo she got to remember her sister. The text read:

Missing: Mariah Bertolini. Mariah cancelled a scheduled visit with her son, which is out of character for her. She seemed to be crying and upset last time she was with family. Mariah left her grandma's residence on Table Rock Rd. with an unknown male in a white truck. She is not answering her cell phone and had not been in contact with her family since 11/07/16. She was wearing black stretch pants, gray boots, and a long gray sweater. Mariah has a tattoo on her left thigh that reads "Danielle" and a pirate lady on her right outer leg.

I targeted a twenty-five-mile radius around Medford—anything smaller would barely reach anyone, as the population up there is pretty sparse. I started cold-calling local businesses to see if anyone had seen her. I also ran Facebook and Twitter ads targeting the cities of Crescent City, Redding, Arcata, and all points in between.

Go ahead and find those places on a map. They are the end of the race for a lot of people running. Even into the 1990s, teenagers from across the country were still landing in San Francisco to dig up the time capsule of the Summer of Love. They quickly realized that dream had rotted in the '70s, been ridiculed in the '80s, and by the early '90s was preparing to be wiped away by the impending Silicon Valley boom. But some of those time-traveling pioneers had heard stories about a place where the dream was still possible.

Shares of the ad on the "Missing Mariah Bertolini" Facebook page were piling up. That's what happens with the missing. You get a lot of shares. People want to help by spreading the word. But tips? People writing in the comments that they have information? Most of the time, the comments are a wasteland.

I was four hours into the search when we got our first spark of hope. Mariah had apparently called her mother from an unfamiliar phone number. She barely said anything and hung up quickly. But Billie Jo was sure it was her. When the last important phone call you remember is the one where you learned your daughter's skull was just found, your mind is going to go to the darkest places. For Billie Jo, hearing Mariah's voice meant she was alive. But it didn't mean she was safe.

She tried calling the number back, but no one picked up. She tried over and over again. She gave the number to law enforcement to trace or ping its location but heard nothing back.

I asked her for the number. I didn't know what I was going to do with it. But I had to try something. She gave it to me, and I promised I would let her know if I was able to get through.

Then I sat there looking at the ten digits. What *was* I going to do?

It's probably a guy she's with, I thought to myself. Maybe a dealer, maybe a player. I couldn't just call him. If I called out of the blue, he would either not answer or hang up just as soon as I got my name out. And any chance I had would be blown.

No. I would text him. And I would be vague. Who would this guy answer a text from? If he was a dealer, he would answer a text from a buyer. If he was a player, he would answer a text from a girl.

I grabbed my burner phone, entered the number, and typed in the vaguest thing I could think of: "Hey."

I pressed send.

Nothing.

I waited thirty minutes and tried again, this time with something a little more specific: "You there?"

Nothing. But the table was set, and curiosity was stirred. After those two messages, if I called, there was a fifty-fifty chance the guy was going to pick up—either to find out if this was some girl he had given his number to or a guy he had met looking to score, or to just put a stop to some random pain in the ass who might continue to bug him all night with texts.

I waited five minutes and called the number.

It rang twice.

And then an answer.

"Hello," said the guy on the other end of the line. He sounded young. No more than thirty.

"Oh hey, it's Billy," I said. "I am looking for Mariah. Is she with you?"

"Um, she's actually not with me right now," he said. "She went to the market."

Who the hell uses the word market? I asked myself. But I kept going. I told him who I was, a journalist in Los Angeles looking for her.

"Can you have her call me back?"

He didn't answer.

"Can you please have her call me back?" I repeated.

"She's actually not coming back here."

"Why? Where did she go?"

He hung up.

I waited ten more minutes, then called the number again.

A woman answered.

"Hey, who's this?" I said.

"This is Mariah Bertolini."

She was safe.

"Well, you had everybody really worried. As you know," I said.

She knew, she said.

I introduced myself, saying I was an investigative reporter in Los Angeles. I asked her where she was.

She responded, "Does it matter?"

She kept trying to get off the phone. I kept trying to keep her talking.

"I worked on your sister's case," I said.

She remembered. "I really appreciate that, thank you."

"Here's the deal," I began. "I'm glad you're safe. You don't have to tell me where you are. But your sister's case. I want to make sure that the guy we all think is the guy who killed her is arrested. I want to see him behind bars. And I need your help. That's what I want to work on now that I know you're safe. I want to work on that. Stay safe, please. That case bothers me so much. And I need your help."

She promised she would call back the next day after she went to Walmart to get a new phone, and we said goodbye. I knew she wasn't going to call back, but I wanted to give her a reason for sticking around this life. I wanted to let her know that I needed her help to solve her sister's murder and to pin the guy we all thought was responsible to the wall. I wanted her to realize that it wasn't just about her. There was something bigger that needed her.

I contacted Billie Jo and was met with a combination of excitement and relief. Finally understanding what she was putting her mother through, Mariah found a police officer, and the two of them called Billie Jo together.

I changed the title of the page to "Update: Mariah Bertolini has been found." I then edited the targeted post:

Update: I just spoke with Mariah and she is safe, I also spoke with Mariah's mom, Billie Jo Dick, and Mariah met with an officer and they both called her mother. Thank you to everyone who took time out of their busy lives to share this post. When we work together, great things happen.

I checked back in with Billie Jo every few days in the week that followed. Frantic had been replaced with frustration. Mariah was in withdrawal. Billie Jo was trying to get her into rehab, but Mariah was on a waiting list for a bed. "She said some pretty horrible things to me yesterday," Billie Jo told me. "I know it was the drugs, but man, it was bad."

After a few more days, she finally caught a break.

"Sunday morning Mariah has a bed in a treatment center in Oregon," she texted. "I'm so grateful."

Helping find Mariah just made my resolve that much stronger to try to put her sister's murderer behind bars—and to maybe help solve the other Humboldt Five cases along the way.

And then something weird happened. Ten days after finding Mariah, I received a private message:

> Hi my name is Jessica Milone and I'm a cousin of Jennifer Wilmer, who you have written an article about and also helped some of her story get aired on crime watch daily. I wanted to thank you for that... I'm trying to get her case reopened even though my aunt had her declared dead well over 10 years ago. It's my life's work to resolve her case for my family.

I quickly wrote back, saying that I would help any way I could. She responded:

> Thank you. I'm actually the little girl in the picture with her that you put in the article you have written about her on your website. Thank you so much for all your help you have no idea how much it means to me. If there is anything I can do to help please let me know I would love to be involved as much as possible.

The little girl that Jennifer was holding in her arms at the beach— the one with the chubby cheeks squinting in the sun as Jennifer beamed that gigantic smile? Fifteen years later, she was writing me. Writing me on Facebook—something that didn't even exist when I wrote the story.

This is what murder does. It consumes everyone around it.

I doubted Jade's case was related to the others in Humboldt, other than the fact that the place was a breeding ground for something sinister. But they are all linked by the name Humboldt Five.

I asked Brenda Condon to make me an admin on the Humboldt Five Facebook page, and I started a campaign, focusing on a ten-mile radius from where Danielle's skull was found. I set up the page, and then as my family was in town, we went furniture shopping for the new apartment I was able to afford with that steady paycheck from *Crime Watch Daily*. We were in Silver Lake, looking for one of those burnt-orange midcentury modern couches when my Facebook messages started to explode. I ran into a store and bought a notebook and pen, then sat on the sidewalk and called one tipster after another.

Many were scared. Most had solid information. They all wanted justice. And they were all pointing to two men.

I got names. Places. Stories about blood in a pickup truck and a drug dealer who had kids lining up outside his house to trade in their iPads and Nintendo DSs for a fix. I called one woman who told me her daughter had overdosed at this guy's house. That she knew Danielle and Danielle had been at the house too. "My daughter left here, went back to Humboldt, and she's dead in a month," she told me. The same story Danielle's mom told me. The same story Jade's mom told me. And there were many stories about Jim Jones.

I talked to the detective in charge who said there still wasn't enough evidence to bring anyone in. I began what I call a "telltale heart" campaign. Any time these two individuals—the drug dealer and the last man to see both Sheila and Danielle alive—would go on Facebook or Twitter or even Google themselves, they might see a picture of Danielle. Her heart would beat under their floorboards. Maybe one day, it would beat loud enough for them to stop being cowards and tell the truth about what happened to her.

I added Danielle's name to the expanding list of murders I was trying to solve using social media. I bought a giant poster board and created a chart to keep them all straight. The names of each case ran down the first column: Danielle, Morgan Bauer Missing, White Boy Q. The next columns listed where I ran the campaigns—Facebook, Twitter, Instagram. Then a space for the best tips that came in. Then two columns that read *Solid ID* and *Arrest* and left spaces for check marks. Those columns were mostly left blank. I added River North Puncher, Nashville, and Chesapeake just to fill out some of the check marks in the last column so when I saw it, I wouldn't get too depressed, which was an all-too-real threat.

I hung the poster board in my office in my Los Angeles apartment, which doubled as my daughter's bedroom for when she visited from college. The cases hung right behind my chair, the same way my dad had hung his painting contracts behind his desk. Next to the chart, I hung pictures of the suspects. If I thought they looked like apparitions in video, printing them out on computer paper made them look even more ghostly. I bought a stuffed animal of *Zootopia*'s Officer Judy Hopps to put on my daughter's bed, hoping to brighten up the room with a little anthropomorphic Disney magic for when she came home. That didn't stop her from referring to where she had to sleep as "the murder room."

The names and blurry faces on the poster board began to add up. But in October, I added one that looked less like a phantom and more like an actual person. The crime had gone cold for the detectives, but it was still fresh in the Sunset Park neighborhood, near Owl's Head Park in Brooklyn. The video was so crisp and the suspect was so distinctive, I knew people would pay attention. People would see him. People would message. He would be identified. He would be caught.

The victim's name was Jennifer Cohen. She was blond and blue-eyed. The lead picture the media ran with showed her with ruby-red lips.

Another showed a more natural appearance, her freckles peeking out in the sunlight. The media loves pretty, white, blond-haired victims. Just like the old monster movies. The creature grabs the pretty blond girl and takes her to his lair, and the people grab their pitchforks to chase after him.

But with Jennifer, the media quickly lost interest, because the pretty blond girl was a drug addict. And the media doesn't like drug-addicted murder victims. Even a pretty white girl.

Jennifer started using as a teenager. In 2001, she found out she was pregnant, and she kicked the habit. She had two children. Boys. Gaetano and Joshua. But by 2010, she was using again. She was in jail. Out of jail. In jail. Out of jail. In jail on September 26. Out of jail. Two days later, she was dead. Her body was found in Owl's Head Park, with "trauma to her head and face," according to the police.

I spotted the case on the WPIX website, which carried *Crime Watch Daily* in New York. I did a search for Jennifer's relatives on Facebook and found her brother, Andrew. He knew his sister was using, but he didn't think she was killed over drugs. Jennifer had scored in the morning, he told me. He had no idea why anyone would do this.

But the police had a video of the man she was with that night. It was clear. I can't emphasize enough how clear it was. It was taken at 2:45 a.m. in the Bay Ridge section of Brooklyn. The man was wearing an Adidas track top, shorts, and a flat-brimmed, snapback hat with a logo on the front and another on its side. He had on a backpack with two straps covering his chest. I watched his distinctive gait as he ashed his cigarette—held in his left hand—somewhat gracefully on a sidewalk grate. His face was angular. A strong, sharp chin, covered with about a week of stubble. Well-defined eyebrows.

The video lasted but a dozen seconds. But it was golden.

I will get this guy in a week, I said to myself.

I set up the campaign. One-mile radius, which in Brooklyn is the population equivalent of a whole damn midwestern state.

Do you know this man? Sunset Park, Brooklyn—seen with murder victim in Sept. Pls msg any info. And pls share.

Tips trickled in—blue-sky tips. One guy said the man in the video was a rapper he had met when visiting New York over the summer. He sent me his Facebook page. It looked promising, and I sent it to the detective. Then it bottomed out.

Another tipster said the man was Egyptian and he had seen him by the halal food stands at Eighty-sixth and Fifth.

I ran an ad in Arabic targeting the area. No luck. I ran an ad in Spanish. No luck.

I kept pressing. Adding more money to the pot.

Around the time the video had gotten more than eighteen thousand views, I checked the post and read the most recent comment. It was only four words.

"That was my mom."

I clicked on the commenter's profile. It was Jennifer's son. I stared at his pictures. Pictures of a little boy growing up without a mom. It shook me to the bone.

My campaigns always have a chance to land in the feed of a family member. I try to make sure everyone involved knows that the campaigns are coming. But never before had I read a comment like this.

Motherfucker. I poured another $1,000 into the campaign, hoping to get any little tidbit of info that could lead to an arrest. I got nothing. Owl's Head Park Man was becoming my white whale, getting away again and again and again. I was not as obsessed as Michelle was with her Golden State Killer, but I was starting to see his face in every person I walked past, three thousand miles away.

11

THE HALLOWEEN MASK MURDER

El Monte, 2016

IN THE SIX MONTHS SINCE I HAD STARTED ON THIS SOCIAL media murder-solving quest, I had gotten one solve (Marques Gaines's attacker in Chicago), one found missing person (Mariah in California), one assist on a murder investigation (getting the ID of Joseph Santillan, the final suspect in the Nashville murder of Teddy Grasset), and a handful of cases where I was pretty sure I had identified the suspect but police didn't have enough to make an arrest (Pacman's killer in Chesapeake, White Boy Q's killer in Tallahassee, Danielle and Sheila's killer and potential accomplices in Humboldt). And then there were the cases that I was striking out on. Dozens of them. Random shootings and hit-and-runs across America.

I knew I was hitting the right neighborhoods, and I knew people with information were seeing the videos or sketches of the killers, but the "no snitch" ethos pervades many communities. On top of fears of reprisal, when you are in a community that has been fucked over by the actions of a few bad police officers, the ripple effects are massive.

In October 2004, seven Milwaukee police officers sadistically beat Frank Jude Jr. outside an off-duty police party. The *Journal Sentinel* newspaper in Milwaukee investigated the crime and published photos of

Jude taken right after the beating. The officers were convicted, and some reforms were put in place. But the city saw an unexpected side effect. Calls to 911 dropped dramatically—twenty-two thousand less than the previous year. You know what did rise? The number of homicides—eighty-seven in the six months after the photos were published, a seven-year high.

That information comes from a 2016 study done by Matthew Desmond, an associate social sciences professor at Harvard University and *New York Times* bestselling author of *Evicted*. He told the *Journal Sentinel* that a case like Jude's "tears the fabric apart so deeply and delegitimizes the criminal justice system in the eyes of the African-American community that they stop relying on it in significant numbers."

With shootings of unarmed civilians being captured on cell phones and shared on the internet, the distrust of the police is not relegated to that local community. The stories of the high-profile wrongful death cases of Tamir Rice in Cleveland or Eric Brown in New York spread fast across the country. We were in a worse place than we were twenty years earlier, when the vicious police officer beating of Rodney King went unpunished and Los Angeles went up in flames. It meant more and more crimes would go unsolved because the police were just not trusted. Why risk your life telling an organization about a crime when you think that members of that organization are out to get you? And how can that ever change?

Those were the thoughts rattling around in my head when I exited the I-110 freeway in downtown Los Angeles and headed toward the Hall of Justice. I was meeting with the Los Angeles sheriffs, hoping to find cases to cover for *Crime Watch Daily*. Cases that were unsolved but salacious enough to get some ratings.

Downtown Los Angeles is riddled with famous crime landmarks, both tall tales and true. I drove past the Bonaventure Hotel, where Secret Service agent Clint Eastwood chased down assassin John Malkovich in *In the Line of Fire* and Arnold Schwarzenegger rode a horse into the elevator in *True Lies*. One block south at Fifth and Flower was where De Niro, Pacino, and Kilmer unloaded bullets in the epic shoot-out in *Heat*. I made a left on Spring, behind the Bradbury Building, where Harrison Ford fought Rutger Hauer in *Blade Runner* and passed the *Los Angeles Times* building, the site of what, in the area, is referred to as the crime of the century: the 1910 bombing by a union member that killed twenty-one newspaper employees. I pulled up to Los Angeles city hall, which pulls double duty in American popular crime culture as both the icon for the show *Dragnet* and as the *Daily Planet* headquarters in the original *Adventures of Superman* TV series.

Across the street from city hall stands the Hall of Justice, where the autopsies of Marilyn Monroe and Bobby Kennedy were performed and the circus-like trial of Charles Manson took place. I walked into a conference room and took a seat at a large table surrounded by a group of Los Angeles County Sheriff's Department's homicide detectives. They were all dressed the same—Men's Wearhouse suits a half size too big, close-cropped haircuts, department-issued facial hair. I was there to talk about their cold-case files. The LASD is the second-largest police department in the country, and they had plenty of bodies that were looking for answers. As we talked, I looked at the detective to my right, whose legs were crossed, and spied the bottom of his shoe. It was worn thin, with three big holes peppered across the heel and sole. Shoe-leather investigating. Door-to-door footwork. I made a joke to the captain, not only about the work ethic clearly on display but also questioning how much our man was getting paid. I got a laugh from the room—and a bit of a sneer from the captain.

The captain handed me off to a helpful sheriff, who brought me into their warehouse at the homicide headquarters a few miles away in Monterey Park. Imagine a Costco, but in each aisle were the stories of thousands of murders, stacked one on top of the other. I went right to the special cage with the high-profile files. Boxes on one shelf held the evidence for the Richard Ramirez Night Stalker case. Nearby was a box with "Sal Mineo" written in Magic Marker on the side, referring to the 1976 West Hollywood murder of the *Rebel Without a Cause* star.

In one corner was a large stack of boxes with *Bradford* written on the side. I knew what was inside. Bill Bradford was a serial killer from the early 1980s who used his hobby as a photographer to lure women to remote locations and murder them. When he was nabbed, police searched his apartment and found thousands of photographs of women who posed for him, clothed and nude and everything in between. The sheriffs identified most of the women, but in the end, there were fifty-four women in the photos who remained unnamed. They held a press conference and distributed the pictures to the media in an attempt to match names with faces. They said that any one of the women could have been a victim of Bradford's. And they were right. Someone came forward when they recognized Number 28 on the list. Her name was Donnalee Campbell Duhamel. Her body was found in 1978, decapitated. Bradford wouldn't talk, but they linked him to Duhamel via a bar called the Frigate in Culver City. He was never charged with her murder, but everyone was sure he did it. He died in prison in 2008. Seventeen women in the photos have still not been identified.

I wondered if a few social media campaigns could help identify some of the unknown seventeen. To my surprise, the detective in charge gave me any files I wanted to take back to the office to make scans and copies. I loaded up a large box with police reports and hundreds of photos of women. Number 26 was a girl wearing a halter top in front of a Confederate flag. Number 27 was in bra, panties, and stockings, posing awkwardly in front of a 1970's-era rec room paneled wall. Number 14 wore an Uncle Sam hat as she stood in front of military equipment, including what look liked a fighter jet.

After scanning them all back at the *Crime Watch Daily* offices, I was getting ready to send them back when I went to my computer to double check the LASD homicide address. For some reason, I searched LASD on Facebook instead of Google, and when I opened the sheriffs' Facebook page, I was met with a video of a woman weeping.

"I miss my son," the small woman, standing at a podium at a press conference flanked by men in dark suits, said between sobs. "I miss him deeply. I don't know what kind of sick person would take him away from me. My son lived with me. We went everywhere together. I know some boys and some moms—they drift apart. My son still called me from work and said 'Mom, I'm going to go to my buddy's. I will call you when I leave his house.' He hasn't come home since he left."

She was shaking, pushing each word out while at the same time trying to catch her breath.

Her son's name was Juan Vidal. He had been shot and killed in an attempted robbery at a Jack in the Box in El Monte, California. Juan was twenty-five years old. He wasn't involved in gangs or drugs. He had just earned a pharmacy technician degree from UEI College and was working the register at Jack in the Box while he was interviewing for drugstore jobs. He wasn't even on the schedule that night but had come in to cover for a coworker. He had also just asked his girl to marry him.

His mother was named Mary. Standing next to her at the podium was Juan's fiancée, Julie Ann, and a Mexican American man with a kind face, Detective Adan Torres. He approached the podium and recapped the particulars of the crime, then played the video of the night Juan disappeared.

The surveillance tape starts with a high-angle shot from behind a fast-food counter. Seven stacks of soft-drink cups sit underneath two empty computer registers. Your eyes are drawn to the double glass doors at the top of frame. You are waiting for something to happen there, when all of a sudden, a man approaches from the right side of the frame, performs a half barrel roll over the counter, and lands in the space behind the registers. He's holding a pistol in his right hand and is wearing a Halloween mask on his face and a baseball cap on his head. Once over the counter, he steadies himself for a second, looks to the left offscreen, seems to point toward the front doors with his left hand, then disappears underneath the camera. In two seconds, he returns, jumps back over the counter, and exits to the right.

When the gunman walked out of the frame behind the registers, he encountered Juan. He demanded money. Juan didn't resist. But the gunman still shot him in the chest. He left with no money. Seven seconds was all it took.

Stick-up robbery murders—the type you see at gas stations and liquor stores—are often some of the easiest to solve. Most establishments have video cameras, and the incidents are caught on tape from both inside and outside the store. They also have those handy height charts you see next to the doors to show how tall the suspect is. But in this one, the perpetrator is wearing a mask, and we don't even have a straight shot of it—just a high-angle shot of a figure in motion. A figure who in one desperate act was about to knock down a set of dominoes and change the lives of so many people in El Monte, California.

El Monte. I had never been there, but I knew it. El Monte has a particular significance in both true and fictional crime. The Jack in the Box where Juan was killed was three miles from the former location of the Desert Inn, the long-gone bar where Jean Hilliker was spotted with "the Swarthy Man," the nickname that was given to the unidentified man who undoubtedly murdered her. Hilliker was a single mother whose body was found near the Arroyo High School ball field after a night on the town in 1958. She left behind a ten-year-old son named James, whose last name was that of his father: Ellroy. James Ellroy employed the demons that stirred that night to launch his career as one of the greatest fictional crime writers in history. Ellroy searched for the identity of his mother's killer in his memoir *My Dark Places*. He uncovered some answers about himself but none about the identity of his mother's killer. The Swarthy Man remains a mystery.

At the Jack in the Box, witnesses said *this* killer ran out of the restaurant and down Flair Drive, where he hopped into a dark-colored sedan that "fled at a high rate of speed." Juan died at the hospital.

"The suspect was wearing a light-blue T-shirt, khaki cargo shorts, and black running shoes," Detective Torres told the members of the press.

"What can you tell us about the mask?" asked a reporter.

"It has a mustache, a real thick mustache," Torres answered. "With black plastic glasses—or remember in the old cartoons, the robbers used to wear just the black band? And a blue baseball cap."

That was the only image we had of the shooter's face—a Halloween mask that looked as if someone crossed Groucho Marx with Cheech Marin, then grossly and comically enlarged and distorted the cheeks, ears, and nose.

Torres spoke directly to the shooter through the news cameras: "Come in on your own and tell your side of the story." He played the short video again.

I ran scenarios in my head. The video would catch people's attention for sure. But could it really lead to an answer to find his killer? In the Marques Gaines cases in Chicago, I had a good idea what the puncher looked like. This was different.

It's early, I said to myself. *Let's let it play out.*

In the audience stood cameramen from most every LA TV station, the *LA Times*, and the local papers in the San Gabriel Valley. They would be running the video on their social media pages. While it wouldn't be as targeted as my technique—and it wouldn't be coming from a dedicated page serving only the one crime and looking for only the one answer—they might get lucky and find someone who knew something about the man in the mask. I decided to wait a week.

But I was still curious. I found Juan Vidal's Facebook page and was greeted by a profile picture of a handsome man with thick sideburns, a Cheshire-cat smile, and a rockabilly-style pompadour. I learned that Juan had a Buick Special Deluxe that he called Christine, and he listed his musical likes as the Smiths and Morrissey. And Blur. I knew Morrissey had a huge following in the Los Angeles Latino community. But Blur? The upper-middle-class Britpop band who sang about "Parklife" and "Girls who are boys, who like boys to be girls?" I liked Juan even though I never knew him. It would not have been a stretch to see me and him sway in the same crowd at the Hollywood Bowl while Morrissey crooned "Everyday Is Like Sunday."

Halloween came and went with no news about the case and the killer. On November 2, six days after the initial press conference, the sheriff's department presided over another briefing to announce that the board of supervisors had voted to approve $20,000 of funds for a reward to solve Juan's murder. The city of El Monte was kicking in another $25,000. That was not a good sign. Sweetening the pot meant only one thing—the police had nothing. They were dangling $45,000 in front of the cameras, hoping someone would pick up the phone and do the right thing.

I checked back in on the case every few days. Two weeks went by with no developments. Juan's murder wasn't the kind of killing *Crime Watch Daily* would readily cover. I would be doing this one alone.

All right, I said to myself. *Let's see if you can help solve the murder of a Morrissey fan.*

I wasn't worried about grabbing people's attention. The video of the Jack in the Box murder was striking enough that people would stop.

People would look. People would share. But we were all going to be dealing with the same problem—we were all looking at a man in a mask.

"Give [a man] a mask," said Oscar Wilde, "and he will tell you the truth."

What was this guy trying to tell us?

Gangbangers don't rob stores with Halloween masks. Kids who watch movies do. Career criminals also don't choose such cash-poor establishments. This guy was desperate. He grabbed what he had on hand. A ski mask is easy to wear on your head like a regular stocking cap, then unfurl over your face when it's time to go bad. But a full-on Halloween mask? This was an amateur. A kid who's seen *Dead Presidents* one too many times.

Watching the video again, I could tell he was young. Few people over forty would jump over the counter with such swiftness. He also had thin, athletic legs. The legs of a young man.

I coupled these body traits with the facts of the case. He entered the Jack in the Box, jumped over the counter, shot an employee, and left with no money. He panicked, which told me he hadn't done this many times before. He was going to be a baby face, probably under twenty-five. He could even be a teenager.

But I wasn't going to get anywhere looking for a guy under twenty-five with thin legs. If I couldn't see his face, the next thing I could look at was his mask. If I could ID the mask, I could run a photo of it along with the video. The campaign would turn into "do you know a guy under twenty-five who owns this mask and might be desperate enough to rob a fast-food joint in the San Gabriel Valley?"

It's all about lowering the odds. Any way I can shrink the pool of who the perp might be gets me closer. And having a picture of the mask was going to be the next best thing to the killer's face.

I typed "Halloween mustache mask man" into Google and hit image search.

It spit out all types of masks: The hippie. The lumberjack. The old-time gangster. The Rock.

I tried again with "human mask Halloween mustache." This time, I got back a crazy-haired Einstein, a blond Viking, and a very realistic Walter White. But scrolling down, I found a cherubic old man wearing a ball cap that looked like it could be close. I clicked on the image and was taken to a site called Grimnation.com. There I learned the mask's name: "Robert No Dinero." Description: "Mask of a male character with large mustache and attached adjustable cap. The mask has great visibility, is adjustable, light weight, and comfortable."

The oversized nose looked right, but the mustache was far too bushy and drooped down far too low over the sides of his mouth. And the hat was a high-crown trucker style. I was looking for a low-profile ball cap.

But Mr. No Dinero, as racist as it was, was the closest thing I could find. I took the photo of the perp and performed a Google reverse image search, employing the favorite tool of the TV show *Catfish* and internet daters everywhere.

Bingo.

Under the "visually similar images" tab was a mask and cap that looked perfect. It was called "Stan the Man." Description: "Show them who's the boss with this Stanley the Man mask. This half mask is comfortable enough to wear all night long. The latex mask features an attached baseball cap and great fit that blends naturally with the wearers face. No glue required."

The detective had said the killer's mask had glasses or a black band like "the robbers used to wear in old cartoons." Stan had neither, but looking back at the video, I wondered if it was the shadow of the cap that was giving him that impression. This was the mask of the killer.

I called costume shops in Los Angeles. A few of them sold the Stan the Man mask. But it was also widely available online, not exotic enough to trace the sale. My best bet was going to be to run the stock photo of the mask along with the video and ask people if they knew anyone who might have worn that mask at a recent Halloween outing.

With that one small victory, I moved on to the question at hand: Who knew an athletic guy with skinny legs between the ages of fourteen and thirty who might be in a situation so dire that it drove him to stick up a fast-food restaurant? There are two ways to target someone that young: go for his friends, former schoolmates, and coworkers. Or go for older family members or friends of the family. I decided to go after the younger set first.

As for the location, I was going to stay local. Although the Jack in the Box was close to Interstate 10—leaving some to speculate that the gunman chose that location for an easy getaway—the facts of the case told me he was local. The gunman was young. He didn't have much time to have lived or worked in multiple areas, knowing the streets and stores to be comfortable enough to try this robbery. Add that on top of his desperation, and I knew a guy like that was not going to drive ten miles out of his way.

I learned another key fact from Detective Torres. The gunman wore a similar mask to someone who had robbed a Subway restaurant in nearby Irwindale two days before the attempted robbery at Jack in the Box. That clinched it.

When this case came up, I was knee-deep in geoprofiling the Golden State Killer, as we were trying to finish the last section of Michelle's book. With GSK, we had dozens of locations that he had struck within such a small section of Sacramento. Michelle had a theory that there was a buffer, or safe zone, in the middle of all the attacks. When plotted out on a map, the crimes formed a circle surrounding an untouched section of a neighborhood called Carmichael. Michelle and Paul Haynes believed the East Area Rapist may have either lived in, worked in, or frequented that area. The idea of the buffer zone was that you would never commit a crime too close to where you lived, also known as the don't-shit-where-you-eat theory. But you also wouldn't commit your crimes too far away, where you might not know any of the escape routes if things went south.

With Juan's murder case, I only had two plots on the map, not even enough to triangulate. But it was enough to start searching.

I reached out to Juan's sister and explained that I was going to use a new system I had created utilizing social media to find people who might know the suspect. I didn't get into the specifics. I just said I was going to try to help. She just wanted the man caught. With the family's go-ahead, I called Detective Torres and explained my plan. He had been looking for answers for weeks and admitted he was stuck. He was willing to take any help he could get.

I called the page the "El Monte Jack in the Box Killer," and for the profile picture, I used the stock photo of a model wearing the Stan the Man mask I was confident the killer wore that night. Close up, free of the blurry images caught on the surveillance video, the mask was sinister. A ball cap sat above two bushy eyebrows. Under the eyeholes were two exaggerated, puffy checks, a large bulbous nose, and a bushy mustache, which on one side hovered over a half-smoked cigar. The mask stopped above the wearer's mouth, leaving his chin fully exposed.

I posted the first ad on November 15, using the video of the gunman hopping over the counter. The video ran for twenty seconds and showed the gunman twice at full speed, then once in slow motion.

For targeting, I selected the zip codes of both Irwindale and El Monte, combined population 115,708 (85,546 adults based on the latest census). With enough money—and the right message that would inspire people to share the post—I could reach almost all of them.

Do you know who shot and killed young man Juan Vidal at the El Monte Jack in the Box on Oct. 21? He is wearing a mask (see avatar, know anyone who has this mask?) but appears to be Caucasian, light complexion Hispanic or middle eastern, 15–30. Please message any info—any info at all. And pls. share.

Less than twenty-four hours later I got a private message from a man named Hector Carillo. "Who are you? How did you know Juan?"

I explained I was a journalist and victim's advocate working with the family.

"The family request that you put your name on the page," he said. "They don't like the way the page is written. Might want to add the search for the el monte jack in the box killer."

I told him my name and attempted to explain my method. There are thousands of "searching for" and "justice for" pages on Facebook. And there are also millions of people trying to grab your attention. Posting with the most direct language possible, even if it sounded like it was coming from the killer himself (as I did with the River North Puncher/Man in the Green Hoodie campaign) was going to get a lot more attention.

Hector responded angrily: "Billy this is an active, non-botched case. Juan was a very good friend of mine and in our group of friends we have a friend that is a CSI for LAPD. please don't fuck our friends case up. you WILL piss off allot of people. This is not a game or an app for us. this is not a cold case trust me."

"Hector, believe me, that is the last thing we want to do," I immediately wrote back. "That is why I check with both the family and the investigator in charge before I start anything. When I asked the LASD if they wanted help, they said yes. If they would have said no, I would have backed off."

The next message he sent was a photo of the rear end of a blue El Camino on a tree-lined road with mountains in the background. In the bed of the El Camino lay a casket.

"He was a car guy," Hector wrote. "We got him his last ride."

Juan was a person, I screamed in my head, that scream I had screamed a thousand times before. *He just wanted to marry his girl, get in his Buick, listen to Morrissey, and drive to his new job at a pharmacy.* And a guy in a twenty-six-dollar mask thought he could kill him and get away with it.

With Juan's friend calmed for a bit, I checked back on the campaign. It was moving quickly. You could tell how it was slipping into pockets of neighborhoods as Juan's friends' comments piled on top of each other. Having a rallying point—a local business most people knew—was key. People had stories about this Jack in the Box, and they wanted to share them. That made the post get in front of more people.

"Oh my God that's so sad why people need to hurt others so bad."

"He may have known where the cameras were he may have been a regular customer so sad to think about if this idiot still goes in like nothing."

"He left a hand print on the counter," wrote another. Which was true, but early on, Torres had told me that there had been so many prints on that counter that it was useless.

"The masked man was going to shoot one of his coworkers so he jumped in front of her pretty much saved her life."

There was action, but it wasn't doing the trick.

At this point, I was learning a lot about how people would react to the campaigns. Empathy has to be higher if a person sees something in a Facebook feed or on Twitter rather than if they're looking at a wanted poster at the post office or a newscast on TV, crammed in the middle of other murders and mayhem. Facebook has life in it. When you watch the news, there is an inherent callus on your brain: Bad things happen; people die. But when you see it on social media, you are unconsciously associating the person who died with your own friends and family. It's all in the same river.

I posted a second ad the next day, this time focusing on the mask. I used the best screenshot I could grab of the gunman from the video and the stock photo of the model behind the mask.

I got a bunch of people commenting that the "guy looks Chinese," thinking that the perp actually posed for a photo with the mask. "It's stock photo, people," I had to write. I tried not to get frustrated. People were trying to help. But after twelve hours of staring at a screen, reaching out to tipsters, trying to track down leads, I was getting whiplash from all my head shaking.

And I wasn't getting anywhere. Was there anything else that might identify the gunman? Cargo shorts are common. Skinny, agile legs pointed to youth. What about his footwear? He was wearing high tops that looked like they might be expensive basketball sneakers.

I requested admission into the subreddit /Sneakers. There was a remote chance that sneakerheads—as detail-oriented about kicks as gearheads are about cars—might be able to ID the gunman's footwear. I asked the moderators if I could post something from an ongoing murder investigation and posted a close-up of the gunman's shoes, zooming in as much as I could without full distortion. They were still pretty pixelated, but I had to give it a shot.

"Trying to identify these sneakers—worn by a man who shot and killed an employee at the Jack in The Box in El Monte in October," I wrote.

I got my first comment within minutes: "JPEG 12's. Limited run."

I actually laughed out loud. "All right, that was clever," I responded. If you're going to troll, at least be funny.

A few more jokes came. I added some more pics along with the video.

"In the first pic they kind of look like Nike Air Max 1s or Air Max 90s," wrote the one sincere commenter. "And in the second pic they look a bit like some kind of Jordan Son of Mars or like a Lebron 10, not really sure though."

Dead end.

I watched the video so many times, I was starting to see things.

Playing it in super slow motion, I thought I saw a diamond-shaped black mark on the gunman's shin as he leapt over the counter. I didn't know whether it was a bandage, a tattoo, or just a bunch of broken pixels from the low-res camera at the Jack in the Box. But I made a Hail Mary post focusing on the possibility of a tattoo.

Again, I got nothing.

A couple of days later, Detective Torres called me. The police were releasing a new still image related to the attack. It was the getaway car. The problem was, it was practically a blur, looking like every late '90s/early 2000s four-door sedan. You know how on *CSI* when they take a blurry photo of a car from a crime scene, press a button, and the pixels all jump around this way and that before coming together and creating a crystal-clear image? Yeah, that doesn't happen in real life.

I enlarged the photo and looked for anything that might identify the car. I had nothing, but I knew someone who might be able to make sense out of the blurs. I emailed the pic to my buddy Adam, who had come to Chicago and shot footage of my quest to find Marques Gaines's attacker. Adam was a car guy. If he didn't have any idea of the make and model, I would go to Reddit along with a few car message boards I knew of.

It took just two hours for Adam to email me back.

"It's a Lexus IS300," he wrote. "Early 2000s. You can tell by the angle of the back window most importantly, the extra brake light that was actually on the side of the bumper at the back of the car."

He included a photo of an early 2000 Lexus IS300 superimposed below the blurry car image still from the surveillance camera. It looked pretty damn close.

I thanked Adam and sent Detective Torres the comparison. He thought it looked pretty damn close as well. I launched a new ad. No video this time. Just the overhead still of the gunman, a still of his legs, the photo of the mask, and the picture of the getaway car.

I also changed the location targets, laying out a two-mile radius around each of the robbery locations. That widened the search into LA suburbs Rosemead and San Gabriel.

The ad read:

Irwindale, El Monte and vicinity: Do you know someone who might drive an early 2000s Lexus IS300? (The possible getaway car). Do you know anyone who might own this mask? (stock photo). This man attempted to rob the Jack in the Box on Flair Dr. in El Monte on Oct. 21 (suspected to have also robbed a Subway in Irwindale) and shot and killed a man. Pls do the right thing. message any info (do not post info in comments). And pls share. There is a reward.

I got a few tips, including a photo of a man next to a car that someone sent me, thinking it might be the guy. I got excited and emailed Detective Torres with the information on November 29. I got a response right back. "Billy, I lost your cell. Can you call me?"

I ran into the parking lot at *Crime Watch Daily* and called him immediately.

"Did that photo look good?" I asked.

"We ID'd him," Torres cut me off.

"Really!?" I said, clenching the phone tightly in my fist.

"Yeah! Someone saw the Facebook ad and called us," he said.

It worked. A video of a killer wearing a Halloween mask and a blurry getaway car. All it took was hitting almost every adult in the surrounding areas of the murder with a Facebook page ad over and over and over again. I had spent about $900 to get it done. If I could bottle what I was feeling, I could sell it for triple the price.

Torres asked me not to say anything to Juan's family. He still had to build the case, and more importantly, he had to make it stick. Other than the gun, that is the biggest thing that separates me from law enforcement officers. I could write a story about the case, get every detail right, and the only three risks I faced were getting it wrong, getting sued, and no one reading it. Torres had to make sure twelve people on a jury would believe beyond a reasonable doubt that this was the man who had killed Juan Vidal. He thanked me for the help, told me he would email me as soon as he got an arrest, and hung up. I was left to do the one thing I am absolutely horrible at: wait.

I busied myself through the holiday season trying my damnedest to ID that man seen walking in Brooklyn with a young mother who was later found dead in Owl's Head Park. People were back home for the holidays. They drink and talk, and hopefully word of the case leaks into their conversation and into the face of the right person. I was spending way too much money trying find him.

I kept my phone with me at the table for Christmas dinner, scrolling through each of my cases in between passing dishes of marshmallow-covered sweet potatoes and green bean casserole. Kendall understood why I had to keep checking, but that didn't make it any less annoying for her. It was beyond a compulsion at this point. The endorphins would rush whenever I got a message to one of the victim's pages. All I wanted for Christmas was my next solve.

The following week, Torres was ready to announce the arrest of Juan's killer. He invited me to the press conference. Out of respect for the family, I put on a suit and drove to the LASD homicide building in Monterey Park.

Waiting in the hall as the TV crews set up, I recognized Juan's mother from the video I had seen months earlier. I introduced myself and was gifted the biggest hug from her, followed by Juan's sister. I was getting paid in hugs. Just like in Chicago with Drexina and Phyllis. I'll take them. They don't pay the mortgage, but at the moment I get a hug from a family member, I don't need anything else in the world.

We walked into the briefing room. Homicide chief Captain Katz began, announcing that an arrest had been made in the murder of Juan Vidal. The suspect's name was Louie Herrera. He was twenty years old. He lived in San Gabriel.

My tactic of widening the search had worked—San Gabriel was just two miles up the road from the Jack in the Box. Katz unveiled a large poster with a photo of the suspect. He had a baby face. He was charged with murder and held without bail.

Torres then walked up to the podium to explain how Herrera was caught. He thanked the media and then turned to me. "Billy Jensen…put together a Facebook page titled 'El Monte Jack in the Box Killer.' Tips started coming in, and eventually, we were able to solve the case."

I was blown away. To get recognition from law enforcement that the work I did resulted in the arrest floored me—especially after the silence of the Chicago police department during the Marques Gaines case.

But Torres told us that the work wasn't done. The getaway driver was still unidentified and on the loose—Herrera wasn't giving him up. A giant cardboard poster of the car was on display. "We still want the driver," he said. "We beg that you guys call and give us tips."

Juan's mother then walked to the podium. "I want all of them to be in jail," she said, tears streaming. She attempted to catch her breath. "The driver needs to be caught too."

After the press conference ended, the local media interviewed me about the case. I hugged Juan's mom and sister again and then went back to work to find the driver. I crafted a new post, centered around where Louie Herrera lived. I also found his Facebook page and began the painstaking task of going through every one of his friends to try to spot a Lexus IS300 in the background of one of their photos or a mention of Louie or the car in one of their posts.

After four hours of digging, I sent Detective Torres an email laying out some of the tips I had gotten. He replied with a stand down. Between the media blitz and the Facebook ad targeting, they had gotten a very promising lead on the driver, and they were working it hard.

The day after the press conference, I got a call from Hector, the friend of Juan who had yelled at me when I originally posted the ad.

"I'm sorry I doubted you, man," he said, referring to the message he had sent me the night I sent up the page. "You're the real deal."

He told me that Juan's family had been getting some threats. I told him I had gotten some doing this as well.

"Listen, I'm a second amendment guy," he said. "I'll take you to the gun range. You definitely have a reason to apply for a concealed carry permit. Let me take you."

I told him thanks, but I'd take a rain check.

Guns scare the hell out of me. I've seen the damage they can do a thousand times over. But that doesn't mean I would never carry one, to go along with the alarm systems and video doorbells, bulletproof panels, and the knife ever present in my pocket—which Dad said to only use if "someone was choking you." I take precautions, everything they tell you to do: No patterns. Driving different ways to work. Giving myself an escape route whenever walking. But I also have to remember what one cop once told me—"Don't be afraid of the bullet with your name on it. Be afraid of the thousand bullets without your name on them." He said that to me ten years ago, and with the number of mass shootings rising in America, I take it even more to heart.

"Okay," Hector said. "But if you change your mind…" We kept talking, and he told me his cousin had been shot and killed in Long Beach a few years back. The police had surveillance video but had not released it and hadn't made any arrests. I told him I would make some calls and see what I could find. We stayed friends on Facebook, like I do with so many other people connected with victims. I keep watching the videos of him restoring 1970s Buicks and dream of one day borrowing one and driving up the coast.

One day. But there was a lot more work to be done. Three thousand miles away, one of my white whales was spotted in New Hampshire. Was I about to get the answers to a thirty-year-old murder mystery? Or would it just rip open another bag of questions in the most perplexing case I had ever tried to solve? Turns out, the answer was both.

12.

THE DEVIL IN PLAIN DARKNESS

Contra Costa County, 2001

IN THE SPRING OF 1986, A MAN NAMED GORDON JENSON AND his five-year-old daughter, Lisa, moved into the Holiday Host trailer park in Scotts Valley, a small California town in between Santa Cruz and San Jose.

Jenson explained to some of his new neighbors that Lisa's mother, Denise LaPorte, had died in a car accident in Texas. He told others that Denise had died in a robbery gone wrong. Either way, he was a single father, working odd jobs, trying to make it in the world with a little girl who was about to start grade school.

He found work at the trailer park fixing VCRs and other electronics. He was earning what money he could, but it just wasn't enough for the kind of life he wanted for his little girl. They were sleeping side by side in the back of a truck covered with a camper shell that was open on one end. Lisa had no toys.

Being the electronics handyman in the park, Jenson interacted with many of the residents. One day, he was visiting with Katherine Decker, who was passing through the park with her husband. As they sat on a picnic table in front of her motor home, Jenson talked about losing his wife, his daughter's situation, and how it had all gotten to be too much for him. He broke down and started to cry.

Decker felt horrible. She told him that their own daughter had been having difficulty trying to get pregnant. Suddenly, Jenson saw a way to help his daughter get a better life. And it was perfect timing. He said he was going out of town for a few days and asked Decker if they could watch Lisa for a three-week "trial" period. If the little girl liked her new home with Decker's daughter and son-in-law in Fountain Valley, maybe they could start adoption proceedings.

The Deckers were thrilled. They took Lisa home with them, and the little girl liked her potential new family. The three-week trial period was a success, but when it came time for Jenson to pick up Lisa and work out the details, he never showed. They searched the trailer park for him, but he was nowhere to be found. Gordon Jenson was gone.

The Deckers didn't know what to do. They attempted to adopt Lisa legally, but when they explained the circumstances to officials, the case was referred to the San Bernardino Sheriff's Department. Lisa was placed in foster care, and a $250,000 warrant was issued for Jenson for child desertion. Upon further interviews and examinations of Lisa, they also charged him with something far more sinister—child molestation.

Police traveled to the Holiday Host trailer park and attempted to gather any evidence on Jenson that they could use for the warrant. They searched high and low for his fingerprints. After checking the usual spots and coming up empty, they dug deeper and discovered a set of prints on the inside of a VCR he had repaired at the park. When they ran the prints through the system, they got a surprise. There was no Gordon Jenson. The fingerprints belonged to a man named Curtis Mayo Kimball, who was arrested in Orange County in May 1985 for drunk driving and child endangerment.

For two years, investigators searched for the dad who had abandoned—and was suspected of molesting—his child. They finally caught up with him after he was arrested for drunk driving in Los Angeles.

Jenson/Kimball was tossed in jail, but the man who had been so talkative in front of Katherine Decker at the trailer park closed up in front of the police. He refused to admit that he even knew Lisa. After a year, he was paroled. He skipped town, violating his parole conditions, and was never heard from again. Lisa was placed with a loving family. Even though she went through a horrendous ordeal, she grew up to have a family of her own. And almost everyone else forgot about Gordon Jenson.

Twelve years later, a forty-three-year-old chemist named Eunsoon Jun was eating at a restaurant in her Richmond, California, neighborhood when she got to talking to the owner. Her roof needed to be repaired, and she was looking for someone to help. Jun was a free spirit, a Korean immigrant, and gifted potter who had a pottery wheel and kiln in the garage behind the house she lived in by herself. But she didn't have the skills to fix a roof. The restaurant owner referred her to a local handyman named Larry Vanner. While Vanner was working on her roof, the two began to talk. His bright blue eyes enchanted Jun. The talk led to romance, and the romance led to Vanner moving in.

Jun's friends were suspicious. Yes, she was a free spirit, but they felt her new beau was less a hippie and more a drifter—a "haggard and stoop-shouldered" street person, Jun's friend Renee Rose remembered. "He smokes a lot. His skin was colorless."

Jun's cousin, Elaine Ramos, said her family had warned Jun to "be careful" when it came to her new man, who was also two decades older than she was. They began to notice discrepancies in some of the things he would tell them about his background. He told them he was a retired colonel. He wasn't. He told them he owned a convenience store. He didn't. But the soft-spoken Jun wanted love, and this man seemed willing to give it to her. She told her friends and family to back off. She was happy.

Jun and Vanner were married in a *Star Trek*–themed ceremony in the backyard of a friend's house in 2001. The marriage was not official, and no records were filed with the state, but they began living as husband and wife, presumably after vows where they pledged to love each other, live long, and prosper.

Less than a year later, Jun was supposed to meet a friend for a lunch date. She never showed. Then she missed a pottery class. Her friends began asking each other, "Have you seen Jun?" No one had.

Days went by. Jun's friend Renee Rose had spoken with her on May 31 and felt she was talking very hurriedly, a drastic change from her typical slow, deliberate manner of speaking. Rose and Jun were planning a trip to Mendocino, a coastal town three hours north of San Francisco, but Jun ended the call quickly. Rose presumed she had had a fight with Vanner and let it go. But the next day, she didn't hear from Jun. And in the days that followed, her friend didn't answer any of her calls. Was the trip still happening?

Rose wanted to know what was going on. She called Vanner. He told her that Jun's mother had suddenly fallen ill, and Jun had immediately flown to Virginia to be with her family.

Okay, Rose thought. "Can I have the number there so I can call her?"

Vanner said Jun was having trouble with her family and was staying at a hotel and he didn't have the number. Rose continued to press. Vanner lashed out. "Renee, I'm sure she has more on her mind right now than wherever the fuck you guys were going."

Rose backed off. She waited a few days for him to cool down and then called back. Vanner told her that Jun had come back from Virginia but had just left for Oregon to work on a cabin he said the two had purchased together. Then he told Rose he was headed out of town to visit Jun, and she was in a fragile state and didn't want to talk to anyone.

None of this felt right to Rose. She kept asking about her friend and kept getting stonewalled by Vanner. By August, she had had enough and called the police.

Contra Costa detectives visited with Vanner. He was willing to go with them to their headquarters to answer questions. Detective Roxane Gruenheid rode next to him in the back of the squad car. He was very chatty, his blue eyes lighting up with the small talk.

Vanner willingly gave his fingerprints. The detectives had a hunch he had been arrested before. But in the years since he had last been through the procedure, things had changed. Live Scan fingerprinting technology had replaced the old paper and ink method.

The Department of Justice (DOJ) maintains the statewide criminal record repository for California. Every person who has ever been arrested gets a record of arrests and prosecutions (RAP) sheet, and the fingerprints they provide at the time of the arrest are attached to the RAP sheet as the unique identifier to show exactly who the person is. Matching the new fingerprints to the ones in the database used to take days. But with Live Scan, it took a few hours. While the detectives were waiting for the results, Gruenheid kept talking to Vanner.

She noticed that Vanner's accent sounded like he might have spent time on the East Coast.

"Your accent's really interesting," she said, trying to keep up the banter. "Where did you grow up?"

Vanner leaned in close to Gruenheid, so close she could feel his breath. Then he growled, "That's none of your goddamned business."

"It was like a flick of a switch, from what his normal behavior was," Gruenheid said. "And then he switched it off again and kept carrying on as normal."

Vanner really didn't want to talk about who he was or where he was from.

When the detectives asked about Jun, he gave what they thought were evasive answers. They also noticed that he referred to her in the past tense. But they really didn't have anything to hold him on.

Gruenheid kept up the idle chitchat with Vanner. Then the results came back.

Vanner's fingerprints matched a profile in the DOJ system. The name? Curtis Mayo Kimball. Kimball had a warrant out for his arrest after he had failed to meet with his parole officer. He was arrested for violating his parole in 1990—after serving time for abandoning a child at a trailer park. That child was little Lisa. It was enough for Gruenheid to arrest him and get a search warrant for the property in Richmond.

Gruenheid drove to the house on Bernhard Avenue in Richmond. She uncovered a home in a strange state. None of Jun's possessions—or any women's clothing or effects, for that matter—were found inside. Over the back fence, she saw a dried-up, dead kitten. She entered a padlocked garage and saw a collection of pottery that Jun had made, next to her wheel and kiln. Passing by the pottery, she walked deeper into the garage until she came upon a peculiar site—a 250-pound mountain of kitty litter piled high next to the water heater. Gruenheid moved the litter around a bit. After a few seconds, she spotted an outline of something hard in the sand. She brushed away more of the litter, and the object was revealed. It was a human foot, connected to a flip-flop. She called in the forensics team. They dug into the kitty litter pile and discovered the body of Eunsoon Jun. She had died from blunt-force trauma to the head. Police said the kitty litter masked the stench of her decaying flesh.

Larry Vanner was arrested for murder. He didn't want to go through a trial. He pled guilty and received fifteen years to life. But the story was far, far from over.

California now had three identities for this man: Larry Vanner, Curtis Mayo Kimball, and Gordon Jenson, all with the same fingerprints. Vanner, the convicted murderer, was the same man who had abandoned his five-year-old daughter Lisa with the couple from the trailer park.

But was little Lisa really his daughter?

"I started to get a really strong feeling—I did not believe that Lisa was his daughter," Gruenheid said. "I was really concerned about where he had gotten her."

In August 2003, Gruenheid requested that Lisa's DNA be tested and compared to Jenson/Vanner/Kimball's. Her hunch paid off. He was not her father. He was not her grandfather. He was not her uncle or cousin. He wasn't related to her at all. Who was Vanner to this little girl? And there was an even more pressing question: where was the little girl's mother?

They tried talking to Vanner in prison, but he denied even knowing Lisa.

Seven years went by. Vanner died in prison in December 2010 at sixty-seven years old, taking his secrets with him. Or so he thought.

Little Lisa was now a grown woman with a husband and children of her own. But she was still left wondering where she came from. Her memories of her childhood were foggy—she remembered only being given away by a man. In 2014, a genetic genealogist, or "search angel," from DNAAdoption.com, worked with Lisa to try to find any of her relatives and hopefully answer some of the questions she had about where she came from. She entered Lisa's DNA into a public online DNA database and found a cousin in New Hampshire. The cousin led to Lisa's grandfather—and to a devastating secret.

Lisa discovered that the name she was born with wasn't Lisa. It was Dawn. And her mother's name was Denise Beaudin. Lisa was happy to connect with her grandfather, but neither he nor anyone else knew the answer to the biggest question that had troubled her for years: where was her mother?

In 1981, Denise Beaudin was living in Manchester, New Hampshire. On November 26 of that year, she attended Thanksgiving dinner at her family home in Goffstown with her new boyfriend, a man she introduced as Bob Evans. A week later, her family went to visit her apartment in

Manchester and discovered the house was empty. The family had heard that Denise and Evans owed money to people around town and thought they were just trying to get out from under the debt by going on the run. So maybe they packed up Denise's six-month-old daughter, grabbed a few clothes, and split.

But her parents never heard from Denise again.

Three decades later, when New Hampshire authorities learned that Lisa's mother was Denise Beaudin, they wondered if it could be a giant piece of the puzzle that could lead to solving the state's biggest murder mystery. Manchester was only thirteen miles from Allenstown. Denise went missing in 1981. And a missing-persons report was never filed.

Could Denise Beaudin be the woman found with the three little girls in the barrels in Bear Brook State Park in Allenstown? Could Bob Evans be the villain responsible for the crime that had haunted them for thirty years?

"The chances are pretty slim." That's what the assistant DA had told me a year earlier when I asked if the case would ever be solved. He told me that six hours before I learned Michelle had died and everything went haywire and sent me on this journey. "Pretty slim." That was a gut punch of a quote. But now there was this. Now there was hope.

Police began digging into the past of Bob Evans. From a tip, they learned that Evans was acquainted with and may have worked for the owner of the Bear Brook Store property dump site, where the bodies in the barrels were found. They learned that he had actually used the site for dumping trash in the past. They learned he had worked as an electrician, and electrical wiring was found in the barrels along with the victims.

In January 2017, New Hampshire authorities announced a press conference concerning the Allenstown Four cold case. Ronda Randall, the citizen detective who walked those woods with me a year earlier, drove up to be there in person. She took with her four rocks that she had collected from the woods years ago. All along, her plan was that when she learned the names of the victims, she would write their names on those rocks. She was finally going to get her chance to do it. I watched a live stream of the conference over Facebook. We were seconds away from finding out the names of the woman and three little girls who were found in the barrels in Allenstown.

Assistant DA Strelzin, New Hampshire Cold Case Unit detective Michael Kokoski, and Manchester Police detective captain Ryan Grant approached the podium. I leaned into my computer, wanting to crawl through the screen to get a better seat.

When the first bodies were found in 1985, many locals' thoughts went straight to eight-year-old Tammy Belanger, who had gone missing while walking to Lincoln Street Elementary School a year earlier. Some thought of twenty-one-year-old Lisa Snyder, who was last seen on July 4, 1985, in Dover, heading to a bar called the Norseman. Or of fifteen-year-old Shirley McBride, reported missing on July 13, 1985, in Pittsfield. Or twenty-one-year-old Page Jennings, last seen January 16, 1985, after her parents were killed.

But one by one, those women and girls, along with thousands of others, were ruled out as the victims.

Detectives drilled deep into the cast of ne'er-do-wells who were around Allenstown at the time. A man named Robert Callahan, who was convicted of sexually assaulting a minor and spent five years in the New Hampshire prison system, lived on the property and was said to have at one point taken in "a woman who had nowhere to go." A Bear Brook Gardens resident named Robert Steffen had been convicted of molesting children in 1985. Pembroke, New Hampshire, produced a child pornographer named Brian Schultz, who might have taken young children from across the country to film bizarre sex acts, including filming them having sex with animals and eating feces. Robert Breest, who was convicted of killing eighteen-year-old Susan Randall and leaving her body under a bridge in Concord, New Hampshire, once lived in Allenstown.

But one by one, those men, along with thousands of others, were ruled out as the killer.

A few years ago, when the victims' DNA was finally extracted and entered into some databases looking for a match, they found nothing. Law enforcement then turned to pollen analysis to attempt to identify where the victims might have lived or traveled. Plants can spread microscopic pollen and spores in the air, which are then carried by the wind and land on the ground—and on people's clothing and hair. Different regions have different types of plants, and there are more than 380,000 different types of plants on earth. The pollen they produce is unique to each region and creates a "pollen print" of their location. You can't drill down to a neighborhood, but you can get an idea of the general area where the pollen is from—the Pacific Northwest, the American Midwest, etc. And pollen is incredibly resilient, sticking to clothing even after multiple washes. Officials were hopeful that pollen could lead to a location where they could concentrate efforts to identify the victims. But the results of the tests were too broad, spreading across dozens of states.

They tried studying the hair, teeth, and bones of the victims, searching for the chemical isotopes they contained. Strontium, carbon, nitrogen, oxygen-18, oxygen-16, and lead can help investigators narrow down where individuals might have lived, based on the food and drink they consumed. Oxygen can point to the drinking water of a specific location.

The isotopes directed investigators to small pockets in Maine, New Hampshire, and northern New York, along with a thick U-shaped pattern starting from interior Washington, dipping down through Arizona and New Mexico and up through the Dakotas. A pretty wide swath. But the results for the one unrelated child were far less broad, showing that she had only lived in the Northeast. To add another piece to the puzzle, the test concluded that all four females did live together in New Hampshire at some point before their deaths.

But after all those tests and theories and Hail Marys, we were finally going to get their names at this press conference. It was finally going to be over.

And then they gave us the news. The woman in the barrel was *not* Denise Beaudin. They still didn't know who she was. And they still didn't who the three little girls were. The mystery was still stubbornly intact. We wouldn't learn their names that day. But we would learn the next best thing. We would learn the name of the man who killed them.

When little Lisa's DNA provided no connections to any of the four females in the barrels, law enforcement then decided to compare the DNA from the barrels against the DNA of the man who had molested and abandoned Lisa at the trailer park, Gordon Jenson.

They got a match.

Jenson was revealed to be the biological father of the youngest girl in the barrels, the girl who was not related to the other three females. Jenson was undoubtedly Bob Evans, the man last seen with Lisa's mother, Denise Beaudin. And remember Jenson was also known as Larry Vanner, the man who killed Eunsoon Jun. He undoubtedly killed the woman and three little girls in the barrels.

He also presumably murdered Denise Beaudin and buried her somewhere between New Hampshire and California. The authorities were not even sure what his real name was. Gordon Jenson. Larry Vanner. Bob Evans. At the press conference, they flashed his picture on the screen behind the podium, and America was introduced to the most horrifying serial killer it had never heard of.

Lisa didn't attend the conference, but Strelzin read a statement she had written. She was thankful she was "reunited with my grandfather and cousins after all these years.

"Currently, I have three beautiful children and a loving husband and would like our presently happy and secure life to remain intact and protected," she continued. "Please turn your focus toward the unidentified victims and other potentially unknown victims in this case."

Assuming Jenson/Evans murdered at least two women (Denise Beaudin and Eunsoon Jun) and three little girls, the miracle in the whole story up to that point was Lisa herself. Why did he give Lisa away instead of "solving" his problems the way he presumably did in Allenstown? Why did Lisa survive?

Giving little Lisa away was what got him in the end, as her DNA, a familial DNA search, and old-fashioned detective work led law enforcement back to him. It was the same way I knew the Golden State Killer could be caught.

We continued to enter the Golden State Killer's Y-STR DNA profile into the public genealogy databases, but there were only about a half a million samples in those systems. And it wasn't his whole genome profile. I know I said this before, but I was sure that the answer was hiding behind those locked doors of 23andMe and Ancestry.com. There were millions of profiles of white European men in their databases. Those people with European ancestry were most likely to order the kit, spit in the tube, and try to find out both where they were from and what diseases they might be more susceptible to. And we were looking for a white male of European descent. Odds were one of his third or fourth cousins spit into one of those tubes. But the doors to those matches were still locked to us.

I had spoken with some geneticist friends of Kendall's, who said it might be possible to extract the DNA from the rape kits collected at the GSK crime scenes and place it in a saliva-like substance to send in the spit tube that 23andMe and Ancestry require. They would be none the wiser. The lab tech would open the box, remove the tube, extract the DNA, and upload it to the database. They would then email us the results, with all of "our" relatives that they found matches to. Then we would work with genealogists to build the family tree headed straight for the killer. We would have his identity in a matter of weeks. It would be violating the company's terms of use, but would it be illegal?

I explained the plan to one of the investigators on the case. They told me flat out, "Billy, if I was retiring next week, I would definitely think about doing that. But I've got a lot more years."

I understood. They couldn't risk their job taking a chance on a constitutionally ambiguous search.

But the family tree worked in New Hampshire. It started with a detective's hunch and an orphan looking for her parents and led to a serial killer. Police were now in a peculiar position—they had the killer of the four females in the barrels but still did not know the identity of the victims. But it was enough to take to the public to ask if anyone remembered the man, and that was what they focused on for the rest of the press conference. They showed a map with all the places (with corresponding dates) that he may have visited throughout the United States. They listed all his known aliases, occupations, and other scraps of information they had compiled. Because he very well may have killed a lot more people.

Myself, Ronda, and a host of citizen detectives online started frantically digging through census reports, newspaper clippings, and old high school yearbooks to learn anything we could about the man they were calling Bob Evans. Any stop he may have made across the country might have been a stop for murder. Did any women disappear near any of the places he traveled?

Strelzin called Evans "cold and calculating" and said that he sexually abused some of his victims. The scenario that became apparent was that of a man who would meet a woman with a child and separate them from their family and friends. He would then kill the woman and abduct and molest the child. Then he would play the part of a struggling father raising a child in an attempt to romance another single mother. Then he would molest her children, kill the woman—and kill the first child—take the new child/children, and start the sadistic circle all over again.

I was focusing on the names *Donna* and *Elizabeth* as possible other victims. Remember when Gordon Jenson told the people at the trailer park that Lisa's mother was named Denise LaPorte and she was killed in Texas? Since he used Denise Beaudin's correct first name, maybe he followed that pattern with other women he killed. He referred to his wife by the name Elizabeth in arrest reports. An October 1986 article in the *San Bernardino County Sun* stated that

> according to authorities, Kimball was married to a woman known as Donna, who works in Orange County as a nurse and who may use the name Donna Walter... Investigators also have received information that Lisa may have a 2- or 3-year-old sister.

Are you ready to follow the trail of one of the most sadistic serial killers the world never knew it produced? The man who would sidle up to a mother and children, molest the children, kill the mother, use the children to lure another set of mother and children into his web, then kill the first children until he "marries" a woman in a *Star Trek*–wedding ceremony, kills her, and buries her body under a 250-pound pile of kitty litter?

I started a campaign in Texas and California looking for anyone who might remember Bob Evans, adding in every fact I knew about the case:

Bob Evans was a white male, five foot ten to six foot one, with a thin build, piercing blue eyes, and brown hair. In most photos, he wore a mustache. He was born anytime between 1936 and 1952. He may have worked at the Manchester, Virginia, hospital as an electrician or mechanic.

He was an alcoholic.

He often lived in campgrounds, trailer parks, and motels.

His vehicles may have included a late '60s red Dodge pickup with a light-colored camper, a White '78 Ford van, and a two-toned Volkswagen van.

He may have attended Lowell Elementary School and North High School in Phoenix, Arizona.

He may have been born in Evanston, Wyoming, as Ulos Jensen. He may have also gone by the names Jerry Edwards Gorman, Curtis Rollin Kimball, and Don Vannerson.

During the 1970s, he may have been in Houston, Texas, working at Brown and Root as an electrician.

During the 1970s, he also claimed to work in Bay City, Texas, repairing instruments.

In 1977, he worked at Waumbec Mill in Manchester as head electrician under the name Bob Evans.

On January 9, 1980, a certified letter addressed to Bob Evans was signed for by an Elizabeth Evans.

Evans was arrested in Manchester in February and June of 1980 and listed his spouse's name as Elizabeth.

Ominously, when he was arrested by Manchester Police in October 1980, he did not list a spouse.

In March 1984, he worked at an electric company in Los Alamitos, California, under the name Curtis Kimball.

In 1984 and 1985, he may have worked in Anaheim, California, under an unknown name.

In May 1985, he was arrested for a DUI in Cypress, California, under the name Curtis Kimball.

In January 1986, he was working at the Holiday Host RV Park in Scotts Valley, California, under the name Gordon Jenson.

In November 1988, he was pulled over in San Luis Obispo, California, under the name Gerry Mockerman, driving a stolen car. The car was registered in Idaho.

In March 1989, he was arrested on warrants for child abandonment. He went to jail.

In October 1990, he was paroled and vanished.

In 2001, he "married" Eunsoon Jun under the name Larry Vanner.

In November 2002, he was arrested for Jun's murder.

In December 2010, he died in High Desert Prison in Susanville, California.

Authorities discovered writings of Evans in which he claimed he was an abused child, the youngest of six, who ran away from home at fourteen. He claimed he was arrested as a teen and spent time in a mental hospital. He claimed to have joined the military, moved to Canada, and met a woman named Denise LaPorte, who he later married in Virginia. There is no evidence any of these stories were true.

In June 2017, police released video of Evans (when he was claiming to be Larry Vanner) being questioned for the murder of Eunsoon Jun in 2002. He is hunched over but not defeated. He is a talker. A manipulator. He thinks he can get out of this. At one point, he says "I've always tried to live by the motto 'There's no defense against the truth.' But sometimes it's hard to find what the truth is." Police were hoping someone might see the video and tell the world what the killer's true name was.

When all we have is a grainy surveillance image, the guy who got away with it can sail into the wind. But if we have his DNA, there is nowhere to hide. For Bob Evans, the race was over. In August 2017, DNA came through again. It was one of his children, a son, who provided the link by entering his DNA into a public database. Unbeknownst to him, authorities were using the database to find the real name of a serial killer, and the two DNA samples collided. The name the killer was born with was Terrence "Terry" Peder Rasmussen. He was born in 1943 and grew up in Colorado before moving to Phoenix and then Redwood City, California. He was a navy veteran, with four children. His wife left him after 1973. Familial DNA solved another mystery that was thought to be unsolvable.

Roxane Gruenheid came with me to New Hampshire so Strelzin could talk to the woman who came face-to-face with the murderer he had been chasing for so long.

I started building a timeline of Rasmussen's movements, trying to figure out every place he had been and if there were cold cases from those areas that showed his handiwork. Who else had he killed?

I met with Pete Headley, the detective who had first handled little Lisa's case in San Bernardino and stuck with it all the way—for more than two decades—helping her work with the genealogist to discover where she came from. And he wasn't done yet.

Pete has what is perhaps the best cop mustache I have ever seen. A perfect salt-and-pepper number that, coupled with his country drawl, gives him the air of a gentleman lawman from a bygone age. We got on pretty well, both of us understanding that familial DNA was the key for not only figuring out who the killer was but for the girls in the barrels, other victims Rasmussen might be responsible for, and thousands of other crimes across America.

Headley and I started looking into other potential related cases in California. An unidentified redheaded woman found in a refrigerator in a ditch near Stockton, California, in 1995 had all the earmarks of a Rasmussen murder. We are in the middle of attempting to extract her DNA to find out first who she was and then if she had ever run into him. There were also unidentified women found in Connecticut in '75, New York in '91, and New Mexico in '96—all wrapped in electrical cords. Could Rasmussen be responsible for any of those murders as well? And there was also the child who was in his car when he was arrested for DUI in Orange County in '85? What happened to him or her?

The Golden State Killer's MO—breaking into houses, tying up the men, raping the women, and then killing them both—was horrifying, but I think Rasmussen might rival him. Using children to attract single mothers with children. Molesting the children, killing the mothers, killing the children when they got old enough to talk. In the competition for most sadistic fuckers ever, these two were running neck and neck.

We still didn't have any answers on the Golden State Killer. Michelle's manuscript had been sent to the printer for a late February 2018 release date. There was no ending. There was no identification of the killer at the end of the book. It was still a mystery. But it didn't matter. We would run the book without an ending. Because the case was so intriguing and because Michelle's writing was so damn good.

While I waited for the book to come out, I busied myself with the questions that were multiplying in my head.

Who was the mother of the two- to four-year-old girl found in the barrel, the one not related to the other three? And was her mother murdered by Rasmussen too? And what happened to Denise Beaudin?

Those questions were right behind who killed Brian Boothe, the man found dead in his New York City apartment on Christmas with a knife in his neck? Who was the Owl's Head Park Killer? Where were the killers from Chesapeake and Tallahassee?

Sometimes you have to travel five thousand miles away and walk through a medieval castle to get one of the answers you're looking for.

13.
___

THE GIRL WITH THE SERPENT TATTOO

Tampa, Florida, 2017

LOCATED IN THE CENTER OF CARDIFF CASTLE IN WALES, seventy-seven feet wide and thirty feet tall, the castle keep was built in the middle of the twelfth century. It sits atop a hill, giving it the best vantage point for the soldiers to see if the Welsh people were going to start rising up again, like they tried to do in 1136.

I was in Wales visiting the BBC show *Crime Watch*, seeing if they would be interested in utilizing geotargeted social media campaigns to help solve the murders they have been reporting on since 1984. Great Britain has an estimated 1.85 million CCTV cameras, a lot of digital eyes for such a small country (in comparison, there are more than 40 million security cameras covering the entire United States, which is forty times as large). Many of the crimes in the UK are caught on tape and could be solved if the footage were seen by the right person.

I watched the taping of the show in the morning and then walked to the castle, killing time before heading north to Manchester to tour the sites of the Moors Murders and the cemetery gates Morrissey sang about. Inside the keep was a grass-covered clearing. I was sitting on a bench looking out at the stones surrounding me, listening to the wind whip the Welsh flag above me, when I got a Facebook message on the Chesapeake

Killer page, which I had launched nine months earlier to identify the tall, thin, dressed-in-black, dreadlocked suspect accused of killing Timothy "Pacman" Croskey in his driveway.

"Hey, I'm just now seeing this video," the message read. "And I recognize this person." They left a phone number.

I did some quick math, figuring out it was only five hours earlier in Florida, and I dialed the number from inside the castle keep.

"This man," the tipster told me, "he's living in Jacksonville, in an apartment with his sister. Darrius Copeland. The sister's name is Dequashia Copeland."

Darrius Copeland was the name I had gotten when I first ran the campaign trying to identify the man with the loping stride walking through the neighborhood right after the murder. I pulled out the souvenir map they handed me when I entered the castle grounds and began furiously writing.

Copeland and his sister were at the Park at Alston, an apartment building in Jacksonville, Florida. The tipster gave me the full address. I thanked them for writing in and immediately shot an email with the new information to the investigators in Chesapeake.

I got back only a curt "received."

Two months later, the U.S. Marshals arrested the two Copelands in Jacksonville. Turns out Dequashia had once dated Croskey and had his baby. The relationship fizzled. Then police say she later wanted him dead. Both brother and sister were charged with first-degree murder. Only 199,997 murders to go.

———————————   ———————————

When I returned to the States, I continued to run my cases while checking the news for new murders I might be able to help solve. I began trading emails with a woman out of Tampa, Florida. Her name was Vanessa Hunt. And she had just lost her best friend. She sent me a video.

A woman wearing a sleeveless top, skirt, and sandals walks slowly through a back alley in the rain. After twenty seconds, a man on a bicycle pulls up to her. He gets off the bike and walks it under the awning to get out of the rain. The woman follows him, walking behind him as she digs for something inside a large purse. The two seem to chat for a few seconds before he follows her down a side alley and away from the camera as the video ends.

When they found Justin Dunn's body, they initially thought it was a suicide. Then they saw the video. What the woman was digging for in her purse was most probably a gun. I could barely see her face, but I could see the tattoo of the serpent on her right shoulder. At least I thought it was a serpent. It could have been vines. Or a chain. Or a rosary.

Vanessa said she was with Justin off and on for five years. But then she was able to kick her habit. Justin wasn't.

"After i got clean i talked to him daily but couldn't be around him cuz I'd start using again," she wrote to me.

Justin was a junkie. But he had dreams like anyone else. He wanted to one day buy an RV and just ride across the country, to live off the grid and eventually leave as small a carbon footprint as possible.

I asked if there was anyone she could think of who would hurt Justin.

"No I can't," she wrote back. "He was the nicest guy ever. He may have been a junkie but he took care of people."

The tips came in fast: "She tricks near the batting cages." "She's outside of the Panera near the mall right now!"

I sent them immediately to the detective. But he couldn't jump on the tips because there was a bigger problem facing Tampa that week: an active serial killer who had shot and killed four random people in the Seminole Heights neighborhood. The detective asked me to help identify him, using the same grainy, faraway video of the killer walking down a side street that every news organization was running. I searched for three weeks. The suspect was finally caught as a result of a tip from his boss at the McDonald's where he worked.

Finally able to go back to the tattoo woman, I targeted females twenty-five to thirty-five who lived within a mile radius of the murder. That's when I got a message. "This might be her," it said. They provided a link to a woman's Facebook profile. I scoured the page, looking at every photo the woman had posted, praying for a shot of her right shoulder. I found her mugshots. She was older than the detective thought, but it could be her. I needed to see that shoulder. I had started cross-referencing her photos with the thousands of pictures friends of friends had taken when I saw it: a photo of the woman and what looked like a serpent peeking out from her right shoulder.

I sent the profile to the detective, along with the name of the motel the tipster said she was living in. But the woman was very mobile and incredibly on the edge. One day, she overdosed, but the detective found out too late that she was in the hospital and wasn't able to interview her before she was discharged. Another time, she got arrested but made bail before the detective was able to see her. The next day, she was in the wind.

She was clueless anyone was on her tail. Can it be a cat-and-mouse game when the mouse has no idea the cat is after her? I would have to wait and hope she didn't kill herself before she got arrested again.

I would continue to email with Vanessa.

"I am checking in," I wrote. "I have sent some tips over to the police, have you heard anything?"

"No darlin', if i had I'd done contacted you and [the detective] Smith… I wish I knew something it's killing me to not be able to help."

"I had someone who I thought looked really good," I wrote back.

"They said they are opening up an investigation on her. But I haven't heard back from them since."

"I truly hope they find her... I always took care of Justin and I feel like I'm failing him right now."

"Never think that. We will find her," I replied.

"Again darlin' thank you for all that you are doing... Words can't express my gratitude."

I asked Vanessa if she was okay with talking about their relationship and drug use.

"I'm ok with that. It's the facts and we are talking about my starshine here. He was an addict yes but more beyond that."

Everyone has someone who thinks of them as their starshine.

Female suspects are rare in the murder world. Eleven percent of killers in America are female. And of their victims, only 11.9 percent are strangers (41.5 percent of their victims are their significant others). Getting a video of a female murderer was unique, but the Girl with the Serpent Tattoo wasn't the first female suspect I had searched for. That would be the girl in the pink top in Albuquerque.

I saw the video on the Facebook page of a local TV station out of New Mexico. It's equal parts grainy and brutal. A man and woman pull up to a gas station in an industrial pickup truck. There is a large spool of wire in the flatbed and what looks to be a triangular flag waving four feet in the air above the cab.

The truck pulls up to the pumps, and they get out. Wearing jeans and a black jacket, the man walks purposefully to the gas pumps to his left, then appears to get into a conversation with another man. The woman gets out of the passenger side of the truck. She's wearing jeans and a pink sweatshirt and has long brown hair. She walks to her right, toward another driver pumping gas, and looks to be asking him a question. Then she heads into the gas station store. The camera cuts to an overhead shot, and you see her more clearly. Her hair is brown, but you can now see her wavy curls. Her top is not just pink but bright pink and low-cut. You watch as she walks back out into the blurriness of the night and climbs into the passenger side of the truck. The driver guns the gas and drives the truck onto the sidewalk directly in the path of a man walking away from the gas station. Twenty-six-year-old Louis Chavez is struck down. He was the man talking with the driver just minutes earlier.

"That video is one of the more brutal things I've ever witnessed on video," Albuquerque police officer Tanner Tixier later said. "There is no doubt that this was an intentional act, which is why we're looking at this individual for murder."

Chavez's sister Jazmine was interviewed on the evening news. "It's horrible. I don't know how you could do that to a person. My brother didn't deserve that. He didn't do anything wrong."

She pleaded with the woman and the driver to turn themselves in. They didn't.

I originally focused on the truck. It looked to be a work truck and had a business logo on the door that I couldn't quite decipher. I searched all the corners of the internet trying to identify that truck, posting photos on Reddit, on electrician's message boards, on oil driller pages, going through every Albuquerque business web page looking for a logo that might be similar. If you want a list of all the commercial electricians in Albuquerque, I'm your guy.

After a month, I learned the truck was stolen. There were no leads on who took it.

With the driver being so far away on the video, I concentrated my focus on the girl in the pink top.

I acquired a new video from the detective, who was looking for all the help he could get. The range of cooperation from detectives runs the gamut, from radio silence to constant updates. But once they understand that (a) I am not asking for money, (b) I am not looking for a reward, and (c) I just want to assist them in getting their collar (the arrest), most of them are very helpful. This new video was longer and had sound. When the female enters the gas station store, there is a man ahead of her at the register, straddling a BMX bike at the counter. The girl in the pink top walks up behind him, and he scoots ahead a few feet to give her room. She approaches the cashier with cash in her hand. "Can I get four on four?" she says, handing the money to the man behind the register.

This video is more defined, and details pop. You see now that her brown hair has blond highlights. Her cheekbones are sharp. Her cleavage ample. Her jeans worn and faded.

I took screenshots of her close-ups and also cut the video so we just saw her approach the cashier and heard her speak. I set up the campaign for a four-mile radius, men and women, twenty to fifty-four. Tips started coming in.

She looks like a girl named Eliza [name changed]. I asked someone I'm friends with that knows her very well and I said 'who does this look like' and she said the same.

False alarm.

Her name is Annett Rodriguez [name changed]. She always seemed rather sketchy, I would sometimes see her walking up and down hotel circle, in that area anyway. I didn't see anything about tattoos but I recognize her for sure.

Same result: nothing.

It seemed like every female in Albuquerque looked like the girl with the pink top.

One person claimed he saw her near the Elegante Hotel in town.

"What made you think it was her?" I asked. "What was she wearing?"

"That same clothes…n body."

"Was she loitering or walking with a purpose?"

"She looked she was on a hurry," he said.

The tips came were coming in fast now.

She has been in jail and still is in jail, my daughter was just saying that looked like her.

She lives in this house with her mom Jennifer Hernandez [name changed]. I have seen her in those boots and that outfit before. She is only 16 or 17 but she is on probation for armed robbery already and has several felonies.

That's my friend on the bike.

Go to Casa Liquors corner of Goff & Bridge. Looks like a girl who used to work there. Talk to the owner John.

Some people were dead-sure they knew her:

When I first saw the video, I thought it looked like her but started questioning myself because she is married to my older brother and I would have never thought her to be with another man (the one in the video) but my brother wasn't telling our family around this time last year she started doing drugs and prostitution behind his back he eventually left her. The man that she's with in the video is NOT my brother (whom she's still married to) I showed the video to several people in my family and every single one of them named——and that included my children. It gave me the chills and I knew I had to say something.

One guy was certain it was his ex-wife.

Someone sent yearbook photos.

"She looks like a girl that took me off to be robbed at gun point and left to die by a guy she picked up," wrote another.

"I see her on Central all the time she's asking for money and beer."

"Where on Central?" I wrote back. "And when was the last time you saw her?"

"About nine-thirty ten o'clock this morning on Central and Eubank."

"By the Walgreens?" I asked, Google maps showing me around a city I have never stepped foot in.

"No Home Depot parking lot."

It was one wild-goose chase after another.

Then someone posted a comment under one of her photos, intimating that she might know who she was. I sent the commenter a direct message.

"Do you know this woman?"

"Ya, I do."

"Could you tell us her name?"

"I forgot her name."

"What can you tell us about her?"

"She is my friend that is a homeless woman."

"Where does she hang out?"

"She goes to St. Martin's here."

She listed the address for St. Martin's. I did a search and learned it was a homeless shelter on Third Street in Albuquerque.

The next day, I got another tip.

"I might know she is. Looks like a girl I know. At least from the camera view. And she has been around that area."

"What's her name?" I wrote.

"First name is [redacted]. I will find out her last name from my girlfriend without raising any suspicion. She lost her kids to the state because of drugs and stealing."

The tipster kept sending information.

"She does heroin and is always stealin makeup now and selling it to make the cash for drugs for her and her girlfriend to get high."

I asked if she had any other identifying features. Scars? A tattoo?

"Yes. One on her breast… It's her I'm telling you."

A tattoo on her breast? That was a sticking point for me. I couldn't see a tattoo on her breast on the video from the gas station interior. I watched it again. After the fifth or sixth viewing, I started to think I was conjuring one up. There was a dark spot on her breast—which I had taken to be a stray lock of hair or a shadow. Might that be a tattoo?

The pictures they sent sure did look like the girl in the pink top.

"I know it's her," the tipster continued. "I heard the voice on the video too. It's her."

"Where does she live?"

"She's homeless now."

"Does she stay at shelters?"

"She never stays at shelters," they said. "But she goes to them during the day for food, etc…"

"Which shelters does she go to?"

"I know she goes to the one on 3rd street."

St. Martin's.

It all fell into place. The last two tipsters were talking about the same woman.

All the police would have to do is wait outside St. Martin's for a day and speak with her when she arrived. I told the detective, and he thought she looked good. But there was a snag.

"St. Martin's staff has not been cooperative with allowing law enforcement onto their property to conduct investigations without a warrant, and I don't have enough probable cause to get one approved."

I would contact the detective every six months to see if he had found her. He hadn't. By January 2018, twenty-one months had passed. They had a record number of homicides in Albuquerque in 2017, and the detective was underwater. But he told me to do whatever I could to see if I could find her.

I called the shelter—they paged her name and said they had never heard of her. I went through back channels to find relatives on Facebook. I got nowhere. She was slipping away.

I asked the detective if I should reach out to her directly.

"Any help that she can provide would be great!" he replied.

I sent a message to her directly on Facebook.

When you send a Facebook message to someone who isn't your friend, it gets stuck in the "Message Requests" folder, where it's often not seen for months or even years. Up until 2016, you used to be able to pay a dollar to Facebook and have your message show up in the receiver's regular inbox, but they took that feature away. I would pay fifty bucks a message to get it back.

I requested a friendship with the woman and sent her a message, hoping she would see it.

Hi. I'm a victim's advocate and journalist living in Los Angeles. Someone reached out to me saying they know you. I was wondering if we could hop on a call this week? Thanks. Billy

Six days later, she saw it.

215

"WHAT IS THIS CONCERNING??"

"Hi, thanks for getting back to me. Someone contacted me saying that she was in foster care with you at some point."

Two hours later, she replied.

"I HAVE NEVER BEEN IN A FOSTER HOME BE4."

"Ok. She thought you went to St. Martins at some point," I wrote. "I'm not from ABQ so am not sure what that is." I saw that she had read the message but had yet to respond. I went for broke. "Someone also said they recognized you from this video as a passenger in a truck involved in a fatal accident at a gas station two years ago."

I pressed send. An error message popped up on my screen:

THIS PERSON ISN'T RECEIVING MESSAGES RIGHT NOW.

She had blocked me.

I hadn't even brought up the hit-and-run to her—she had blocked me as soon as I mentioned the shelter. Two different individuals who didn't know each other ID'd her as both the girl in the pink top and a woman they know who goes to St. Martin's. It seemed like I might be on the right track. I spoke with the detective. He thanked me for giving it a shot and said he would look into the Facebook page. I was left to wait again.

Back in Los Angeles, I was working with Pete Headley to identify any of the other victims of the Allenstown Four killer, who we could now at least call by his real name: Terry Rasmussen.

After finding little Lisa's family—and then identifying Rasmussen—Pete had been chasing down every West Coast lead that might be connected to the killer and looking into using familial DNA to put all the pieces together.

There was one unidentified murder victim he liked in particular: the

Lady in the Refrigerator. She was found on March 29, 1995, inside a fridge that had been dumped in a ditch in Holt, just outside Stockton, California, in San Joaquin County. She was killed by blunt-force trauma to the head and was tied up with electrical tape. All the earmarks of Rasmussen.

This wasn't a robbery—she still had a diamond ring on her finger. Her hiking boots were expensive. She wore a Victoria's Secret bra, a blue sweatshirt, and Levi's shorts. Her teeth were pristine. The tape was determined to have been bought at a surplus store in Oakley, California. A bag of ice found in the fridge was produced by the Glacier Ice Co. out of Freemont. The refrigerator was from the East Bay. Rasmussen lived in the East Bay and lived behind a convenience store. If we could trace the ice to that store, the woman in the fridge could very well have been another female who stepped into the killer's path.

But in order to see if she was a victim of Rasmussen, we first needed to find out who she was. We needed to pull DNA from the woman and run it through a public DNA database like GEDmatch, hopefully find a relative, then interview anyone who knew her to see who she was with at the time. If one of those people was Terry Rasmussen, there was a good chance he was the one who had killed her.

There were other possible victims. Headley gave me a list of Rasmussen's AWOLs from when he was in the navy. There were half a dozen. I had places and dates and was searching for any missing persons or unsolved murders that might match up.

We knew he was seen with a woman and a little girl in Anaheim. We still didn't know where Denise Beaudin was. And we were still trying to find the identity of the victims in the barrels.

We would try to use familial DNA to get answers for almost everything.

Pete had found Rasmussen using whole genome DNA and entering it into a public database to search for family members. He was lucky that the killer's blood had been drawn—and stored—before his death. You needed a good bit of DNA—sometimes close to 250–1000 nanograms—to get the whole genome. That's still less than a grain of sand. (With GSK, Michelle was just using the Y chromosome—one chromosome out of the twenty-three pairs of chromosomes that make up the whole genome—and getting nowhere.) To solve a crime or identify a body via familial DNA, you have to find the right case, evaluate what DNA you have, and extract the DNA. If you are attempting to identify the perpetrator, hopefully they left enough DNA at the scene to process. If you are attempting to identify a body, you want to pull DNA from flesh or hair. Bones left out in the sun have a lot of bacteria, and getting a proper DNA strand from them is tough but not impossible. When you have your DNA, you send it to the genealogy lab, upload to a database like GEDmatch, see what matches you get, then consult with a genetics genealogist who will start building a family tree using all sorts of resources, from Facebook pages to census records. After that, you start eliminating people from the tree based on what you know about the crime or the body in question—locations, time periods, physical descriptions from witnesses or victims. From there, you will hopefully find someone who looks good.

Of course, when it comes to a crime, the chain of custody for the original DNA—the unadulterated trail that is supposed to make a beeline from the crime scene to the crime lab to the courtroom—has now made a slight detour. A defense attorney might try to latch onto that detour in an attempt to muddy the waters and discredit the case. So if police have a solid suspect who is still alive, they need to be sure they have the right person and need a direct sample to compare to the crime-scene DNA. They follow the suspect around until they discard something with their DNA on it—a cup, a napkin, chewing gum. Lonnie Franklin Jr., the Los Angeles serial killer known as the Grim Sleeper, dropped a pizza crust. Then they test it and see if it matches the original sample. If it does, they get a warrant and make an arrest.

It's coming down to criminals vs. science. Facial recognition software technology is getting stronger, and in the future, some of the videos I've been using to find murder suspects might be able to be matched to a facial recognition database. But without a doubt, the ability to use familial DNA matches to find rapists and murderers is the biggest single tool to catch violent criminals the world has seen since the discovery of DNA itself.

Some throw up the privacy balloon, claiming that the unsuspecting genealogy buffs who entered their DNA into the databases never consented to a law-enforcement search. But for most departments, the stumbling blocks are money and resources. Getting loud is the only way the backlog of thousands of rape kits that have been sitting in police evidence lockers across the country will be processed. Getting loud should force every agency to take the DNA found in every rape kit and at every murder scene and run it through familial databases, 24/7. We are at the precipice of being able to solve more cold cases than ever before. If the police claim they don't have the manpower to build the family tree, we need to get loud. Start fund-raisers. Recruit volunteers. You reading this book are deputized. Go get a megaphone.

Theoretically, with all the technology we have—the interconnectivity of social media, every person carrying around a hi-definition video camera in their pockets—we should be able to solve the bulk of murders. But people are people. Crime investigations are messy and complicated. And there are just too many bad guys out there with too many guns and too few people willing to tell the police when they have information about a crime. There is no reason that with all our tools, the United States solves only 61.5 percent of all homicides every year. Japan clears 95 percent. Germany between 88 and 94 percent. England and Wales clear 85 percent. Canada clears 75 percent.

The politicians must deliver the resources to allow police departments to utilize crowdsourcing and familial DNA searches to find these criminals and ensure their capture. The answers are there. Science is catching up to the bad guys. It's up to people to make sure it's put to good use.

Allenstown and Golden State were getting me trapped in a maze of chromosomes. I didn't get into this to do science. I've watched *Jurassic Park* fifty times and love the little animated Mr. DNA that explains how they made the dinosaurs. But I also got a C in biology in high school.

I needed a drink and an old-fashioned video search, getting back to the one thing I had finally found some success with.

On the morning of June 10, 2017, San Jose police officers responded to a 911 call and found an adult male with a stab wound outside a home on Everglade Avenue. The victim, Samuel Choi, died the next day. Police released video of the murder in August 2017. The image of the suspect was pretty clear—a Hispanic male walking down the street, his hands in the pockets of his hoodie. The video was in color. It was blurry, but you could tell he had a beard. He was wearing red shoes and carrying a khaki backpack.

I called up the San Jose PD Homicide unit and talked to Sergeant John Barg. I gave him my spiel, and he was intrigued, much more than most detectives I cold-called. I asked if I could have the raw video, and he said he would check. But his mind was on something else.

"I have a murder suspect who fled," he told me, introducing me to a whole 'nother case. "Do you think this could work to find him?"

"I really just focus on unsolved cases," I said. "I don't do fugitives."

Fugitive searches are a different beast. For instance, on the TV show *America's Most Wanted*, the producers had the name, height, weight, profession, hobbies, and, most importantly, a clear photograph of the person they were looking for. They would present the murderer's

CHASE DARKNESS WITH ME

photo on screen and say "Joe Smith is five feet eight inches tall, 160 pounds. He is trained as an electrician, and he likes to bowl." Then one of the millions of people watching the show would register all that info and say to themselves "Hmm, that guy kinda looks like Phil from the Thursday night league down at Bellmore Lanes." And the hope is that person would pick up the phone and call the toll-free number. The hope worked. The national dragnet of *America's Most Wanted* nabbed more than one thousand fugitives, including seventeen people on the FBI's Ten Most Wanted List.

With a fugitive search, you are up against the skills of the individual you are hunting. Did they alter their appearance? Did they have the resources to hide out overseas? Did they die in a ditch?

What I was doing was different. What I had was simply the blurry image and the location of the crime. That was it. A specific needle in a haystack full of loads of other needles. In my crimes, the police had already gone to the media and struck out. Leaving the family waiting for a miracle. Waiting for a confession that was doubtful to come.

Barg kept pitching me his fugitive. "Just let me send you his information. He killed a father of two, and we've been looking for him for over a year."

I gave in.

"Okay."

Then he told me where he "thinks" the killer might be, and my face went straight into my palm.

14

THE CANTINA SCENE

Los Angeles, 2017

MEXICO.

Fuck.

Barg had just told me the murder suspect he was looking for, the one who killed the father of two in San Jose, was hiding somewhere in friggin' Mexico.

This was going to be impossible.

He said he was first going to issue a press release. If that couldn't find him, he would hit me up. The release went over the details of the crime. On the night of November 8, 2016, a fight broke out in the streets near the corner of West Alma Avenue and Mastic Street in San Jose. Joseph Miller chased his victim for over a block. When he finally caught up to him, he crushed his skull in with a concrete block. When police arrived, they found fifty-one-year-old Alfred Perez with blunt-force trauma injuries. He died at the scene.

The release went out. They got no response.

Two weeks later, Barg contacted me. "Howdy, Billy." He asked if I was still willing to help.

"Yes," I said.

I was hoping he would now give me a more detailed location on where the suspect was hiding.

"We think he's staying in one of two areas in Mexico—Mazatlán or Puerto Vallarta," he said.

Two cities, with a combined population of 750,000 people. A campaign in Spanish. Terrific.

"That's a big area," I said, trying my best to not be a downer.

"Yeah, I know," Barg replied. "That's one of the reasons we haven't been able to find him. But that's all we have. Here's a photo of the suspect."

I opened up the attachment, and my mood changed. The light from the heavens opened up to a feeling I can only describe as "glorious."

The suspect was a ginger. Red hair. Pale skin. In the photo, he's standing in front of a house, wearing a baggy white T-shirt and baggy jeans. His right hand is holding a cell phone, and he's throwing up a gang sign with his left hand—which is a good thing, as it let us clearly see the Chicano script-style of the tattoo on the back of his hand. It read "Daddy." And then Barg told me the best part—he didn't speak Spanish.

I didn't have a local store or bar to pin him to. I didn't even have a city we were for sure he was in. But a redhead with a tattoo on his hand who didn't speak Spanish? He would stick out like a sore thumb. People would notice him in Mexico.

I wrote up the campaign in English, and Barg had his Spanish-speaking partner translate:

Mazatlán: ¿Has visto a este hombre? Es buscado por un asesinato en San José, California, durante el mes de noviembre del 2016. Se sabe que está en el área de Mazatlán. Él tiene el pelo rojo, ojos azules, mide 1.8 metros de altura con un distintivo TATUAJE en su mano izquierda. Su verdadero nombre es Joseph Miller. Si lo ha visto, envíe un mensaje a esta página, o llame al Departamento de Policía de San José al 408-277-5283. Por favor comparta esta información y se ofrecerá una RECOMPESA.

[Mazatlán: Have you seen this man? He is wanted for a murder San Jose, California in November, 2016. He is known to be in the Mazatlán area. He has red hair, blue eyes, is 6 feet tall with a distinctive TATTOO on his left HAND. His real name is Joseph Miller. If you have seen him, please, please message this page or call the San Jose Police Department at 408-277-5283. And please share. There is a REWARD.]

I duplicated the same campaign in Puerto Vallarta.

But I still didn't know where or who I was going to target inside each city. They were big places. I needed some type of anchor. I looked at his picture again. A gringo, a shade paler than me, in two tourist towns. Where would he go? I searched for a Hooters.

Unfortunately, the one Hooters in Puerto Vallarta had closed. I then searched for a cluster of sports bars, ones with American names. Any place where expatriate and tourists might congregate. I jammed my flag down in the middle of a handful of somewhat douchebag-sounding bars like Nacho Daddy and Players Sports Bar and circled a mile radius with a small, sixty-dollar buy.

There was just one small problem—if anyone wrote to me, they would be writing in Spanish. I don't speak Spanish. I took four years of Italian in high school, and much to my mother's chagrin, I can't speak a word other than "molto bene." I downloaded Google Translate onto my phone, took a screenshot of the ad, and sent it to Barg, and on November 14, 2017, I was using my system to hunt my first fugitive. Then I needed to get out of the house and into the world.

Being present is a constant struggle with a new case around every corner and a new tip ready to pounce in every Facebook comment. My son was now a senior in high school, applying to colleges. My daughter, now in her second year of college, had just declared her major would be plant protection. Our dog, a beautiful bull mastiff named Maisy, had just died of cancer. I would play hockey on Tuesday nights and get into the odd scrap to feel some semblance of being alive. Kendall would come visit in LA and drag me away from the investigations long enough to go have a drink at the Three Broomsticks pub inside the Wizarding World of Harry Potter at Universal Studios. That I had to go to a fairy-tale land in order to feel more human wasn't lost on me.

I pressed *publish* on the campaign to find Joseph Miller and headed to a bar called Frank 'n Hank in Koreatown to pregame with my fellow Hollywood Manchester City supporters before a Liam Gallagher concert. The former Oasis front man played "Live Forever," "Rock and Roll Star," and "Cigarettes and Alcohol," and I got to pretend it was 1995 for the night.

I woke up with a moderate hangover to a message from one tipster. He had seen him, all right. In Mazatlán. A ginger. Tattoo on hand. Didn't speak Spanish.

Another wrote me.

Then another.

I quickly learned the Spanish word for "reward." Almost everyone asked about the *recompensa*, something very rarely mentioned by tipsters in the States.

"Buenas tardes."

"Se dónde vive en Mazatlán."

"Yo lo conozco y se donde vive."

They had seen him on this beach. They had seen him at this bar. They had seen him in the stores around town.

All in Mazatlán.

Dime donde obtener informes acerca de la recompensa y yo junto a dos amigos lo buscamos y si lo encontramos lo retenemos hasta que llegue alguien por el.

I copied and pasted that last one into Google Translate. It spit this back at me:

Tell me where to get reports about the reward and I, together with two friends, look for him and if we find him, we hold him until someone arrives for the reward.

Mexico was a different, helpful, frightening beast. I forwarded the tips to Barg.

On top of the willingness of the tipsters to abduct the wanted man and hold him for the authorities (Barg was able to talk the tipster out of that plan), there were other surprising benefits to the Mexico campaign. No one was asking for a clearer picture of the killer. No one was crying foul over the police conspiring against him. No one was saying the typical and tired "snitches get stitches" that would come up once or twice during every campaign I ran in the United States. No one was even cracking jokes, saying it looked like this friend or that. Everyone was on board. And it was going viral within that one-mile radius.

I wrote my responses in English, had Google translate to Spanish, and then pasted them into Facebook Messenger, asking questions about where exactly they saw him. When was the last time they saw him? And most importantly, where was he right now?

I got their phone numbers and texted them to Barg, who called each tipster. We got women he had hit on. We got the apartment he was staying at. But we were still not sure. No one was mentioning the tattoo. Or his name. We needed proof that this was not just another ginger on holiday or someone trying to shake us down for *recompensa*. We needed a photo.

My workday over, I headed to a new pop-up bar on Hollywood Boulevard called Scum and Villainy, which was supposed to be a convincing replica of the Mos Eisley cantina from the original *Star Wars* movie. In the Uber, Barg texted me that he was on the phone with one of the tipsters I had sent him and asked me to check the private messages on Facebook. The tipster was going to send a photo of the man he thought to be the guy we were looking for.

I walked into the cantina, ordered a blue milk, and settled into the back booth. A Jawa scuttled in front of me, holding a crimson-colored cocktail. An imperial officer sat at the corner of the bar, talking with what looked like a smuggler. The Instagram-model-esque bartenders were dressed like space pirates, fake blasters in holsters slung low on their hips. And I sat in the back booth like an antsy Han Solo, waiting for the photo to arrive.

Like most kids born in the '70s, when Luke Skywalker walked out of the blinding bright of the desert into the dark menagerie of the cantina, I crossed the threshold from the known into the unknown. Every one of us has had that moment. But the cantina also means something else to me. Before I learned how to solve murders, if you googled my name, the story that would come up first was a *Star Wars* mystery I had solved.

When Obi-Wan Kenobi entered the cantina with Luke on Mos Eisley looking for a pilot, his first choice is a space pilot sporting arched eyebrows, killer muttonchops, and a black-and-white space suit more akin to an astronaut than a fighter pilot. While we cannot hear their dialogue, it is obvious that Kenobi asks him for a ride, and for whatever reason, the space pilot says no.

And for whatever reason, no one ever knew what the actor's name was. Kenobi went on to meet Chewbacca and Han Solo, launching a million action-figure battles on the rug in front of Dad's La-Z-Boy. The other pilot, who we later learned was named BoShek, faded forever into the darkness of the Mos Eisley bar.

I learned all this while attending Star Wars Celebration in Anaheim with my daughter. We were sitting in a panel called "Secrets of the Mos Eisley Cantina" when the speakers stated no one knew who the actor actually was. This was the most analyzed, most catalogued, most obsessed-over movie in history, and there was a mystery hanging out there.

I turned to my daughter.

"I'm gonna find this guy."

"Yeah, right," she said.

"I'm telling you. I'm going to find BoShek."

After months of talking to *Star Wars* extras, ancient casting companies, posting on all sorts of cinema fiend message boards in an attempt to get the crowd to help me, I woke up one morning and found myself gazing into the dark eyes of BoShek, sporting an incredibly spiffy shirt and those killer sideburns. His name was Basil Tomlin. His grandson saw one of my posts and contacted me. Unfortunately, Basil had passed away. But I had found him.

I wrote a story about the quest on my website, and articles about the discovery in *Gizmodo*, *A. V. Club*, and dozens of other blogs made me a minor hero of geeks everywhere.

Back at the cantina, I downed my blue milk in the booth, thinking about that incredibly geeky quest and how it might have actually been my very first missing-persons solve. It was nerd training wheels for what I was doing now.

I ordered another drink and kept refreshing my messages on my phone, waiting for the photo of the fugitive murder suspect the tipster was supposed to be sending. After twenty minutes, I got it. He looked very, very good. I quickly opened up the picture Barg had sent me of Miller, then placed the two side by side. It was a perfect match.

We had him.

I used an app to paste the photos side by side and sent it to Barg.

"That's the same gringo," I wrote.

The detective sent me back three responses in quick succession.

"Hell yes."

"Holy shit."

"I'm speechless."

This is actually working! I thought to myself. My first fugitive case, and we found him within twenty-four hours. In a whole 'nother country! I was becoming the world's first digital consulting detective. I had solved a half-dozen homicides. Now I was finding fugitives. This was going to be my life.

There was just one problem. Now we had to actually get him. And in Mexico, just because you know exactly where a fugitive is doesn't mean the police will go pick him up.

The next day, I got a text from Barg: "Turn off the juice—he's running."

The federales didn't act fast enough, and our fugitive was on the move. I deleted the ad.

The next day, we thought he was probably headed out of town and going back on the run. I went to a Harry Potter–themed birthday party that day, where a bunch of twentysomethings were wearing robes and playing quidditch beer pong and making wizard staffs out of their empty beer cans—which grew taller and taller throughout the night.

I kept checking my phone to see if the tipster had written back. He hadn't.

I shook off a somewhat large hangover the day after and played hockey, checking my phone in between shifts. Nothing.

I was getting concerned. This was Mexico. This was a killer. What if he found out and turned on the tipster?

I sent the tipster another message and waited. The next day, I finally got a message back. Sometimes tipsters take the day off too.

But he had no new info.

"He likely knows about the ads and that's what prompted him to leave the area of Mazatlán," Barg said to me.

"Can we follow him?" I asked. "Can we trace him? Can we get the federales to go in as soon as we get his hotel address?"

We had just found a needle in a haystack, and he was slipping away.

Barg was frank. "Mexican law enforcement is so challenging to work with that I think a strategy of attrition is a good one. If we make him feel like he is being pursued, then he will either run back to the U.S. or screw up and commit a crime in Mexico and get himself arrested—which works in our favor."

Barg and his partner, Wayne Smith, met with the U.S. Marshals in an attempt to light a fire under local law enforcement.

The tipsters kept talking. But Miller was running. We could be back to square one. Barg was optimistic. "We will bag Miller," he told me, sensing the urgency in my texts.

The undoing of a person's life is as easy to accomplish as the justice is hard. All it takes is the squeeze of a trigger. But justice? So many things need to fall perfectly into place for justice to find its way.

First, you need to identify the perpetrator. That's the hard part. Then, you need to find them. No easy feat. That's where we were at in Mexico. Next, you need to arrest them. Who knows what is waiting on the other side of the door when police bang on it, warrant in hand? And finally, you need to build a case so strong that it will convince twelve perfect strangers that the man or woman you identified, found, and arrested is guilty beyond a reasonable doubt.

All four steps must fit neatly together. Something you have to always tell yourself whenever you're yelling at your computer screen "Why can't they find this guy already?" or "We know he did it. Why can't they just arrest him?"

Barg and Smith were able to identify the murder suspect—Miller. That in itself is difficult. One third of murders in America don't even get that.

Then the suspect jumped to another country: 761,600 square miles filled with 129 million people who speak another language.

Barg tried a press release in Mexico. Nothing happened. I started a campaign looking for him in two cities, with a combined population of 750,000. We found him in one day.

And yet we were helpless.

We needed to be on the ground. Knocking on doors. That's what these social media campaigns are: knocking on a thousand doors. Efficient. Concise. They're not going to hit every door, of course. Not every person has an active Facebook, Instagram, or Twitter profile. But for the people who do, with the right wording of a post, a compelling picture, and the right amount of cash, you can hit almost everyone in town. It's like having a team of detectives swarm a neighborhood and talk to everyone within a few days. I can't get the body language, facial cues, and speech patterns that police will pick up on when they come face-to-face with a neighbor who might know something. But I'm also not threatening. I'm just a post nestled in between pictures of your sister's baby and your uncle complaining about Trump. Any place where people are looking for human interaction, this system can work.

Barg was still optimistic. But it seemed like Joseph Miller had turned back into a ghost.

I couldn't wallow in self-pity. I was gearing up for a Thanksgiving push on all the cases I hadn't been able to solve. The holidays are a good time to reactivate older campaigns to try to get some new answers.

I was betting $500 that would happen. I started with a case I had covered for *Crime Watch Daily* over the summer. The bodies of two women were found within a month of each other, dumped in fields outside Columbus, Ohio. Like many young women in southern Ohio, they had succumbed to the opioid epidemic that had taken over the area. Dozens of bodies of young women were being found across the state. Some were "body dumps"—people who overdosed and whose "friends" dumped their bodies instead of calling 911. But some of the women had signs of trauma indicating they were murdered. There was at least one killer lurking in southern Ohio using the desperation of women trapped in the opioid epidemic to feed their bloodlust.

> Do you live in Fairfield County? This Thanksgiving, please discuss with family and friends. Do you have any idea of who might be capable of killing these two women? A guy who likes to go into Columbus and pick up girls murdered Lindsey Maccabee and dumped her body on Lake Road near Pleasantville. Danielle's body was found dead along Allen Rd. Four little girls lost their moms, and they need answers.

I posted pictures of Danielle and Lindsey and shots of the locations where their bodies were found.

Next, I tried to find anyone who might remember the Allenstown Four killer from when he was living in Texas.

Ingleside, Texas: For Thanksgiving, please discuss. Do you remember this man? He was born Terry Rasmussen, but also went by other names. He lived in the Casa Del Rey Apartments in the late 70s. He was convicted of one murder and died in prison, but we know he killed many more.

I posted photos of Rasmussen from when he was younger.

I also reposted Owl's Head Park man walking down the street, ashing that cigarette in the sidewalk grate.

I timed them to start on the Wednesday before Thanksgiving—typically one of the biggest drinking days of the year for young people—and run through Sunday morning.

At this point, they were all Hail Marys.

I struck out on all of them. Christmas came, and I tried again. Got a few interesting leads, but nothing solid. January was a wasteland.

Michelle's book, *I'll Be Gone in the Dark*, was released at the end of February 2018. I figured I would try to use my new school method and tossed up a couple of campaigns in the hopes of finding someone who might recognize the man in one of the many sketches of the East Area Rapist/Original Night Stalker. I targeted everyone over sixty years old across the world who had once lived in East Sacramento or Goleta. Another Hail Mary.

The book debuted at number one on the *New York Times* bestseller list. Paul Haynes, Patton, and I held a live event at Skylight Books hosted by Karen and Georgia of the *My Favorite Murder* podcast. It seemed like everyone in the audience, including the devotees of the podcast, who lovingly refer to themselves as Murderinos, had all jumped down the rabbit hole with Michelle to try to see if they could solve the case. Across social media, readers talked about double-checking their alarm systems, jumping at every bump in the night, and warning others that it was a really, really bad idea to start reading the book after dark.

When Michelle passed away, the world was introduced to the name the "Golden State Killer." But only now was the world really learning what he was all about. The way he slithered into the houses and tied up the men, placed dishes on their backs, and told them not to make a sound before raping the women. The way he graduated to murder. The way he slithered back out of the houses and into history, at least twelve murders and forty-nine rapes in his wake.

At the book events, some people asked why there are no more serial killers now like there were in the '70s. Well, science has caught up, so most sociopaths can't get to the numbers we saw back then. But they are still out there, many preying on the opioid-addicted sex workers who take every chance imaginable to get their next fix. Maybe some become terrorists. Or CEOs. Or decide killing one person at a time is inconvenient and become the monster that has replaced the stranger offering candy in modern America—the mass shooter.

Meanwhile, word was getting around police departments that there was a guy who could help them with cases. I started getting more and more requests and turned none of them down. I had the robbery squad asking for a campaign to catch a serial burglar. A coworker had a friend whose daughter had gone missing and was asking for help finding her. One detective was looking for a Chinese rape suspect possibly hanging out in a town outside LA, and I started my first campaign in Mandarin.

I was up to thirty active investigations. I was running out of money. The TV shows I had been trying to start had not worked for one reason or another but mainly because they were about unsolved crimes and didn't have any guaranteed endings. I had one kid in college and another getting ready to start in the fall. I didn't want to stop. But I got an idea. Other than my wife and the detectives I was working with, I hadn't been telling anyone what I had been doing, solving these crimes. Maybe if I wrote a story, I could not only make a little money, but it would put the word out and maybe I could get some help. I daydreamed that Mark Zuckerberg might see the story and, in a Daddy Warbucks–like gesture, give me a line of Facebook and Instagram ad credit so I could run a thousand campaigns at once. Or more likely, a police department might be willing to pay for the ads and start a pilot program.

I began writing a feature for *Los Angeles* magazine about the Halloween Mask Murder in El Monte. While fact-checking the events, I started to wonder why it was taking so long for the case to get to trial. I asked the detective what was up. "Hold off," he told me. "If you write something that contradicts the facts we presented to the DA, it can hurt the case during trial. The case is a death penalty case and will be severely scrutinized."

The death penalty. That shook me.

I hate the guy who got away with it because he takes life away. Now, I had just learned that what I'm doing—the thing that's taken over my life—could directly lead to the taking of another life. It should've occurred to me, but it never did. The work I do is supposed to be about justice. But not like this. The man in the Halloween mask made a horrific decision and tore many lives apart. When I looked him up, I learned he was an army veteran who had escaped the streets but got sucked back in when he came back. He was a bad guy, one who needed to be locked up for a long, long time. But not this. Not death.

You want bad guys to be snarling, spitting beasts, showing their fangs dripping with blood or twirling their mustache as they tie the damsel to the tracks. But they're not.

It's hard not to see the world in good and evil colors when all your heroes wear capes or carry lightsabers. Baked within us is the ability to identify the villain within five minutes of watching a Disney movie. But the grainy, fleeting image you chase is every shade of gray.

There are sick, twisted sociopaths out there, to be sure. But very rarely is there a situation that presents that Manichean dividing line between good and evil. Axis and Allies. Empire and Rebels. It's all shades of gray. Sometimes they are the heroes in someone else's movie. They are often desperate or drugged or drunk. Or just dicks. Or just had a bad day. That's still no excuse for shooting someone in the face, and every single one of them needs to be brought to justice, to serve every waking moment of their lives in prison, hopefully devoting the rest of their time to a cause that can help others. To offer some redemption. Some of the victim's families want those killers put to death. I can't imagine the pain the Tate or LaBianca families felt when they turned on the TV and saw Charles Manson giving an interview, or Kimberly Leach's family when they saw Ted Bundy's smiling face. I would never stop the families from getting what they wanted. The death penalty is just not something I believe in. And now a suspect I helped catch was facing it.

In the summer of 2018, when a writer was doing a feature on me for *Men's Journal*, the detective wavered on whether it was the social media campaign that brought in the tip or the original press conference. I don't know why he changed his tune. Right after it happened, he told me, "We got him. Someone saw the Facebook page and called us." Then he invited me to the press conference. Then at the press conference, he gave credit to me at the podium.

On top of that, after the success of El Monte, the detective wrote to me, "You've been a great help. I've already started passing the word around the floor to other investigators." From there, I started getting emails from detectives to help with a half dozen other cases. I actually set up a campaign for another murder in the very same town of El Monte. Within a week, I had identified the girlfriend of the suspect, then found a photo of him on her Facebook page and got his name. The detective wrote me a letter of recommendation to tell other investigators about the success, as I was attempting to build this system into something more widespread among police departments.

In the letter, he wrote:

> *In February of 2018, I was provided information of a gentleman, Mr. Bill Jensen, who assisted with posting specific information on social media (Facebook) to assist investigations for any detectives. I provided limited information and a photograph of a possible suspect that was being sought in the investigation. I advised Mr. Jensen of the location of the incident, to hopefully target a specific area/neighborhood, so specific individuals were targeted. The information being posted was to stimulate the possible suspect(s) to reach out and/or to assist in identifying a positive name of the suspect. The information provided through the help of the website, yielded the identification of a suspect and possible gang affiliation. The help that Mr. Jensen provided was useful, and I would use his assistance on future cases if I believe it will help in solving the case.*

That letter was more proof that the system was working—and being readily utilized by the sheriffs. Maybe I should have had the detective write a letter right after the first el Monte solve. But to tell you the truth, I was actually relieved he was wavering on acknowledging my help with the Halloween Mask Murder. I didn't want this one, even though it was proof that it worked. I didn't want it on my conscience that it could lead to the death penalty.

But it was all still out there. Along with the missing-persons cases filled with long-lost romances and love triangles and family members pointing fingers at each other. The 3:00 a.m. Facebook messages from a father who has been thinking about his murdered daughter so much that sleep was not coming. A sleep that is often the only refuge from the thought of his little girl's dead body lying behind a cornfield.

He writes me asking for answers. Asking for updates. Asking for anything. Asking for just someone to talk to. "Who killed my child?" shouted into the darkness.

I welcomed the late-night changeover from investigator to grief counselor. At least there was a human on the other end. At least there was something real. Talking to a family member searching for answers was an escape from the false leads, red herrings, and blind alleys that were crowding my thoughts. I had solved or helped solve ten by now, but every time I got another arrest, I saw five more I needed to work. Rape kits with DNA that I was positive could be matched through genealogy databases were piled up across the country. The forty thousand unidentified human remains that were untouched and untested were waiting for us to give names to their owners. I walked to the convenience store down the block and bought a lottery ticket, hoping I could win the $500-million-dollar jackpot and put it all toward a quest to extract their DNA, find their relatives, and give all of them back their names.

I'm not chasing people. I'm chasing shadows, phantoms that flit in and out of a surveillance video. That's on a good night. On the other nights, I'm chasing darkness.

The ginger fugitive in Mexico. The Owl's Head Park Man. The Girl with the Serpent Tattoo. The Golden State Killer. The Villain with a Thousand Faces. All still out there. Their wicked club gaining thirteen new members every day as the unsolved murders in America grow. So many cases. So many victims' families asking for help.

There is a way to solve these murders. I needed money to sequence

DNA and run it through databases. I needed money to run a thousand more campaigns on social media, looking for that someone who knows something.

I need a hundred of me. A thousand of me. I need an army of me.

Something has to give.

15

THE MONSTER AT THE END OF THIS BOOK

Chicago, 2018

IT'S 2:00 A.M. I'M IN BED IN A HOTEL IN CHICAGO. I DON'T know if I'm dreaming or not.

I'm writing this in present tense. Because it's happening right now. Right. Now.

Patton is sleeping in a room on a lower floor. I'm debating running down and banging on his door.

I'm in Chicago because Patton, Paul Haynes, and I just put on an event for Michelle's book in Naperville, hosted by Gillian Flynn, the author of *Gone Girl* who also wrote the foreword for the book. It was the first time all four of us were in the same room together. And Michelle's family was there too. Naperville sits just thirty miles west of Michelle's hometown of Oak Park, Illinois. It was also the first day of shooting for a documentary HBO is making on *I'll Be Gone in the Dark*, so cameras were following us around. The event went well. The crowd loved the book, as usual. During the Q and A section, we got the same question, as usual: "Do you think he will ever be caught?"

"Yes," I replied, ramping up to my stock answer. "Because we have his DNA. And he will be caught at some point from a familial DNA match... We'll ID him within five years."

Someone then asked another question we got on every stop: "Do you think he's still alive?"

Paul took that one with his stock answer. Based on the life expectancy of baby boomers, which the killer was, there was a good chance he was.

We talked about how Michelle thought she was one step away from solving the case so many times—and how she was devastated when that step became a hole she fell through.

"I got him!" she would say. She matched his DNA to someone on a Y-chromosome public database. She found cuff links being sold online that might have been stolen during one of the attacks. In person, she would be beaming. I talked about how I was never there for the letdown, when she found out that she *hadn't* got him. That whatever she had uncovered was a red herring. A false clue. A dead end.

But I just found out. She may have just gotten him. Him. The Golden State Killer.

Twenty minutes ago, Paul Haynes texted me with a tip from Mike Morford, a blogger who Michelle and I had on the *Shadowpulp* podcast five years earlier. Back then, we were talking about the Zodiac Killer. Morford had since moved on to the Golden State Killer. And he was plugged in. He said that there was a press conference tomorrow in Sacramento. All very hush-hush.

Now I'm texting and emailing anyone I can think of who might know what's going on. I haven't heard back from Erika Hutchcraft of the Orange County DA's office or Paul Holes. Holes just retired a few weeks ago. I'm sure he would know what's going on. I'm sending a message to Debbi Domingo. Debbi's mother was killed by the Golden State Killer.

"Hi, Debbi, has anyone contacted you?"

It's 12:50 a.m. Chicago time.

Debbi writes back. "Yes, but basic details only. I am in shock."

"Who reached out? Was it someone official?"

"Yes, Anne Marie," Debbi writes, referring to Anne Marie Schubert, the Sacramento district attorney. "All she told me was that he is in custody and they'll do the press conference at noon."

He is in custody? If he is in custody, that means he's alive. The Golden State Killer is alive and in a jail cell. This was bigger than just some announcement about new information about the case. Or even identifying the killer but announcing that he had died of cancer in South America a few years ago or something. They actually had someone in custody?

A DA would never tell a victim's family member without being sure they had the guy. But I needed another source.

I'm scrambling. I finally hear back from a producer friend of mine who also worked on the story. She got word from top brass at Sacramento that she should come up tomorrow for a press conference. Confirmation number two.

He is in custody. The East Area Rapist. The Original Night Stalker. The Golden State Killer. He is alive. And he is caught.

I send out a cryptic tweet: "If you've been following the Golden State Killer case, stay tuned. We will be having a rather large announcement tomorrow. #michellemcnamara #IllBeGoneInTheDark #stepintothelight"

"Oh my god Billy!!" Karen from *My Favorite Murder* tweets at me. "What do you think? Is it real?"

"Put it to you this way," I tweet back. "We're all staying in the same hotel tonight in Chicago, and I'm debating waking Patton up."

"I just keep getting chills. Congratulations!!" she replies.

Karen was not the only one telling me congratulations. I guess I understand why. I helped finish Michelle's book, where she hunted a supposedly uncatchable killer for close to five years. They can't tell Michelle congratulations. So they are telling me. But I still think I'm dreaming.

Fifteen minutes ago, I found out he was in custody. Now, I have just learned his name. Joseph James DeAngelo. My heart just sank a little.

That doesn't sound right. The DNA told us we were looking for a Germanic or British name. I remember that three-week period when I was digging up family trees with eighteenth-century British census reports. DeAngelo? That can't be right.

I just checked Michelle's hard drive. Nothing. She had thousands of names of possible suspects. But no DeAngelo.

Now I'm searching through online newspaper archives. People are sending me articles they are finding from the hidden corners of the web. A marriage notice. A small story about Joseph DeAngelo enlisting in the navy.

We always thought he might be military. And a sailor.

But I'm still not sure. I just don't know.

I keep digging through the newspaper archives online. And I just found this article from 1979. The headline reads:

AUBURN POLICEMAN DISMISSED IN SHOPLIFTING ACCUSATION. *Joseph DeAngelo, the Auburn policeman...* the story begins.

A cop. We always thought he could be a cop. The way he evaded all the patrols as the East Area Rapist. He had to at least have a police radio. But Auburn? Auburn was thirty miles from East Sacramento. We were sure he would either live, work, or play in East Sacramento.

The story continued.

Joseph DeAngelo, the Auburn policeman accused of shoplifting...

Shoplifting? That's weird. He was caught shoplifting as a cop? What did he take?

The story continued.

Joseph DeAngelo, the Auburn policeman accused of shoplifting a can of dog repellent and a hammer at a Sacramento drug store...

Ho-ly shit.

This is it. Dog repellent. A hammer. Things a burglar would carry. Things he wouldn't want anyone to know he was buying.

Joseph DeAngelo, the Auburn policeman accused of shoplifting a can of dog repellent and a hammer at a Sacramento drug store last month was fired this week. Auburn City Manager Jack Sausser said DeAngelo failed to answer any of the city investigations and did not request an administrative hearing so was dismissed Monday.

What kind of a cop doesn't request a hearing? A cop can shoot an unarmed man dead in the street, and within seconds, the police union is right beside him, ready to fight tooth and nail for their man, dragging a case out for months. This guy was arrested for shoplifting and just walked away?

This was the guy. This *had* to be the guy.

I am writing this as it's happening. I know when you write in present tense, you are supposed to make the reader believe everything is happening right then. But in reality, you're really writing in the future and faking it.

But this is happening right now.

'Cause I can't sleep.

'Cause we came to Chicago for a book event, but it was in this strange, giant church an hour outside of Chicago. And there was a coffee-house inside it, and I had a weird green smoothie. And the Gone Girl was there. And Michelle's family was there.

'Cause after the event, we went to a party at a bar but didn't even stay for a drink, and we drove back to Chicago.

'Cause when I got back to the hotel, I decided to walk the ten blocks to the spot where Marques Gaines was killed two years ago, but the chill in the air and the threat of a 7:00 a.m. flight forced me to turn back around and go to sleep.

'Cause there was this camera crew here to film a documentary. And I just texted Liz Garbus, the director. "I know we just met six hours ago, but I think we got him," I wrote, hoping she wasn't thinking, *I just took on this project with this lunatic, who for the next year is going to be texting me at all hours of the night with claims that the killer was just caught.*

'Cause I think I am going to wake up from this dream and not remember any of it. So I am writing it all down.

'Cause I just saw his face.

I did a search on Classmates.com for Joseph DeAngelo. An entry came up: Folsom High School, 1960–64. There was a link to his yearbook from 1962. He was just a sophomore. His cheeks are chubby. His hair is curly, styled in a modified, low-key pompadour. Not the feathered hair from one of the East Area Rapist composite sketches, which we tried to compare to the pictures in the Sacramento high school yearbooks from the late '70s, where every boy we looked at was a carbon copy of the next. Another picture was emailed to me, a darkened shot from a newspaper above a story about his navy service.

I wrote Debbi.

"You've seen the pictures?"

She hadn't seen them.

I paused before writing back. "Do you want to?"

"Yes please."

I sent her his photo. It's the first time she'll see the face of the man who police think killed her mother.

She wrote back. "Thank you."

I know she will send out the photo, along with some of the articles I sent over, to the sisterhood survivors. Jane Carson, victim #5. Michelle Cruz, the sister of Janelle Cruz, the Golden State Killer's last known murder victim. And Margaret Wardlow, his youngest survivor, who he attacked when she was just 13. We're all going to be together in a week at CrimeCon, the convention for true-crime fans, in Nashville. We're supposed to be putting on a presentation about all the clues we think have the best chance to lead us to solving this thing. Well, those plans just went to hell.

I'm thinking for a moment about the conference, and something strange just happened. After I confirmed to myself that this was the guy, the guy we have been chasing for so long, I think I gave myself maybe thirty seconds of happiness. Amazement transformed into a fist pump, then turned back into amazement.

And then a switch flipped in my head.

"Build a timeline. What else has he done?"

The details of the cases we had pored over for years. The General Custer homework and the hand-drawn map found at the crime scene in Danville. The caliber of gun used in the Maggiore murder. The patterns of the china he stole. Those cuff links. The minute details of the twelve murders and fifty rapes. They all just wiped away, and I yanked the wheel of the thousand-mile-an-hour race car hard to the right, tires screeching below me.

Where has he been? Summer camps? School trips? Second jobs? Weekend furloughs in the navy? Family vacations when he told his wife he was going for a walk and then did something evil? I need to build a timeline. Build a map. And match it up with any unsolved rapes and murders from those dates and locations. This guy did more than those twelve murders and fifty rapes. How many unsolved cases will find the monster at the end of their story to be this guy, Joseph James DeAngelo?

But I knew one guy who was just going to be happy.

I let Patton sleep another hour, then sent him a text at 4:30 a.m.

"She got him. Suspect is in custody per two sources. Press conference at noon pst time."

"Is it HIM?" Patton wrote back. "They're sure it's him?"

"I can't see how they would announce a press conference and say they have someone in custody if they didn't have a DNA match," I wrote.

"WOW!!!!!" Patton replied. "THIS IS FUCKING AWESOME!"

At 5:00 a.m. I reluctantly stopped searching for more archived stories about DeAngelo, got dressed, and rushed down to the lobby to wait for the car to the airport.

I caught Patton's reaction when he walked out of the elevator.

It only makes sense for it to go down in Chicago. After seeing her family. After being together for the first time. Sleeping in the Sofitel, the same hotel Michelle and Patton stayed in for the last ten Christmas vacations. Might as well rename it the Victory Motel.

At the airport, as we waited to board the plane to New York, our giddiness betrayed any lack of sleep.

"I really got hung up on the name," I said to Patton. "The DNA was pointing us to an English or German name. It was like in *Murder on the Orient Express*, when Bianchi recalls the time he heard the name of Daisy Armstrong's killer: 'I remember feeling ashamed that he had an Italian name. Cassetti.'"

Inadvertently, I had just wound Patton up, and for the next five minutes, we were quoting the 1974 movie version of the Agatha Christie novel.

"Mr. Ratchett, I have made enough money to satisfy both my needs and my caprices," Patton began, in a pitch-perfect Albert Finney as Hercule Poirot. "I take only such cases now as interest me, and to be frank, my interest in your case is, uh…dwindling."

Like I said, giddy.

I was going back to New York to continue what was supposed to be a workcation. Kendall was scheduled to give a talk about her Parkinson's disease research at an investigator's meeting at the Michael J. Fox Foundation, and I was tagging along. I had bought us tickets to see *Harry Potter and the Cursed Child*, as well as *The Iceman Cometh* starring Denzel Washington. I missed New York and wanted a Fribble from Friendly's. Crinkle-cut fries from Nathan's. And a soft pretzel from a street vendor. Those plans were all going to go to hell.

We landed in New York and started doing interviews on the fly with various news outlets as we waited for the press conference. Patton had a prior engagement downtown, so at 3:00 p.m., we went with the film crew to an office near the World Trade Center and huddled around my laptop to watch the press conference, which was streaming from Sacramento.

One by one, district attorneys from Orange, Ventura, Sacramento, and Contra Costa counties took to the microphone and said little about the case. I could see Paul Holes in the background. It was evident halfway through that they weren't going to let him speak. The press conference seemed less about giving out information and more of a victory lap in an election year with the hopes that this arrest might be able to drum up some votes.

They talked about the groundbreaking method of finding DeAngelo with DNA. But they didn't mention familial. But I knew that was how they got him.

They didn't mention he was a former cop, burying the lede many newspapers would run with.

Then they opened up the floor to questions. After five or six, a reporter asked, "Did the new book, *I'll Be Gone in the Dark*, generate any new leads in the case that helped with the arrest?"

Patton got off the couch he was sitting on and pressed his face close to my laptop's tiny speaker. I leaned in with him.

"I'm glad you asked that question," Sheriff Scott Jones said. "Because that's a question we got from literally all over the world in the last twenty-four hours. And the answer is no. Other than the fact that it kept interest and tips coming in."

He couldn't wait to say no. The room was deflated for a brief second, then we both shrugged. What else were they going to say?

Patton reminded us that Michelle never wanted any credit. She just wanted him caught.

When the conference was over, I called Karen and Georgia for a special episode of *My Favorite Murder*. I put it out to all the Murderinos to join in helping me build the timeline and solve cold cases DeAngelo might have committed. I also snuck in a story about my desire to set up a pilot program to deputize citizen detectives to data mine and help solve cold cases. I did a couple more interviews, then stumbled back uptown.

On the steps from the subway, one hour of sleep in the last forty-eight, I caught a glimpse of red in the corner of my eye. I turned and saw Curtis Sliwa, the founder of the Guardian Angels, wearing the iconic red jacket and beret of the civilian volunteers who patrol the subway stations, keeping them safe. One of the original citizen crime fighters. I must have ridden the subway a thousand times, and the one time I see him is the day the Golden State Killer is caught.

I asked if he heard the news.

"Yeah," he said in his thick New York accent, simultaneously handing me a business card. "He was a former cop."

Ever a critic of the police, Curtis didn't bury the lede.

I reached my Times Square hotel and fell into bed around midnight.

The next three days were a blur. I was answering rapid-fire questions from George Stephanopoulos on *Good Morning America*, tear-inducing questions on *20/20*. NPR, BBC, CBC, *48 Hours*, *New York Times*, *Times of London*. I said no to the *Sun* newspaper in England and yes to Swedish Public Radio, because I thought it would be a fun thing to say I did.

Toward the end of each interview, every reporter had the same question: "Do you think the book had anything to do with the capture of the Golden State Killer?"

I fumbled with the answer at first. "Of course it did," I'd say. "Michelle named him 'the Golden State Killer.' Saying her book had nothing to do with the capture of the Golden State Killer when she was the one who actually gave him that name is a bit disingenuous." My righteous indignation matched the sheriff's. "And Paul Holes referred to Michelle as his partner, and both pressed for familial DNA testing. Would you really say a detective had nothing to do with the capture if she passed away suddenly and her partner later solved the case they had been working on for years?"

But on Thursday night, walking out of the CNN building through Columbus Circle on a quest to get some Nathan's fries, I realized what my answer should have been. It wasn't Michelle's book that led to his capture. It was Michelle's death.

The tribute I wrote about her was all about her dogged quest to find the identity of the Golden State Killer and less about her being the wife of a beloved comedian. And once Patton tweeted out the tribute, reporters were introduced to the investigator and author Michelle McNamara, the woman who wrote the story about her quest for the killer in *Los Angeles* magazine. And they in turn wrote stories about her laser-focused drive to find him. The East Area Rapist/Original Night Stalker, who Michelle thought had such a hard time being noticed because of branding, was introduced to the world right alongside her. Stories about Michelle McNamara and the Golden State Killer appeared in *People* magazine, *Time*, the *Daily Mail*, *USA Today*, the *Washington Post*, and countless others.

Powerful people take notice when there are international headlines about a citizen trying to solve a crime that happened in their own backyard.

Two months after she died, a press conference was convened in Sacramento, with DA Schubert announcing a renewed effort to find the killer, where her office would be devoting a lot more resources, as well as a stronger cooperation with the FBI. And there would be a new $50,000 reward.

In his answer, the sheriff confirmed all this. "That's a question we got from literally all over the world in the last twenty-four hours." The whole world knew about the Golden State Killer because of Michelle. And the work she did pressed powerful people to find him.

I posted that tribute to Michelle on April 23, two years to the night before we flew to Chicago for the book event. That was also the twentieth anniversary of my dad's death. On that night in New York, Kendall and I had dinner at Delmonico's Steakhouse, because that's where the protagonists convened each night to try to catch the serial killer in Caleb Carr's novel *The Alienist*. And also because my dad always loved a good steak.

On the train back uptown, we got off a stop early at Penn Station, 'cause it always reminded me of Dad and him taking me to Madison Square Garden to see Andre the Giant or to the Thanksgiving Day parade to see the big balloons or to Greenwich Village to get me a fake ID.

We walked down toward the Long Island Railroad terminal. Forever totemistic and nostalgic, I wanted to buy a comic book at the big newsstand Dad always took me to, the one across from the long ticket counter and train tote board. But when I turned the corner into the terminal, the newsstand was gone. Replaced by a drugstore. I was bummed. I dragged Kendall all over the station, looking for another newsstand. I finally found a bookstore that was open across from the Amtrak station. They had a small shelf of graphic novels. I bought one with a story about the Teen Titans being all grown-up, fighting crime in Manhattan before having to work together with their mentors to battle an unseen foe.

In the middle of the whirlwind, I got a text from the detective in Tampa who I was helping search for the Girl with the Serpent Tattoo. He had written me earlier that the woman we thought might be her was back in prison with a high bond. He was finally going to be able to visit her before she made bail and see if the tattoos matched up. I was sitting in a chair behind a desk, pretending to be on the phone while they shot B-roll for the *20/20* story when he emailed me.

Not her… Back to the drawing board. Tattoo of cross on her left shoulder. No tattoo on back. Chinese symbol upper right shoulder.

Fuck!!!!

I said that in my head. They still run sound with B-roll.

But seriously. Dammit. Well, I guess two in one week was asking for too much. I would start the campaign again—after the Harry Potter play.

Two days later, back in Northern California, Paul Haynes and I were standing in front of the East Area Rapist's first known crime scene in Rancho Cordova. It was the first time we got to walk the same streets that the man, now known as the Golden State Killer, had prowled.

We had just had coffee with Paul Holes. He gave us the inside story of how he caught him. Sure enough, he entered his DNA profile—this time a full genome profile, not just the Y chromosomes—into a public database, GEDmatch, and got a hit on a third cousin. From there, he and a volunteer genealogist built a family tree and looked for someone the right age who lived in the Sacramento area. He saw DeAngelo, and he looked good, but he was a lot older than what he thought he would be.

"I drove to his house and was sitting outside in my car," Holes told us. "I was a day from retiring. I just wanted to know. I was thinking to myself: what if I just knocked on the door and asked him for a swab?"

Holes was very close to getting out of the car. But the background check on DeAngelo said he had guns. A lot of them. Paul Holes decided against it and retired the next day.

The police then staked out DeAngelo's house and waited for him to discard an item containing his DNA.

They tested a tissue found in his trash, and it was a match to the DNA of the killer.

They had him.

In the last few days, Paul Holes had been on TV constantly and had been transformed from retired investigator to true-crime heartthrob. The hashtag #HotForHoles was making the rounds, spurred by the Murderinos.

As we were wrapping up, Paul asked me what else I was working on. I told him I was still investigating the Allenstown Four, creating a timeline for Rasmussen, to see where else he had been and what other crimes he might have committed, just like I was starting to do with DeAngelo. And I said Pete Headley, the San Bernardino detective who was working the West Coast portion of the Allenstown Four case, and I were working with a geneticist to amplify the degraded DNA of each girl in the barrels. We still needed to find their identity.

"You know, I was on a conference call with Pete Headley in February 2017," Paul said to me. "He told me about little Lisa and how they used a familial DNA match to find out who she was, which led to the killer. About creating the SNP profile, getting an extraction, and using the whole genome."

"Really?" I said, dumbfounded.

"Yeah, I just wasn't allowed to tell you at the time. I remember you telling me about the case at Michelle's memorial," he said. "Then we learned that it was connected to the Larry Vanner case. I told you I responded to Eunsoon Jun's crime scene in Contra Costa, right?"

Paul had learned from Headley how instead of just using a Y-STR profile (just one of the twenty-three pairs of chromosome that make up the human genome), which we had been using all these years and had led us down the road of an English or Germanic name, they should sequence the whole genome of the killer and upload it into the database.

The two cases—Allenstown and Golden State—were destined to be forever linked in my mind ever since that night in Boston, when I learned Michelle had died just hours after I walked the woods where the bodies were found in the barrels. But I had just learned they were actually linked. For the whole world. Lisa, the little girl abandoned at the trailer park, the one who helped solve the Allenstown Four case and lead investigators to the serial killer Terry Rasmussen, actually helped catch the Golden State Killer. And in turn, she would help catch thousands more killers who thought they got away with it.

Michelle had a saying. She didn't believe in things happening for a reason or some divine fate. Everything was random, and the best we can do is be nice to each other. "It's chaos. Be kind," is what she would say. But there was some cosmically aligned chaos going on.

That night, Paul Haynes and I had drinks with Ken Clark, one of the lead investigators on the case with the Sacramento Sheriff's Department. While Paul Holes was the scientist, Ken Clark was the detective. He has worked over two hundred homicides, but the GSK was as much his white whale as any of them. The drinks flowed, and Ken, a magnificent storyteller, told us about coming face-to-face with DeAngelo. About how when they arrested him at his home, he told them he had a roast in the oven.

I mentioned how crazy it was that at almost the exact moment that we were in Chicago answering questions about whether he would ever be caught, Clark was actually catching him.

Ken then told us a story about Chicago. He was once there for a conference, and he and a detective friend went out drinking late one night in an empty bar downtown. At one point during the night, Ken peered out the window of the bar toward the barren sidewalk and spotted a large man looking in at them. Ten minutes went by, and he checked again. The guy was still there. Ken knew for sure: this guy was menacing; he was casing them. He was sure they were going to get jumped once they got outside.

"And we had left our guns at the hotel," he said. "And this was a big guy. At least six foot four. Angry-looking."

Ken picked up a knife from the table.

"So I told the bartender, 'I'm going to take this knife. I'll bring it back.' And I slide it up my sleeve, holding the blade like this." He showed us how he carried the knife.

The two cops walked out of the bar. The large man gave them an intimidating stare, but he didn't try anything. They got back to the hotel, and Ken, true to his word, returned the knife to the bar the next day.

"When was this?" I asked.

"About four years ago," he said.

"And downtown Chicago? The tourist area?"

"Yeah," he said.

I took out my phone and started swiping through photos, past the pictures of DeAngelo, close-ups of the Girl with the Serpent Tattoo, the truck from the hit-and-run in Albuquerque, the girl with the short shorts from White Boy Q's murder in Tallahassee, the killer in the Halloween mask in El Monte.

I finally landed on the one I was looking for.

"This is crazy, but could this have been the guy?" I asked.

He looked at the still photo of the Man in the Green Hoodie that was sent to me over Twitter the night I was trying to find Marques Gaines's attacker.

"Yeah," he said. "That totally could be him."

Okay, odds are it wasn't him. But I liked the way the chaos was feeling this week.

———————————

After Sacramento, it was off to Nashville and CrimeCon, where Paul Haynes and I were set to deliver two presentations with the Sister Survivors on the Golden State Killer. Right before I boarded the plane, I got a text message from John Barg, the San Jose detective I was working with on finding the ginger murder fugitive who ran to Mexico. We had been playing a cat-and-mouse game with him for six months, ever since I found him while I was sitting in that back booth of the *Star Wars* cantina on Hollywood Boulevard. We would locate him, but the federales wouldn't act, and he would relocate. Over and over. Barg said now it might be different.

> Billy. New info and new issues with JM. I think we need a new ad. I will spare you the long-winded back story, but basically we believe we have found JM in a neighborhood in Guadalajara. A neighborhood called Santa Cruz Del Valle, north of the airport. Please check this area out and let me know what you think.
>
> We have been assured by the feds (hold your breath) that they have boots on the ground ready to react to real time information that we receive about JM and his location in Guadalajara.
>
> Our goal is to activate an ad campaign in this area and then respond to leads immediately.
>
> We would like to flip the switch Tuesday morning.
>
> How do you feel about all of this and can you help?
>
> Thank you
>
> JB
>
> PS: When I read about the use of open source DNA on the Golden State case, I thought you might be involved…

"Let's do it!" I wrote back. "I'm at the ready for Tuesday morning."

"Super," he replied.

Santa Cruz Del Valle: ¿Has visto a este hombre?

I listed all the murder suspect's specifics. His red hair. His height. His tattoo. What he was wanted for. The phone number for the San Jose police department and, of course, the *recompensa*.

The ad was ready, waiting for Tuesday morning to hit *publish*.

I navigated through CrimeCon and the two thousand predominantly female attendees who packed the ballroom to hear our Golden State Killer talk. The biggest problem with true crime has always been its imbalance of villains to heroes. True crime is full of supervillains: Manson, Bundy, Gacy. But the superheroes are rarely acknowledged. They are anonymous civil servants. I always wanted that to change. And I wanted to give Paul Holes the rock-star introduction he was denied at the press conference. We brought him out, and he got a standing ovation.

The rest of the convention was not quite Beatlemania, but it was close. The last night, a bunch of podcasters fled the theme park–like atmosphere of the convention center for a meet-up at a bar on Broadway in downtown Nashville. After a couple of hours, I made an Irish exit and walked to the loading docks of the Country Music Hall of Fame.

I found the exact spot the surveillance video was trained on when Teddy Grasset and his friend were walking before the car with the glowing blue license plate holder crept up behind them. I followed the steps they ran as they were chased by the two men. They must have run right past a sprawling Johnny Cash mural, its peeling paint chips littering the sidewalk below, before Teddy was murdered.

The next day, I was back in Los Angeles. On Tuesday morning, I got the go-ahead from Barg. I hit *publish*, and the campaign to find our fugitive was live.

Three hours later, I got a series of texts from Barg.

"Shut it down now, buddy."

"Right Now."

"We have a live one."

He sent a new photo. It was Miller, staring straight into the camera, almost attacking it. He was a lot thinner and had what looked like white powder on his nose.

"Roger that," I replied. "Did they see the new post?"

"Oh, yeah. The phone lines exploded. I don't want to get him spooked."

I quickly deleted the ad. We had gone through this exercise before: we didn't want any of his friends or family to see the post on Facebook and warn him that the search was heating up. So it was gone.

Four hours later, Barg wrote back.

"Bad news. Our guy went sideways. Let's crank it back up. We need more tipsters."

I created a new ad, set the parameters, and boosted a run for two days at two hundred bucks. This was a short game. I wanted to give it all we had. I just wouldn't eat a steak for a while. The small radius meant we would hit about 80 percent of the Facebook users in the area.

Barg texted me three hours later.

"We have new intel. Can we re-center the location of the ad? Close, but a few blocks over."

He gave me the coordinates, and I shifted the ad over about a half mile.

Tipsters started calling in again. Some asking for money up front. Some obviously fakes.

I kept checking the messages on Facebook. I had gotten very little. Everyone was using the phone number.

Then I saw a message.

It was in Spanish. I began talking to the tipster, jumping back and forth between the Facebook app and Google Translate. After fifteen minutes, I was able to convince them to give me their phone number. I texted it to John.

"They want you to call them."

John rustled up his partner who speaks Spanish.

"We are calling him now… He sounds nervous… My Spanish speaking partner is smiling and giving me a huge thumbs up. So that's a good sign."

Ten minutes went by. John texted back. "Great info. Positive ID. He gave us the neighborhood. We are waiting on the exact address and phone number."

Then I waited. And waited. The day turned into night. I guess the info wasn't that great.

But the next morning, I didn't get a text from Barg. I got a call.

He didn't even say hello.

"We got him," he said.

Hell yes!

"You have no idea the shit we had to pull together to make this happen," he said. "It was ridiculous. But all started with that ad in Maz… Great job and thank you."

No one would know about this one. No press conference. No fanfare. No *Good Morning America*.

He is suspected of killing a father of two. Not the numbers of the Golden State Killer. But he ripped a family apart. One of fifteen thousand that are ripped apart every year by a callous killer.

Later in the day, Barg sent over a photo of the fugitive, black handcuffs sitting atop the tattoo on his hand.

"A beautiful sight," I wrote back.

───────────────

I was exhausted. It had been ten days of little sleep and lots of celebratory toasts. I collapsed on my bed.

I woke up at 2:00 a.m., as usual.

I went to open up YouTube to watch some more unsolved murder videos, searching for another case to work from my bed. I was going to miss all the hubbub of the last few weeks. Not only for the solve but just for being around other people. I was back to doing this on my own again. Starting up another Facebook campaign to identify another murder suspect. Adding another few hundred to the $13,000 balance on my credit card. Wondering if this idea of crowdsolving would ever catch on and I could get some help to solve those 199,990 unsolved murders that I haven't gotten to.

But first I opened up my Twitter feed. I had seen my follower list spike since the news of the Golden State Killer's capture, and seeing all the retweets and comments from people was satisfying after tweeting for so long into the darkness to just a few thousand followers who were probably mostly bots. I read all the comments, then opened my messages.

Inside the inbox, I saw notes from friends. People offering congratulations and wanting to go out for more drinks to celebrate. One victim's daughter from an older case, my first editor, John Mancini, a theme-park designer friend of mine.

I was about to open up YouTube to search for my case when I looked over at the "Requests" tab inside Twitter messages. If you don't know the sender, this is where their messages go. Few people really ever check it.

I clicked on it. And my page lit up.

Hi Billy! I've been a Computer Forensics Investigator for four years. I have an MS in Cyber Forensics. I really support the work you are doing to encourage all of the able and willing sleuths interested in helping to solve cold cases! I would love to be a part of what you are doing.

Hi Billy, I heard you talking about a pilot program you were hoping a state might try out in which citizens who pass a simple background check do data mining work on a volunteer basis for cold cases. Can you please get back to me with more info about this? Perhaps I will propose it to my superiors as draft legislation for a future legislative session here in Connecticut.

Hi Billy. I'm an entrepreneur and run a software company and would love to help on the project any way I can.

Hi Billy. I have become fascinated with what you've promoted as "internet sleuthing." I'm an engineer and a masters student and have found myself with a lot of time on my hands. I want to do something productive with it. My brother was killed and his killer was never brought to justice, so I know first-hand how it feels to be a family member with no closure. I'd like to help in any way that I can.

There were dozens of them. All people with skills. All wanting to help. Mini Michelle McNamaras everywhere, all wanting to spend their every waking moment to help solve a crime. The army, the one I needed to take on the villain with a thousand faces, was going to happen. I was no longer going to have to do this alone.

I wrote all of them back, telling them that we would start working on building something that could bring a lot more justice to the families who need it. If we could do this right, we could solve so many unsolved murders.

Then I opened up my computer and ran through my cases.

I still needed to find the Girl with the Serpent Tattoo. And build the timeline for Rasmussen. And uncover all the places Joseph DeAngelo has been. And find the Owl's Head Park Killer. And on, and on, and on.

The End.

No. It's not the end. There can never be an end to this story. We still have more than hundreds of thousands of murders to solve and tens of thousands of missing persons to find. So come on. Let's start.

But for the purpose of this chapter, I'll play along.

The End.

EPILOGUE

Los Angeles, 2018

IT'S WELL PAST 1:00 A.M. ON A WARM TUESDAY NIGHT IN MAY, and I'm rifling through old newspaper archives, searching for any information I can find about Long Island tattoo parlors that have since gone out of business. In 1997, the torso of a woman with a tattoo of a heart-shaped peach with a bite taken out of its side was found in Hempstead Lake State Park, not far from where I grew up. She was still missing a name. The detectives called her "Peaches."

I first covered her story in 2002 in the *Long Island Press*. I would check back in on her every few years, but she remained nameless.

Then fifteen years after the story ran, there was a glimmer of hope.

They tested her DNA against bones that were found in 2011 near Jones Beach State Park. It was a match. Someone had killed Peaches and distributed pieces of her across two parks in Nassau County, New York.

They still didn't know her name, but at least two mysteries had now become one.

Until they got another match.

The DNA of the remains of a toddler found near Jones Beach lined up with Peaches. She was a mother. And she was murdered along with her child. And detectives believed they were now both part of the Long Island Serial Killer investigation.

That was in December 2016. And tonight, we still had no idea who they were or who killed them. I broke out the credit card and entered the paywall of *Newsday* archives, going through old advertisements of tattoo parlors, hoping I might be able to track down someone who might have worked there and see if they could recognize Peaches's tattoo. It's a shot in the dark, something to do before I can convince the authorities to let me help connect them with someone who could perform a familial DNA search.

Three hours of looking at grainy newsprint images, and my brain began to wander.

I started looking at the other stories on the pages: students arrested in protests, ads for *Jaws*, Commodore desk calculators, and fancy, big-lapelled suits.

I was ready to call it a night when I decided to look for something else. That article my dad had told me about during that bedtime story when I was six. The one where he punched a detective and was arrested and refused to give his name, so they ran his photo with the headline Do You Know This Man? I had looked for it before but never found it.

I couldn't search under his name, since the fact that his identity was unknown was the whole point of the article. I had to try keywords. *Unidentified. Punched. Detective. Arrested. Teenager.* I came up empty-handed. I remembered the tattoo-covered kid my dad had bought the driver's license from before he ran away to California. I tried "Chris Keer." "Christopher Keer."

Still nothing.

Maybe I had the date ranges wrong. Maybe it was in another news-paper. Maybe my dad was telling me a tall tale just to get me to go to sleep. I was about to give up, when it occurred to me that I had no idea how Chris Keer might have spelled his name.

I searched *Christopher Kear*, K-E-A-R, and got one result.

I clicked on the link and came face-to-face with my dad.

His intense eyes were burning through the black-and-white photo, his expression at the same time both scared and angry. It was the only picture I have ever seen of him without his mustache. CHRISTOPHER KEAR? read the caption. POLICE STILL NEED NAME read the headline.

"Suffolk detectives yesterday hit another big roadblock in trying to find out who the real Christopher Kear is. It seems that the FBI doesn't know either.

"First Squad detectives said an FBI report they received said the bureau had no record of the fingerprints of an arrested man who claims to be Christopher Kear of 25 Elwood Ave., Hicksville. Police said the Christopher Kear they tracked down at that address is currently in Kings Park State Hospital. And he's got fingerprints and the testimony of relatives to prove it.

"Consequently, police still have a man who claims he is Kear in jail awaiting a hearing next week on a third-degree assault charge. When first arrested Aug. 26 by First Squad Commander Det. Lt. John Biscardi for allegedly punching the officer in the face, the man identified himself as Christopher Kear, 20. But during a preliminary court hearing Wednesday, he refused to give his name or address."

The cops didn't have a clue who he was. The FBI didn't have a clue who he was. They turned to their last resort to find out who he was. They turned to the crowd. I printed out the page and hung it on my wall, my dad's face looking down at me in the middle of all the pictures of the men I'm trying to find.

I smile every time I see it.

ADDENDUM

So You Want to Help Solve a Murder?

> "I am not the law, but I represent justice so far as my feeble powers go."
>
> —Sherlock Holmes

IF YOU'VE GOTTEN THIS FAR AND WANT TO KEEP READING, I'm guessing you may be interested in helping to solve a murder. You might be the type of person who walks down the sidewalk and spots a piece of paper with handwriting on it and picks it up because it *might* be a clue to a crime. Or you see a single flip-flop underneath a sixth-floor balcony, look up, and wonder when exactly its owner jumped.

You dig into every crime story you hear. You put pieces together and think you could deliver to the police the exact picture of what happened. Well, are you ready to get messy? Are you ready for long days of no answers? Ready to bite your tongue when you want to lash out?

Are you ready to shout into the abyss?

Did you answer *yes* to all these questions? Fantastic. You've taken your first step as a crimesolver.

Did you answer *no*? Well, ride shotgun with me, and maybe you'll change your mind.

But if you're looking for a casual hobby, this ain't it. Attempting to solve a crime will consume a good chunk of your time. The intense nature of the subject and the stakes will take their toll on your relationships, your job, and your faith in humanity. But I truly believe citizens like you can help solve the backlog of unsolved murders, violent assaults, and missing persons.

And if you're in any sector of law enforcement or public policy and you are scoffing at the idea that ordinary citizens can solve a crime, I'm asking you to suspend your disbelief and hear me out.

The professional detective has only been around for two hundred years. Police departments were formed in the early nineteenth century not to investigate but to control mobs and riots. Before that, serious crimes in most areas were solved by private citizens or the local doctor or judge.

In America, the clearance rate for murders dropped from 93 percent in 1960 to 62 percent in 2017. Stranger murders, a transient population, lack of public willingness to talk to the police, drugs, and a lot more guns are the main reasons for the decline.

Murders are much harder to solve today. That means investigations take longer and use more resources. And ask any police department why so many crimes go unsolved, and the answer you will receive more than any other is this: we don't have the resources.

"What's going to happen is that you're going to have fewer police trying to solve just as much crime," criminologist Jay Albanese of Virginia Commonwealth University told the *Christian Science Monitor* in 2008. "If that's the scenario, you can't just continue doing what you're doing now, or you'll continue to slowly slide backward." We are in the middle of that slide.

But there is hope. The most talented and educated retirees history has ever seen—the baby boomers—are searching for a pastime with a purpose. So are their Gen X children and the millennials. Many are more than willing to donate their time and considerable skills to help clear cold cases. Law enforcement needs to use them. Set up a civilian liaison in your local police department, and get volunteers to digitize old handwritten police reports and locate newspaper clippings, giving your detectives the ability to locate particulars and suspects of older crimes with a database search instead of spending days thumbing through the files in the basement. We are not talking about ancient crimes here—there are some departments who have crimes from the late twentieth century still sitting in old boxes, waiting to be destroyed by a flood or thrown away during the next move of police headquarters.

Why should all the details of these old crimes be digitized? Every day, thousands of people are adding their DNA to public databases. But those third-cousin familial DNA matches we're all chasing since the Golden State Killer opened the floodgates will only be as good as the post-match genealogy and background research of the family trees. Amateur genealogists know how to build family trees; they can connect that long-lost cousin from one part of the world to the killer you are looking for just a few miles away. The genealogist can then give their findings from the family tree to the detective, who can search the database for the names on that tree and potentially come up with a match, a suspect from a list of a hundred suspects that they had a hunch about a few decades ago but didn't have enough evidence to make an arrest. From there, the detective can work to get a sample of the suspect's DNA and match it to the sample from the crime scene. Then an arrest can be made.

That evidence sitting in evidence lockers and old files is a bonfire of hope, burning ridiculously bright now that familial DNA matches are in play. The needles in the haystack are now buzzing, glowing, bouncing up and down, screaming to be found. We just have to look for them using these new tools.

But why train citizen volunteers? Why not just hire an army of data entry personnel?

First off, many agencies don't have the money to pay their detectives, much less pay a bunch of civilians to work on older crimes that were not committed under the current administration's watch and aren't included in their annual crimesolving reports.

That's the practical reason—money. But there is also precedent for using volunteers in our criminal justice system.

Our entire criminal justice system is constructed on a foundation of crowdsourcing. It is put into practice thousands of times each day in America. Housewives and grocery clerks and IT workers and farmers are called upon to take part. It's called the jury system.

And while the system can be manipulated, cajoled, twisted, pulled, and stretched every which way, after forty-four thousand years of civilization, it is the best humanity has come up with when it comes to determining someone's guilt or innocence. Twelve ordinary people in a room, presented all the facts in the case by trained professionals, and then asked to render judgment. The jury system is a marvel, as inefficient as it is fair. Inefficient because in a case of murder, if eleven people say guilty and one says innocent, you have to start the whole thing all over again. And yet it has worked better than anything else.

These twelve people are not required to pass a test on forensics or police procedure or the constitution, nor do they have any skills or background in the subjects presented to them. In fact, having knowledge and skills—being a former police officer or journalist, for instance—will often get you tossed out of the jury pool before they ask if you've read any news about the case in question.

Most every murder case that goes to trial ends with crowdsourcing via the jury system. And yet coming up with excuses for not participating in the process has become a tired punchline in an America filled with people who are too busy to go participate in this system but wonder why the murder clearance rate is at an all-time low.

If you've ever avoided jury duty, here's what I'd like you to do. Close this book or press stop on your phone or tell Alexa to pause, turn it on its side, and hit yourself square in the nose with it. Then come right back to this location.

I'll wait.

Nothing is more important than making things right—or at least as right as they can be righted. Remember that sting the next time you get that jury summons. And the government should treat jury duty like short-term disability—no one should ever lose salary or be threatened with the loss of their job by doing their public duty.

The person out there with information about a murder or missing person who refuses to say anything is a sibling of the jury dodger. You cannot rely on the next person to do it.

Now then, where were we? Ah, yes. You want to solve a crime.

First, let me ask you. What is your call to adventure?

The question I get the most—after "Do you think you can find the Zodiac Killer now?"—is "Why do you do this?"

I never think about it, except when people ask. The best answer I can give is a question.

"How can I not?"

I simply cannot fathom that one person believes they can have such dominion over another that they can take away a life. And I cannot fathom that person living life free of consequence. If people didn't kill each other,

I would go build playgrounds and theme restaurants or invent the Happy Meal of the future or something. But I do this. Because how can I not?

There are a lot of people like me, both professionals and amateurs, invested in solving crimes. And every one of us has that one case. You probably have one. That one case that grabbed you by the throat one day and still hasn't let go. We have different names for that case. "My obsession." "My favorite murder." "My white whale."

Okay, I'll admit, I have a few. The Rainbow Murders. The Humboldt Five. The Allenstown Four.

But since I've started the crowd-solving endeavor you just read about, my white whale has been the Owl's Head Park murderer.

I didn't just wake up one morning and get obsessed with the case. It built with every sentence I read about it. With every frame I watched of the suspect. Every pause. Every screen grab. Every enhancement.

This guy walking the streets after allegedly killing a woman, not a care in the world.

But all the time and effort and hate and money spent isn't the reason. The reason Owl's Head Park is my white whale came in the form of that four-word Facebook comment the campaign received one day.

That was my mom.

That little boy lost his mom to a monster. When I saw that, I knew I was going to be looking for that monster for the rest of my life.

Your white whale is different from your origin story. Michelle's white whale was the Golden State Killer. But her origin story can be traced back to her childhood, when she knelt down in an alley in her hometown and held in her hands the pieces of a shattered Walkman that a murder victim had left behind.

My origin story goes back to my dad showing me the front page of the newspaper with the word CAUGHT! over the photo of Son of Sam and him telling me, "They got him."

Your origin story is tucked somewhere in the recesses of your mind. Go ahead and think about it. Ask your parents about events you might have forgotten. If you bought this book, you probably have an origin story that's implanted within you.

Then you have your call to adventure. The moment that pulled you out of your regular life and thrust you into a whole new world.

You can have more than one. The death of Michelle, fueled by my search of the villain with a thousand faces, coupled with seventeen years of writing stories with no endings, all shook me out of place. They stood on top of each other to reach the light bulb above my head when I came up with the idea of merging my day job and my night passion and using social media to solve the crimes you just read about.

You are going to be thinking about your origin story. Your call to adventure. And eventually, you will have a white whale. God help you. 'Cause they can all lead to obsession.

You might want to go down the familial DNA/genealogy road on your own. You will find information on how to sign up for the pilot programs I am working on creating in various police departments on my website, billyjensen.com. If you cannot find a local program, try to start one, volunteering to do everything from data entry to hand-digitizing old police reports. Each department will have their own rules and requirements—you may have to be sworn in, undergo background checks, etc. Or you can also try some of the techniques I'm going to show you to try to solve a murder yourself.

But we need to lay down some rules.

Crowdsourcing can be the most powerful tool next to DNA to help solve cold cases. But all it will take is one mistake to destroy the opportunity.

If you want to be a hero, you have to have a code.

Rule Number 1: Never Name Names in Public

When you're investigating potential suspects, never name names on Facebook, Twitter, Instagram, or blog posts. Under no circumstances should you name someone or provide a link or a photo of a person you "think" might be the man or woman who committed the crime you are trying to help solve. This is the biggest rule. If you don't follow it, you are not only going to hamper an investigation but also potentially ruin an innocent person's life.

Say you're working a murder case. You have a surveillance video of a man who killed a woman in an alley behind a liquor store. You set up a campaign and get a tip with a photo of someone who looks a lot like the suspect in the video. I mean, he's a dead ringer. You see on the man's Instagram account that he had tagged a photo from a bar near the crime scene the very night of the murder. You take screen grabs of the video and compare them with his Facebook profile pic. You look at more pics, watch the video again and again, and each time, you get more and more excited. *This is the guy!* you say to yourself. You want to yell it to the world.

Don't. Take all the information, write it up in a clear and concise manner, and deliver it to the detective in charge.

Say two weeks pass, and there is still no arrest. Check back in with the detective and inquire. But *do not post anything about the person you think may be the suspect*. If you are right, they might run. If you are wrong, you might be ruining a life, possibly your own.

Say you are running a social media campaign, and a commenter posts a link to a profile of a person. "Could it be this guy?" they ask atop the link. Take a screen grab of the post, delete the post, and message the commenter directly. Take the conversation off-line.

If the police don't make an arrest, there is usually a reason. If months and months go by and they have not even verified that they got your information, you could go to a journalist. Or email me, and we can strategize.

Naming names in public—or worse, actually messaging the person you suspect is responsible for the crime—crosses the line into irresponsible and dangerous vigilantism. And there is a clear line between what we want to do and being a vigilante.

Even though the vigilante and the establishment are after the same aims (peace and justice), the establishment rejects people taking the law into their own hands. Self-policing could work in a smaller society in which every member is educated and trained and has a common belief system. But in a large society, it invariably leads to chaos. Look at any comments string below a crime story on Facebook and that will become tragically clear:

Kill him, no trial!

It's a mental health issue.

You don't know what your talking about.

Learn how to spell "you're."

You see? Chaos.

"But aren't a lot of our superheroes vigilantes?" you ask. "Batman is always called a vigilante. And I want to be Batman."

Yes, we all want to be Batman. But you can't be the rogue Batman who plays by his own rules. You have to be the Adam West Batman. The Batman who is a stickler for the laws laid out by the society he serves. If you don't like the laws, then vote to change them. But if this is going to work, he's the example we must follow, old chum.

In the last five years, people have become more analytical and more detective-like than ever before while digging into real-life crimes.

Information on the cases, along with the contact information for the people involved, is spread across the internet. You can snoop from afar, but you can't insert yourself into anyone's lives, because it can lead to pain and danger.

In that crowdsourcing panel Michelle and I delivered at SXSW in Austin, we talked about the most notable crowdsourcing failure. In the aftermath of the Boston Marathon bombing, members of Reddit created the subReddit group /findbostonbombers, tossing a dragnet across the internet and catching both good and bad information in the process. The crowdsourcing effort was able to identify some clues even before the FBI, but it also faltered when members started publicly naming names. A web search had revealed a Facebook page and YouTube video of a family desperately searching for their loved one, a Brown University student named Sunil Tripathi who had gone missing a month earlier. When the FBI released photos of the suspects that Thursday after the bombing, one had a passing resemblance to Tripathi. Users started typing their suspicions out loud that Tripathi was the bomber. Mainstream media picked up on the conjecture and published the name. Tripathi's body was found on April 23, floating in the Seekonk River in Providence. No foul play was suspected. He had nothing to do with the bombing.

Whenever someone attempts to start a debate on the merits of crowdsourcing investigations, a detractor tosses in the Boston bombing as a conversation ender. Only positive examples of real results can change that. A bunch of people reading this book and repeating those mistakes will only keep more cases in the cold—and a hurt a lot more people.

By 2014, the public was ready to wrap their arms around true crime, which led to readers and listeners and watchers no longer being content with just sitting on the sidelines. They wanted to solve the crimes themselves.

The podcast *Serial* told the story of nineteen-year-old Hae Min Lee, a high school student in suburban Baltimore who went missing one day in 1999. Her body was found a month later in a haphazardly made grave. Suspicion was leveled at her ex-boyfriend, fellow high school student Adnan Syed. Syed was arrested, tried, and convicted of her murder. He was found guilty not with an abundance of physical evidence but rather on the damning testimony of his friend, Jay, who said he helped Syed dispose of the body after Syed murdered Lee over a breakup.

Once-passive listeners had morphed into detectives, plotting the routes from the library to the park where Lee's body was found, investigating if the local Best Buy really did have a pay phone, the billing patterns for a 1999 potential butt dial, and how it could have affected the Nisha call.

The seed was planted. By the time *Making a Murderer* hit Netflix in 2015, the citizen sleuth was addicted. Thousands of people scoured the internet for every sliver of evidence they could find. *The Jinx. The Keepers. My Favorite Murder, Case File, Last Podcast on the Left...* The public knows *a lot* more about crime and investigative techniques than they did before the Boston bombing. But we need to harness that skill and not make any mistakes.

And even if the person you found *is* guilty, do you really want to post something that could lead to a horrible outcome?

When sixty-three-year-old Brenda Leyland was found dead in a hotel room in Leicestershire, England, police searched for her name online and found it on a website called McCann Hate Exposed. Much like JonBenét Ramsey's parents in the States, the McCanns have been subject to immeasurable internet trolling since their daughter went missing from a Portugal holiday apartment in 2007. Using the handle @sweepyface, Leyland took to Twitter at least forty-three hundred times to talk about the crime and implicate the parents of little Madeleine. The McCann Hate Exposed page had "doxxed" Leyland and twenty-six other Twitter users who had been trolling the parents of Madeleine McCann. The site published Leyland's private information for anyone to see.

After a TV news crew showed up at her door to ask her about the trolling, Leyland fled town, checked into a hotel, and killed herself.

Finding out information about someone you think is guilty is what we are trying to do. Publishing it on the internet for all to see, exploit, and possibly use for nefarious deeds is not. Collect the information and send it to the detective in charge.

Rule Number 2: Do Not Expect to Get Credit

"Okay, I'll follow the rules," you say. "But what if I do all this work, get a great tip, send it to the police, and they make an arrest? No one will know I got the guy. What if I don't get credit for helping solve the case?"

My answer to you: I feel your pain, but get in line.

We all want credit. You will be spending hundreds, if not thousands, of hours on cases if you go all in. You will experience failure after failure. When you finally see something come to fruition, you will want to shout it from the rooftops. If you can get credit, that's great. But whether you do or not is entirely up to the detectives. Some are willing to say that the success of the job was a team effort with multiple factors and multiple people pitching in, and others will take all the credit for themselves or their internal team. If they don't thank you or call you out, don't take it personally.

So be pragmatic when it comes to credit. The bad guy is in bracelets. That's the most important thing. The victim's family will know how much work you did, and so will you.

Rule Number 3: Be Safe

Investigating crime is not a game. It can get very real, very quick. You need to take precautions and know when to say when.

Set up new Facebook, Twitter, and Instagram accounts separate from your personal accounts. Do not share information about yourself, other than the fact that you are a victim's advocate helping the family. And never go "undercover."

Marie Parent was a Scottish grandmother living in Quebec and taking a private detective course. When it came time to choose a final assignment, she looked into the case of Louise Ellis, a journalist who went missing in 1995. Parent cozied up to the main suspect in the case, Ellis's boyfriend, Brett Morgan, already a convicted killer. She spent time with him at his house. She recorded conversations. Police learned of Parent via the wiretap they had running on Morgan's phone and asked if she would go undercover to catch him. She agreed. She got close. Too close. She kissed him "four or five times," she said. He finally took her to where he dumped Ellis's body.

In those woods, Parent thought she was going to be murdered herself when Morgan put his hands around her neck…to tie a bandana around it as a gift. But she had uncovered enough info to nail him. Police offered her a reward of less than $5,000. She couldn't even find a job as a private detective afterward, saying that she had "showed up" all the PIs in the area. This was some *Silence of the Lambs* shit—using a trainee to catch a killer.

Dr. Maria del Rosario Fuentes Rubio was not so lucky. Rubio was a general practitioner living in Reynosa, Mexico. But on Twitter, the thirty-six-year-old mother used the pseudonym Felina (Catwoman) and posted detailed information about the drug cartel violence that was taking over her city. People followed her less to rubberneck than to know which areas to avoid getting trapped in if a shoot-out erupted. She often sent out her reports in real time, as they happened. The cartel felt this put their members in peril, not to mention the fact that Rubio often tweeted out cheers when cartel members were struck down.

The cartel told her to stop. They threatened her life. She didn't back down.

In October 2014, they kidnapped her and commandeered her Twitter account. "Friends and family, my real name is Maria del Rosario Fuentes Rubio," they tweeted. "I am a doctor. Today my life has reached its end. I have nothing left but to say to you all, don't make the same mistake I have. You will gain nothing by it. To the contrary, today I realize that I have found my death in exchange for nothing. They are closer to us than you think."

"Shut down your accounts," read the next post. "Do not risk your families' lives as I have done."

Her captors posted photos. One showed the face of a woman, clearly understanding that she was going to die. The next showed the same woman with a bullet in her head.

If you are threatened, tell the police. Being a citizen investigator is not worth dying over.

There are your three rules. They should, of course, work in tandem with the rules you should be living by every day: Be kind. Be true. Don't be an ass. Use your head.

And don't be rude or dox other citizen detectives you encounter on Twitter, Reddit, or other message boards that you don't agree with. Don't show up at people's houses or places of work.

If you want to grab a bunch of friends or your book club and tackle a case, that could be great. Get that one friend or family member who spends too much time analyzing the *Bachelor* or *Real Housewives* (they know who they are) and pull them in as well. Create a private Facebook group, split up tasks, pool your money to start a campaign, drink some wine, and who knows, maybe you might actually solve one.

How to Choose Your First Case

So you have your rules. But there are five thousand unsolved murders every year in the United States and fifty thousand missing-persons cases. Where do you start?

Start in your own neck of the woods. Location is key to so many crimes, and you're going to know the ins and outs of your town or city or county. If you are effective within your city/county/state, you will begin to earn the trust of law enforcement. It's a great feeling when you don't have to cold-call a department every time you have a case you want to work. And if you help them clear some cases, they will start contacting you, looking for help.

Start by scanning local news websites for unsolved crimes for which police have released a photo or video of the suspect or persons of interest but still don't have any answers. Don't just stick with murder. For many people, murders in your town may, thankfully, be few and far between. That doesn't mean you can't help. Hit-and-runs, sexual assaults, robberies—these are all crimes you could go after if the clues are good enough.

Set up Google news alerts for terms like *police*, *identify*, *surveillance video*, and *suspect*, plus the names of all your local towns and counties. If you want to be on the alert for missing persons, the alert should read *last seen* and *missing*.

You might want to sign up for a new dedicated Gmail for all your alerts to keep them separate from your personal account, as they will add up.

When you get an email alert, open the link and check out the story. Watch or read it a bunch of times. And then wait. Monitor the story. Set up a Google alert for the victim's name. But let it breath for a bit. I typically only act after three to four weeks from the time the story ran or the police asked the media for help. Then I call the detective. By that time, if they are still looking for answers, it means they are probably stuck.

A quick scan of a recent Google alerts looks like this:

PD: MAN ARRESTED FOR MURDER OF MOTHER, STEPFATHER LINKED TO 7 OTHER PHOENIX-AREA MURDERS

BODY DISCOVERED ALONG MONTEBELLO BIKE PATH; MURDER INVESTIGATION UNDERWAY

POLICE REQUEST PUBLIC'S HELP IN LAWRENCE MURDER INVESTIGATION

The story about the man arrested and linked to seven other murders in Phoenix was caught in this alert thanks to the keywords *police*, *identify*, and *surveillance video*. But it is clear: they have already caught the guy.

The body on the bike path is a next-day story about a body found with head trauma in Montebello, California. There is no video and not many other details. I could open a campaign, but there is not really much to go on to both capture someone's attention in the split second you need to on social media and to get that someone to contact you with actionable information.

The last one, about police needing the public's help in a murder investigation in Lawrence, Massachusetts, is much more promising. A click on the link reveals a story about twenty-five-year-old Mindy Tran, who was found shot to death in a crashed car on Hillside Avenue on November 26, 2017.

The accompanying video looks to be shot with a black-and-white surveillance camera, pointed toward a private yard with a street in the background. At twenty-seven seconds, two individuals enter the frame from the left, walking in the street. One is wearing light pants and looks to have his hands in the pockets of a dark hoodie. The other is wearing a light-colored top. By thirty-eight seconds, they are out of the frame. At forty-two seconds (the footage has been edited), you see the two individuals again, this time as blurs running from left to right and then out of the frame again.

The video isn't great. Someone wouldn't be able to identify the people if they just casually knew them from the neighborhood. And we have no rallying point, such as a store or restaurant where people often go and would have stories about that they would want to share. But if the persons of interest are walking in this neighborhood, they might very well be local. And the police aren't looking for a car, which doesn't generate nearly as many comments as videos of people, even if they are far away.

I would run this as a one-mile radius friends/family/enemies campaign. It would be geared less to find people to identify the individuals from the video and more to catching a person who might have heard something in the neighborhood about someone who was shot to death in their car and might have a hunch about who the shooter could have been. But we're getting ahead of ourselves. First, we need to ask the family and the police for permission.

Reach Out to the Family

The family is hurting. They want justice. And they are angry. Find them via Facebook or through a Google white pages' search. Introduce yourself as a victim's advocate. Don't call yourself a journalist or a blogger or a citizen detective. Tell them you are sorry for their loss. Explain your method. A lot of them won't get it. Say you want to help and you are not charging them any money. Repeat, you are not charging them any money. And you will not collect any reward. The reward, if any, is for the tipster. (And don't ask them to pay for the ad. This is all out of your pocket.) Tell them it's worked before—describe it as a digital wanted poster that can hit every Facebook or Twitter or Instagram user in town. Tell them the odds aren't great, but it can only help. If they tell you no, reply "Thank you for your time, and again, I'm sorry for your loss," and move on to the next case. If they tell you yes, ask them to inform family and friends that they will be seeing images of the people who killed their loved one on their social feed if they live in the area. It can be a real shock to them if they aren't warned.

Next, do the same thing with the detective working the case. He might stop you right there and say "we don't need any help."

That's great. Yes, you've just spent a few hours going through cases, finding one, looking at the video, and finding the right detective to call. It's happened to me a lot. Be happy. The bad guy is on his way to being caught.

But if the police need help, tell them you don't charge anything. Tell them that there is this guy who has had success with this technique and wrote a book about it and thinks a lot of murders can be solved this way. Tell them you don't want a reward. That you do this to help victims' families. Tell them that you will send any tips that come your way.

If it is a missing-persons case, they often will jump at the chance for any help. They want to spread the word far and wide, and they are more comfortable with you putting up what are tantamount to smart digital missing-persons posters than trying to find a killer. In fact, in my experience, there was only one time a family declined. If you do start a missing-persons campaign, you have a huge responsibility. It is a 24/7 job. Someone who might have information might make a comment or send a message, and you need to respond immediately and get the information to both the family and the authorities. It is not for the faint of heart. If you cannot devote the intense time, please don't do it.

Build Your Campaign

First, you need a Facebook profile. Facebook is on the outs with young people, and I kick myself every day, wishing I had come up with this idea eight years ago when the kids were still active. But people still use it more than any other website outside of Google and YouTube. It is where they organize their activities and communicate with others. Facebook also had the forethought to buy Instagram, which is where many young people have migrated, along with Snapchat.

But our hub is going to be Facebook. From your Facebook page, click on the triangle at the top right of the page and scroll down to the *create a page* link. After you click, you'll be presented with two options: create a business page or a community page. Click the *get started* button under the community option. You will be asked to name your page. In the same way you first look at the sender whenever you get an email, your name is one of the first things people will see, and you need to make it count. "El Monte Jack in the Box Killer" was clear and concise. It gave people the town, the location, and the jarring effect of *Killer*. "River North Puncher" was close, but to be honest, I should have mentioned 7-Eleven or the intersection in the title. "Inkster Shooter at Fast Franks Party Shop" was another I used to find a killer at a local—and notorious—liquor store in Inkster, Michigan. For the Girl with the Serpent Tattoo, I used "Justice: Searching for Tampa Bay Tattooed Female," just to try to get everyone who saw it to rack their brains for all the women they know with tattoos, then they would look at the image and see where the tattoo was placed.

For one that caught a killer in Southern California, I used the names of two neighborhoods, then a question: "La Puente/Bassett: Do you Know Me?" You are grabbing the users' attention by mentioning their neighborhood. Then you are giving them a call to action.

If you are looking for a missing person, use "Have you seen" or "Where is" then the missing person's name. "Have you seen Jamie Harroun?"

Then you have to pick a category, which is a new Facebook requirement. I often choose *website*. If you choose something else, they will start asking for things like addresses.

Now you need to add a profile picture. For Marques Gaines's case in Chicago, I spent about ten minutes trying to grab the perfect screenshot of the Man in the Green Hoodie before I captured the best one to use. It's not always going to be perfect. It just has to be the best one you can capture that someone might see and say, "Hmm, I might know that guy." If you have a sketch, roll with that.

For a missing person, use the most recent photo that the family is using. So often, I have seen people use older photos of missing persons, either because they are the quickest ones to access or their missing loved one looks the best in them. The pictures going out into the world need to be the best representation of what the person looks like right now. As I did with Morgan Bauer, ask for video of the missing person to use in the ad. People can change their hair, but they rarely change their voice or mannerisms.

Upload the pic. Facebook will ask you for a cover photo. Here, I like to use a map of the area I am looking for information from. You could also use Google Street View photos.

Upload, and your page is set. Now you have to build your post. This is the most important step.

Start writing a post and adding a video or photo as you would on your personal page.

Your words are key. You need to grab people. You need to be conversational. But the image—either still or moving—is most important. Marques Gaines in Chicago, Pacman in Chesapeake, White Boy Q in Tallahassee, the Halloween Mask Murder in El Monte. All had engaging copy and compelling video.

For Marques Gaines's murder in Chicago, I took on the persona of the puncher himself, the Man in the Green Hoodie. This was my first, and it's a technique I use sparingly.

This is the video where I punch a stranger—a stranger who later dies. It was taken 4:20 a.m. on Sunday, Feb. 7 outside the 7-Eleven on State and Hubbard in River North, Chicago. I am the man in the green hooded jacket and white sneakers. (The man who died is in the blue shirt. He just went to the store for some chips.) If you know my name or anything about me—anything at all—please message me here or leave a comment. If you don't have any information, but have friends in Chicago, please share. His family desperately wants answers.

With Pacman's murder in Chesapeake, I gave the reader a task:

Watch the way this man walks. Look at his thin frame. He is a murder suspect, wanted in the killing of a good man in the South Norfolk neighborhood of Chesapeake, VA in early August. Do you recognize him? Maybe someone who you haven't seen around for a while, who left town in August? Please message with any information, no matter how small. Please.

Teddy Grasset's murder in Nashville was the same. You, the reader, have a job:

See these two men walking? In a few seconds, one of them will be dead. See that car pulling up behind them? Do you know anyone who recently drove a Silver Chevy Impala with a glowing blue license plate holder? Watch the two men get out of that car. Do you recognize them? This happened behind the Country Music Hall of Fame in Nashville on Sept. 25. Please message with any information. And please share.

But the key is this: you are not looking for the suspect. You are looking for people who might know the suspect.

That's a small but significant difference. It opens up your search from one person to around two hundred. When I look at a suspect, no matter how blurry they are, I ask that one question: who might know him?

So write the post and add the photo and video, but instead of hitting *publish*, hit *boost post*.

You will see a pop-up screen titled *boost post*. From there, it will ask you to choose an audience through targeting. (Or at least this is how it worked in the winter of 2018. Facebook often tweaks their dashboard and changes some steps, but it should be pretty close.) Hit *edit*, and here is where the magic happens. You can choose from gender, age, things people like (or have mentioned or commented on or liked), and, most importantly, locations. Enter an address closest to where the murder occurred. Then shrink it by whatever you can afford. One mile, two miles. It will tell you how many Facebook users you will reach inside that area based on the money you will spend. So you need to drill down as much as you can.

With the Halloween Mask Murder at the Jack in the Box in El Monte, I knew I had a white or Hispanic male (from the paleness of his legs), who was very fit (as evidenced by the vault over the counter). I was able to narrow down the age to below twenty-five, within a mile of the two crime scenes he was spotted at. Then I tried to reach his peer group but also elders who might know him. Former bosses. Teachers. Location is always going to be your biggest threat, and if Facebook let you drill down to a quarter mile, it would make my life a lot easier. A mile is okay, but that can get very expensive. A mile radius in a big city could mean five hundred thousand people. You don't have the money to hit all of them. You have to pick your spots. You then set the budget and duration. I usually go ten days, making sure I hit both weekends. You can also choose to run the ad on Instagram, which is owned by Facebook. If you have a good image, do it. You will hit the younger crowd that way, and I have been using it more and more. Though it is impossible for something to be shared and go viral, the ad buy will get it in front of the right people.

Then you have to enter your credit card information.

Hit *boost* and hit *publish*, and you will wait for Facebook to approve the ad. Usually takes a couple of hours. Then you're live. Inform both the family and the detective that you are boosted.

Now you are using two social media platforms. If you want to use Twitter, you need to launch a whole new Twitter profile, which means launching a new Gmail account. It's tedious, but Twitter led to my first solve, so I won't discount it. Use the same strategies, albeit with more brevity. Write a tweet and search for locals with large followings and ask nicely for a retweet. That's how I ended up with the video of the Man in the Green Hoodie.

You'll be running on three platforms now. The last of the quadfecta is Snapchat, which only offers ad buying around a specific radius, which can be very, very small and specific. You can draw a circle around just a couple of businesses and present an ad to anyone who tries to post a photo from within that circle. But it costs a big chunk of change. There is also Google, which I have used for a "telltale heart" campaign, betting that the guilty party is going to be googling the victim's name, searching for new information. When they do, they would be met with the ad and their photo or sketch staring right back at them. It's a long shot, but if you're working on your white whale, toss that harpoon.

Make sure your phone is sending you alerts from the platforms if you get a message. If someone direct messages you, reply as fast as you can—within five minutes if possible, so they don't change their mind or sober up. If they ask who you are, don't give your name. Just say you are a victims' advocate working with the family.

As tips come in, compile them in a Word document and send them to the police, at the most once per day. If there is something pressing, like a tipster saying they see the suspect "right now!" call the detective. Take screen grabs of interesting/unusual comments. If someone makes a comment saying they know the person, direct message them from the page and then delete their comment.

You will get a lot of people commenting like idiots. Don't mind them. They are helping your algorithm and getting the campaign seen by more people when they comment. If they make threats or name names, screen grab and delete.

Bottom line: you are getting the image of the suspect in front of more people than television and newspapers and local news websites combined. You are canvassing the neighborhood, hitting up everyone with a Facebook profile. They will all see it. Whether they are willing to write you with information is up to them.

The People Who Will Contact You

The consequences of holding on to a murder or missing-persons secret differ from religion to religion.

Eternal damnation for some. Karma for others. Instant karma for John Lennon devotees. Catholic shame. Jewish guilt. And then there is the telltale heart of a secret beating underneath the floorboards of your brain.

The secret your ex-boyfriend told you that one night. The hit-and-run you and your friend vowed to never discuss again.

It beats. Beats. Beats.

If you have information about a violent crime, tell someone, anonymously if you have to. Stop the guilt from beating. The theater for the movie of your life is reserved. Will you want to sit in the front row or watch through your fingers in the back?

People who know each other. Those are the crimes that most of the time get solved. So many of the ones you will work are stranger crimes. That doesn't mean someone doesn't know something.

You first have to find them. Then you have to make a campaign compelling enough for them to message you.

You will get friends of the victim, friends of the suspect, family members, local busybodies, local media.

Treat everyone with respect. Tell them nothing except what has been publicly released about the case. And again, refer to yourself as a victims' advocate helping the family.

You will also get jokers, time wasters, and lonely people writing in. You can't get mad. Just suss them out, and you'll be able to tell if they are just yanking your chain or claiming to have psychic visions. People will tag their friends, saying it looks just like this friend or that friend. Send them a direct message asking them if they have information about the case. Nine times out of ten, they will say something like "I was just messing around." But I have gotten great information that has led to arrests from comments that on the surface looked like utter bullshit. You have to check them all out.

How to Act

If the families ask you for updates, you have to be vague. You can't say "We got the guy!" or even "We're close!" That's up to the detective to tell them. Just say tips are coming in or say "It's slow going" if they aren't. If the police have decided not to work with you and the family are frustrated, then you can start opening up with the information, sharing tips, and coming up with strategies.

If the family calls or emails you a lot, never say "You know, I have a lot of other cases. I'm very busy." They don't care. They want to know about their case.

It's easy to bad-mouth the detectives to family members. Don't. You are seen by these families as a symbol of hope. Superman didn't fly around complaining about detectives not calling him back. It will seem like a Sisyphean task running a dozen investigations at once. Watching twelve boulders tumbling down toward your chest is never a good feeling. But you cannot let anyone you are working with feel your frustration. And not just because whatever you are feeling is nothing compared to the hurt the family is feeling.

When psychologist Martin Seligman conducted an experiment putting animals in stressful situations seemingly beyond their control, they gave up trying to escape—even if a clear escape route presented itself. Seligman called the phenomenon "learned helplessness." The point he wanted to make was that when some people are in a bad situation, they don't try to make it better, because history has proven time and again that it is futile and they're helpless.

Keep at it. Like the poster my dad had hanging on his wall: "Nothing in the world can take the place of persistence." The only thing you can control is how you react. Keep checking the comments and messages on the page you have created, even after your ad has stopped running. You can keep putting money into the ad, open up the radius, try to narrow down the demographics. Get new information and hit up other locations. But at some point, you will want to stop buying ads, unless you are independently wealthy. It hurts, but you have to do it. The page might have gotten a lot of likes, so you can keep making posts and asking for shares. And keep answering the family's queries. Anything can happen. Remember, my success rate is around 15 percent. I lose a hell of a lot more than I win.

Even though information will almost always be a one-way street—you will give the detective everything you have, and they will give you nothing in return—the squeaky wheel always gets the grease. But it's not your job to keep drilling a detective. Guide the family or friends of the victim to do that. And anyway, unless you have a solid relationship with them, the police will be more willing to talk to the victim's family or friends than to you.

That's what Sheila Wysocki did.

In 1984, twenty-year old Angela Samota was raped and murdered inside her Dallas apartment. Her friend and former roommate, fellow SMU student Sheila Wysocki, waited twenty years for answers. She said the police told her "some cases just aren't meant to be solved." So she took matters into her own hands. She got a private investigator's license, set up a "war room" in her home, and traced her friend's final steps on earth.

Samota had gone out barhopping that night with two friends. After visiting the Boardwalk Beach Club, Nostromo, and the Rio Room, she drove her friends home around 1:00 a.m., went to visit her boyfriend at his apartment, then went back home.

A little later that night, a man knocked on her door and asked if he could use her bathroom. Samota let him in. Seconds later, her boyfriend got a call from Samota. She told him about the man she had just let in to her home. Then the phone went dead. Her boyfriend rushed to her apartment. On the way, he called the police using the mobile phone in his work truck. The police got there before him. When they opened the apartment, they found Samota's bloody, naked body on her bed, dead from multiple stab wounds.

DNA testing was in its infancy. All police could say was the semen collected on the scene was that of a nonsecretor. Samota's boyfriend, Ben, was a secretor, so he was eliminated. The police suspected one of the friends she was out with, a nonsecretor, but they couldn't place him at the scene. The case went cold.

Twenty years later, the determined Wysocki took up the case. She called the Dallas police more than seven hundred times, trying to get them to pay attention.

It worked. A DNA search was run again, and this time, it came back matching a convicted sexual predator named Donald Bess, who was out on parole at the time of the murder. Wysocki attended the trial. Bess was given the death sentence.

Wysocki didn't solve the case, but it's doubtful it would have been solved without her. Calling a police department more than seven hundred times over the course of two years gets their attention. Cold cases are a giant train with more than two hundred thousand wheels. The squeaky wheel is going to get the grease. Work with the family and friends and strategize how to be in consistent contact with law enforcement.

Go Bigger Than Just One Case

You have to get loud. Do not take lack of resources as an answer. Push for a volunteer citizen-detective genealogy pilot program in your community (you can find the nuts and bolts on this in the PDFs that came with the book). Crowdfund to extract DNA from a hair fiber of an unidentified murder victim, and present the cash to the police if they claim they don't have the funds to do it themselves. If they fail to act, contact the local media. Get loud.

In the hall of fame of citizen detectives, it's the ones who saw a hole in the system and worked hard to plug it that shine brightest.

Meaghan Good of the Charley Project (named after one of the first high-profile abduction cases in American history, the 1874 kidnapping of four-year old Charley Ross in Germantown, Pennsylvania) has written close to ten thousand profiles of missing persons—all for free. Her writing is crisp and to the point, and the profiles of each missing person are extremely user friendly, with relevant information and multiple pictures.

Good also lives with autism and bipolar disorder. She runs by the motto "Do what you can, with what you have, where you are."

"Autism is a pain in the neck," she told *Vice* in 2017, "and I wish I didn't have it, but I wouldn't be able to run the Charley Project without it." Good found what she was good at—researching, being meticulous and organized, and put those skills to good use for justice.

Todd Matthews was a factory worker who became obsessed with

finding the identity of "Tent Girl," an unidentified murder victim discovered by his father-in-law in the woods of Kentucky in 1968.

Tent Girl was Todd's call to adventure. He eventually used an online classifieds site to find her identity. She was a twenty-four-year-old woman named Barbara Ann Hackmann-Taylor.

He found the answer. But Matthews didn't stop there. He worked on building the volunteer missing-persons site Doe Network and had so much success that the government asked him to help create the National Missing and Unidentified Persons System (NamUs). It is the only centralized database in the country for missing persons and unidentified remains. The database could be much larger, but most police departments are not required to enter missing persons or remains into the system. It's all voluntary. There's another thing you can get loud about.

If you don't want to spend money or devote all your free time to a cause, you can still solve a crime. You just need to keep your eyes and ears open.

In May 2014, a nurse in a Quebec hospital told new parents that she had to take their newborn baby girl, Victoria, to another room for a few routine tests. She never brought Victoria back.

Caught in every parent's nightmare, the mom and dad called the police, who then issued an Amber Alert—be on the lookout for a red Toyota.

That's when boredom became an ally of justice. Four friends with nothing to do on a Monday night saw the story about the phony nurse. One of the friends looked at her photos and thought the woman looked like someone she knew. They drove to that woman's house, confirmed the hunch, and called the police. Baby Victoria was back in her mother's arms that night.

In December 2016, Uber driver Keith Avila picked up a male and two females—one of whom looked very young—and drove them to a hotel in Elk Grove, California, just outside Sacramento. During the trip, he heard the male and female coaching the younger woman: "Okay, when we get there, the first thing you're gonna do is give the guy a hug and you're gonna ask if he has any weapons." Avila dropped the three off at the hotel—then immediately called the police. Turns out the young woman was a sixteen-year-old girl being sex trafficked by the couple.

That same year, Carmen Moreno was picking up garbage in a park in Seville, Spain, when she spotted a pile of bloody tissues. A woman had just overdosed in the park, and the police who were called to the scene had haphazardly left some debris behind, including the tissues. But Moreno had watched a lot of *CSI*. She wondered, *If it was an overdose, why was there so much blood?* So she took out a plastic bag and carefully collected the tissues. The tissues led to an arrest. The woman didn't die of an overdose. She had been raped and murdered.

Stay aware. Stay alert. You can help.

What's In Store for You
If you do decide to try to solve a murder, you must prepare yourself to be beset on all sides by multiple factors of the case.

In front of you are the bad guys. And they multiply every day. Thirteen new unsolved murders every day.

To your left is time. And boredom. The quest for answers and finding none. The no-snitch policy, less about a code on the streets and more about what people have co-opted from movies and songs.

To your right is your bank account, rapidly depleting. Your credit card statement charting upward. Your family wondering what is taking so long as they wait for you to come to dinner.

But behind you is the family of the victim. The late-night email from a woman still wanting to know what happened to her husband. The one she picked. The one who picked her. After every bad date and crappy relationship. Every teenage crush and heartbreak. She found him. They built things. They saved. "We can't go to Disney this year. Maybe when the kids are a little older."

And then someone wipes it all away in the blink of a muzzle flash.

Why? is replaced by *Who? Who?* is replaced by *Where? Where?* is replaced by *How?* How will we find this man who took everything away?

Without the survivors behind you, you will fall down. They push you forward. When a promising lead turns out to be a crushing red herring, you fall backward. But you never hit the ground. Because the survivors are already there. They have already hit the ground. They have already lost so much and are still charging ahead.

And then if you stay at it and catch a little luck, you get the euphoria. I'm not going to lie. It is euphoric. Seven months of searching for an answer every day, and then getting a call from a detective: "We got him." It's euphoric.

But that's not why you do it.

You do it because how can you not?

Now if you will excuse me, I have to go: I just got a tip about a killer I'm trying to identify in Dallas. I have to send the info to the detective. He looks pretty good.

IN CONVERSATION WITH
BILLY JENSEN AND PAUL HOLES

On an afternoon in November 2018, Sourcebooks sat down with Billy Jensen and Paul Holes as they were on a break from shooting a TV docuseries in San Diego, California. As the two drank from a bottle of whiskey aptly named Writer's Tears, we asked them about the future of detective work and crowdsolving.

I'd love to hear about what you guys are up to and your process. First of all, can we talk a little bit about the Golden State Killer and DeAngelo and how you're feeling watching the progression of that investigation over the past several months?

Paul: Since DeAngelo has been in custody, I've been paying attention to the court process to see where things are at. Of course, I'm absolutely thrilled that that case is solved and the fact that the tool that was used in that case has proven to be highly successful in solving other cases—I think about twenty at this point.

Billy: Right, now it is about twenty. But to have it be *this* case as the entry point for using familial DNA to solve crimes, *that* was important because we knew that there was going to be some sort of a privacy backlash. And I remember the day it was announced that it was solved, Pete Headley called me up and said, "How bad is it?" And I was like, "What do you mean how bad is it? We just solved this thing." And he's like "How bad's the backlash?" And you know what? There were people writing little op-eds about privacy, but no one was gonna want to be on the side of protecting a guy that has killed at least twelve people and raped at least forty-nine women. So it was great that it was *this* case. And now all of these dominos are falling in these cases that a lot of people never thought would be solved. It's just the tip of the iceberg, though. We've got a lot more work to do.

Paul: I did get a little bit of backlash after DeAngelo. A fair number of journalists were calling me up saying I was becoming the poster child for the law enforcement guy that was violating everyone's privacy. But especially with some of the journalists that I've talked to, the concern now is that law enforcement are going to try to use [familial DNA] as a routine tool on lesser crimes. I think you're going to start seeing legislators coming forward to see if they can't do something legally to possibly limit its scope.

Billy: I mean, listen, we still have so much of a backlog of rape kits they haven't even processed, much less try to use familial DNA. So, the idea that you might get some weird police department that has a [Breaking and Entering] or something and is like "Let's use familial DNA to solve this burglary case…"

Paul: Exactly. The amount of resources it takes to do this technique when you're starting with bad matches or distant relatives—no agency is going to put those kinds of resources on a smaller crime.

Billy: That was the most frustrating thing when Michelle [McNamara] was working on the case—that we knew the answer was behind that locked door at 23andMe. The answer was there. And now we're going to see a lot more crimes being solved because of it.

Apart from familial DNA, do you have any thoughts about how the process of crime investigation is going to be changing over the next five years, whether it's through technology or just how people are using information that's already available?

Paul: During the last five years, there has been a shift. Law enforcement always lags behind the private sector when it comes to implementing new technology. So technology that has been out there with the social media world and with locational aspects tied to your phone, law enforcement is just now catching up and implementing that in a more robust way. And that's just going to continue to drive developments. People may not appreciate how much information they put out about themselves in their social media. We find out so much about somebody by looking at their Facebook page and their Twitter accounts.

Billy: Five years ago, I would talk to certain police agencies and they weren't yet looking at people's social media. And I was like, "Come on, guys, their entire social network is right in front of you!" My concern now is that a lot of young people aren't using Facebook. I kick myself for not coming up with this system five years earlier, when Facebook was really humming. Now younger people are abandoning it. That's why I started using Instagram more now, but on Instagram you can't really share a post or anything. I think there's two ways to use social media. One way is to push knowledge of the crime out there and geotarget people who might have seen something. And the second is looking at the profile of someone who has been killed and seeing who's connected to that person. And you're gonna see that hopefully happen more and more, because the police are wise to it and they see that as a great investigative tool.

Paul: Back in the day—and it wasn't that long ago—if we wanted to find out about a group of people, a family, a gang, or just friends, we would have to sit on the house and watch who's coming and going, talk to people that we had confidence wouldn't go back and burn us. Now, we go to the social media accounts. We can, from afar, develop intelligence that helps guide us in terms of how we're going to deploy resources on whatever the circumstances of that particular investigation are.

Can you talk about any of the cases that you're actively working on now and using these methods on?

Billy: What we're doing with *Murder Squad*, our podcast, is introducing people to cold cases that we feel like we can pick back up and do something with. There are so many listeners for podcasts like *My Favorite Murder* or *Case File* that have all this knowledge and want to be a part of something. So we are interviewing people that were involved in an old case, then putting that out to the public and saying, "This was somebody that was doing this in the early '80s, late '70s. Show this to some people that might not be on social media, go share this with your uncle or aunt who lived in Southern California or wherever at the time." Being able to utilize social media and people's connections and telling them, "Remember your great aunt? Why don't you send her a message over Facebook and say, *Hey, do you recognize any of the people connected with this case?*" It sounds like it's a shot in the dark, but if you have enough people doing it, you're gonna get answers.

Paul: In many ways, it's targeted crowdsourcing. The people listening to the podcast obviously have an interest in true crime, and there's going to be a percentage of those people that want to do their own little investigation. So now we're going to have an army of individuals that are out there trying to find the answers and feed them back to us or back to the investigating agency. I think it's going to be a lot more effective than a law enforcement agency holding a press conference and saying "Hey, you recognize this person?"

Billy: That's the main reason why I started the Facebook thing in the beginning with the Marques Gaines case. When you have a press conference, it might get shown on TV, but guess what? Nobody really watches TV anymore. But they are on social media, and they're opening up Facebook multiple times a day. That's where you have to hit these people if you want to get their attention.

Paul: Law enforcement is now starting to set up their own social media accounts, whether it be a Facebook page or Twitter—but how many people want to follow the county sheriff's office?

Billy: What we're trying to do is move the true-crime fan—who has got all this knowledge and has been sitting on the sidelines—and we're trying to push them now to the front lines, obviously in the right way and following the rules. A lot can be done because we have the tools right here. We just need to have the resources. And whenever you ask any police department, "Hey, why didn't you solve this case or that case?" one of the biggest things they're going to say is lack of resources.

Do you think that you have an advantage over active law enforcement officers in your ability to run investigations in unconventional ways?

Paul: There's no question that now that I'm outside of the law enforcement sphere there is a fair amount of flexibility I didn't have before. Of course, you lose something when you don't have access to the law enforcement resources, when you don't have the police officer powers to be able to compel somebody to do something for you, get search warrants, whatever. But with Billy's skill set and my experience, together we possess a lot more knowledge than most departments have.

Billy: I've certainly been able to talk to certain suspects who won't talk to the police. We're at a point right now that distrust of the police is pretty high. That cascades down to things like if you know something about a murder, you're not going to say anything. A lot of people don't want to get involved with the cops unless there's a reward.

What trait or quality in yourselves have you found most useful to this kind of work that you're doing?

Paul: Obviously, I spent twenty-four years on one case and had lots of failures, and so one trait that I will pat myself on my back over was the persistence. To just keep going and keep it moving. I've also developed a broad area of expertise across multiple disciplines used in investigations, whether it be forensics, behavioral, or other investigative components. And so I can look at a case using that breadth of knowledge. Oftentimes, a detective knows nothing about forensics, can't even read the reports, and so he has to rely on somebody to tell him what the report means. Then later if he stumbles across something in his investigation, he may not put two and two together and think, "Oh! Hold on, I understand the science behind this particular investigation, and I just ran across a witness who's telling me something that matches up."

Billy: For me, it's definitely the persistence. It's the one thing that you can control when you know you're going to hit so many dead ends. If you had a Paul for every crime, a lot of them would eventually get solved. If there are five thousand unsolved murders in America every year, that's thirteen a day that aren't going to get solved. And there's only one way to solve a crime, and that's to just keep pushing forward no matter what gets in your way.

Do you feel like there are changes that could be made within our law enforcement agencies that would give more room for that kind of focus and persistence that maybe we're not fostering right now?

Paul: The biggest thing I see that hampers a lot of these investigations is the reality that there are always more cases coming in. So somebody may be highly motivated to work a select case, but once that case starts to get a little bit older, they're going to catch more cases. Then the case they were working starts getting less and less attention until eventually there's nothing happening to it. That's how they go cold. And the reality is that there are more cases than you have bodies to work them. And I just don't see an answer to that.

Billy: It comes down to money; it comes down to resources. In the same way that there's a lot of knowledge out there with some citizen detectives, you could think about bringing those people into police departments to work on old cases. One thing that takes forever is taking old files that are handwritten and typing them up so they're searchable. And you know those files are gonna get lost at some point. They're going to get destroyed in a flood or you'll go looking for something and they'll say, "Oh, that was the old building, we threw everything away." We've heard that so many times. But with everything we're talking about, familial DNA and using social media are the two biggest things that are going to be able to help to solve a lot of these crimes. I just hope that there's a couple police officers out there that are willing to put this stuff in the budget and try and see if it works.

What would be your number one piece of advice for those people that are out there and are interested in getting involved in citizen investigations?

Paul: If they really want to maximize their impact, they need to kind of always treat it as a profession, and they need to educate themselves as best they can about all aspects related to a crime and criminal investigations so they can better understand what they are seeing, what they are reading. You have to get up to snuff in terms of your knowledge base.

Billy: You have to stay on it. A lot of people might start a website for a missing-persons case and then forget all about it. We see that a lot. If you're really into true crime, and if you want to take it beyond the kind of soap-opera aspect of it that you see on certain TV networks and really want to get into the nitty-gritty and solve it, you have to do your research. You've gotta find a case that speaks to you and a family that wants help. And you can never give up.

What do you see yourselves doing in ten years? Are you still going to be running these investigations?

Paul: You know, I've been doing it now for so long that it's just part of me. People have asked how I feel now that the Golden State Killer is solved, and one of the biggest things that I feel is a void since that case was such a big part of me, and now I'm not doing it anymore. So I don't see myself ever getting away from being a part of criminal investigations, although now it's going to be on the media side.

Billy: Michelle [McNamara] used to worry about what would happen to her when the Golden State Killer was solved, after she spent five years looking only at that case. I talk about this sort of White Whale. Once you catch the White Whale, what do you do? And the key is to use all that experience that you used in catching that White Whale and apply it to the next case. What we do, telling stories, investigating, trying to help people, those are things that don't really have a time limit or an age limit. There are a lot of cases people ask us to look into. It's just going to be a matter of picking the ones that we feel that we can help with, and also training a lot of other people to do it to solve as many as we can. I'm gonna ask Paul here—what's the one case that you would want to solve? We know the granddaddy of them all is Jack the Ripper.

Paul: Jack the Ripper would be interesting. Obviously Zodiac is a big one right now. Many people are very interested to know who that guy was. Of the most notorious cases out there, that's probably the one I would like to find out who that was. Just to understand him. Obviously, we want the solution for the victims' families, but we gotta understand that guy because he was somewhat different. Now, I've said, compared to GSK, the Zodiac is a coward, and the types of crimes he was just committing were just not as scary, he was doing lovers' lane stuff. But the ego, the narcissism reaching out to the newspapers and wanting that attention is an interesting aspect about him for me.

Billy: He was very much a supervillain. He had his own outfit. He had his own logo. He talked in ciphers. This guy is right out of the Batman essential casting. He toyed with the police; he toyed with the media. He wanted that attention. Then he faded away. There are so many other murders to solve, but Zodiac, Jack the Ripper, the Cleveland Torso Murderer—those stories are always going to bubble to the top when people talk about unsolved cases. We want to see them unmasked. BTK was like that. But then we saw him, and he was just a pathetic little worm. These guys are not supervillains in the end. Quite frankly, I just wish they were identified so we can focus on all of the other ones. If solving those would give us the opportunity to solve a hundred other ones, I would go for it.

READING GROUP GUIDE

1. Billy's passion for true crime developed early in life as a result of his dad pointing out newspaper articles about local crimes. Do you remember any crimes that happened in your town or region during your childhood that affected you deeply? Do you think it's common for people interested in true crime to often come to it during childhood or adolescence?

2. *Chase Darkness with Me* covers a wide spectrum of cases, some solved and some unsolved. Which ones do you find most compelling?

3. Billy's current method of investigation relies heavily on social media and reaching out to the networks of victims to seek information. Do you think he opens himself up to any kind of risk through his unorthodox techniques? If he were to contact you about a crime committed against a friend or family member, would you be willing to share information with him?

4. Are there any investigative techniques, involving social media or otherwise, that you think Billy could adopt? What other opportunities does the internet open up for people interested in solving crimes?

5. One of the main points Billy highlights in *Chase Darkness with Me* is that our current law enforcement institutions are severely limited by a lack of manpower and resources. How do you think law enforcement is going to need to change in order to continue to be relevant and effective as technology becomes a bigger part of our lives?

6. The man accused of being the Golden State Killer was identified through familial DNA. What are your thoughts about the ethics of private organizations like 23andMe refusing law enforcement access to the DNA information they have collected? How would you feel if a distant relative were convicted of a crime as a result of DNA evidence you had submitted?

7. What crime would you call your "White Whale"?

8. Billy posted a soundtrack playlist to this book on Spotify ("Chase Darkness with Me" by LonesomeCowboyBill) and every song, from the Beatles to Bowie to Prince to Public Enemy, has a specific reason for being on the playlist, along with a reason for being in the order in which they are presented. Some are actual moments from the book, while others have lyrics or moods that match up with major moments. Can you guess what songs match up to which events in the book?

9. Many true-crime fans struggle with the ethics of enjoying media that explores other people's tragedies, while a lot of true-crime writers and journalists frame the work they're doing as seeking justice for the

victims. Have you experienced this internal conflict at all? How do you view the balance of privacy and dignity for the victims and their families versus raising awareness and seeking justice?

10. Have you ever thought about helping to solve crimes yourself? If so, where would you start? Do you have a particular case in mind that you think you might be able to contribute to?

ACKNOWLEDGMENTS

We are all supporting actors in each other's movie. I can only hope I am as much help to you as you all have been to me.

To my literary agent, Marc Gerald; Andrew Eisenman and the entire Audible Originals team; and Anna Michels and the entire Sourcebooks team. Thank you for believing in me, my story, and this new idea of crimesolving.

To John Mancini, for teaching me how to write a killer lede.

To Lisa Gregorish-Dempsey, for answering a cold message on Facebook and, instead of calling the police, gave me a job with television wizards Scott Eldridge and Jeremy Spiegel and the entire *Crime Watch Daily* crew.

To Patton Oswalt for letting me and Paul Haynes help complete Michelle's book and for thrusting your grief into the light to help so many others. To Paul Haynes for being an excellent copilot in the *I'll Be Gone in the Dark* whirlwind. And to Liz Garbus, Elizabeth Wolff, Julie Gaither, and the entire Moxie Firecracker team, who I know will cement the legacy.

To Paul Holes, for being a fantastic partner—we are just getting started. And, of course, thank you for gifting me the ending of this book by solving the Golden State Killer case along with Barbara Rae Venter, Ken Clark, and Erika Hutchcraft, and all the others who never gave up.

To Karen Kilgariff, for your wonderful friendship and for not calling security on me when we first met (I was not wearing a trench coat, btw). And to Georgia Hardstark (and Steven Ray Morris) and all the Murderinos, for keeping all of these stories out of the darkness.

To all the bookstagrammers, for using a visual medium to share your love of the written word.

To @Super70sSports, @DinosaurDracula, @HamillHimself, and @MJMcKean, for making me laugh on Twitter when I need it.

To every hockey player who has ever punched me in the face. I never took it personally.

To John Barg, LASD, and all the detectives who were willing to take a chance on a crazy idea and let me help them solve these homicides and find these fugitives.

To Alexis Linkletter, for helping me soar, and Jac Vanek, for keeping me grounded.

To Lenora Claire, Camille Dodero, Doron Ofir, Alicia Kozakiewicz, Paul Thompson, Ashley Hammen, Tom Forman, Jon Beyer, Adam Davis, Jeff Ross, Kevin Balfe, Nancy Miller, Mike Lacey, Jed Morey, Robbie Woliver, Owen Michael, Bob Mohler, Stephanie Schwartz, Denise Chandler, Dawn Friedman, Cori, Stacie and Mom, Gary Dellabate, Morrissey, David Bowie, Chuck D, Lenny Dykstra, Clark Gillies, Adam West, Jack Webb, and Rowdy Roddy Piper, for your friendship and/or inspiration.

To Carol Schweitzer, Angeline Hartmann, and everyone at NCMEC for never giving up.

To Rhonda Randall, Carl Koppelman, Todd Mathews, and all the citizen sleuths out there burning the midnight oil inside their various rabbit holes.

To Drexina Nelson, Hector Carillo, Scott Greene, Billie Jo Dick, and all of the friends and families of the victims.

To Kendall, Zoe, and Will for everything. Seriously, everything.

To Michelle McNamara. If there's a heaven, you are there, solving an unsolved murder. It's a different version of heaven than most people envision. But that's your heaven. You are the patron saint of citizen detectives everywhere.

And to Dad, for teaching me how to throw a punch, take a punch, and never, ever give up. This is all still a rip-off, but I'm trying to make the best of it.

ABOUT THE AUTHOR

Billy Jensen is a true-crime journalist focused squarely on unsolved murders and missing persons. But after seventeen years of writing hundreds of stories with no endings, he was fed up—and decided to try to solve the murders and find the missing himself. It worked. Combining the shoe-leather investigative tenacity and skills he learned reporting crime with radical techniques honed from his day job as a digital executive, Jensen has solved or helped solve ten homicides and helped locate missing persons. Law enforcement agencies now reach out to Jensen to help in cases that have them stumped, using him as a "consulting detective." He was friends with Michelle McNamara and, after her sudden passing, helped finish her #1 *New York Times* bestselling book, *I'll Be Gone in the Dark*, about the hunt for the Golden State Killer. He was a senior producer and investigator on the Warner Bros. show *Crime Watch Daily* and cohosts with Paul Holes the podcast *The Murder Squad*.